KENT

A Chronicle of The Century

Volume Four: 1975-1999

by Bob Ogley

The fourth volume of Bob Ogley's *Kent Chronicle of the Century* takes us through the final 25 years of the 20th century. It embraces the inward-looking seventies and the realisation that Kent has a heritage that really is worth preserving. We remember the silver jubilee year, how we hailed a Wimbledon champion, saluted the success of our county cricket team but suffered together through those "winters of discontent". The eighties bring social upheaval. Chatham dockyard closes. So does Ashford's great railway works and the East Kent collieries become industrial tombs. Who can forget the tragedy of Zeebrugge, the IRA bomb that devastated the Royal Marines School of Music and that windy night in October 1987? The map of Kent is redrawn again in the nineties with a tunnel to Calais, a bridge to Essex, a great dome at Greenwich and an information superhighway that guides us to the millennium. Here then is the last chapter of the century for you to enjoy with the help of almost 200 illustrations.

 Froglets Publications

Froglets Publications Ltd

Brasted Chart,
Westerham,
Kent TN16 1LY
Tel: 01959 562972
Fax: 01959 565365

Volume One
ISBN Hardback 1 872337 24 4
ISBN Paperback 1 872337 19 8

Volume Two
ISBN Hardback 1 872337 84 8
ISBN Paperback 1 872337 89 9

Volume Three
ISBN Hardback 1 872337 16 3
ISBN Paperback 1 872337 11 2

Volume Four
ISBN Hardback 1 872337 06 6
ISBN Paperback 1 872337 01 5

Boxed Set Hardback 1872337 15 5
Boxed Set Paperback 1872337 75 9

© Bob Ogley

Front cover illustrations
The Millennium Dome, (MNEC QA) Princess Diana, Josie Russell and Eurostar (Topham PA)

Originated by Froglets Publications Ltd.
Scanning by CK Litho, Whitstable.
Printed and slot bound by Thanet Press, Margate. Casebound by Green Street Bindery, Oxford.

Jacket design by Alison Clark &
Richard Barker

FOREWORD

With the publication of this book — the fourth volume of the Chronicle of Kent, covering the last 25 years of the century — I have completed my millennium project. It's been hard work but great fun and the many hours of studying small print on library microfilm have been rewarded with the discovery of some real gems. Kent's story, throughout the last 100 years, has never lacked drama or excitement.

In guiding you through the century I cannot claim to have spotted every major historic detail; that is impossible. My mission was to capture the highlights — reportage rather than analysis — and allow you, the reader, to compare the pattern of life today with that of the beginning of the century.

As usual I am indebted to many people. Librarians especially, museum curators, newspaper editors and particularly cameramen and women, whose photographic skills are an integral part of the success of this series. As an added bonus Radio Kent has allowed me to review each year of the century on the Pat Marsh Show. I will miss my weekly trips to Sun Pier, Chatham and particularly the jolly host and his friendly researchers!

I would particularly like to thank the following: Mike Pearce of the Isle of Thanet Gazette, Terry Butler of the Medway News, Gary Sawyer of the Kent and Sussex Courier, Roger Perkins of the Sevenoaks Chronicle, Bob Hollingsbee, Gordon Luck, Frank Chapman, Gordon Anckorn, Alex Watson, Mark Davey, Chris Taylor, the Kent cricket archivist, Tom White of Kent's Fire Brigade Museum, Terry Tullis and the helpful staff at Topham Picturepoint.

All four volumes would not have been possible without the help and encouragement of the staff at Froglets — Fern Flynn, who was involved in all stages and took many of the modern pictures, Avril Oswald, who read the text and compiled the index, Francesca Wade who helped with the research, Mark Laver who searched for literals and Sonja Whittle who came to our rescue in the final stages.

You will find, on page 194, details of the first three books in the series and how to order them from Froglets Publications if you so desire. You will also discover that boxes or slip cases are available for the four volumes and these can accommodate hardback or paperback. May I suggest that a signed full set may make a special "millennium present". Please let Froglets know your wishes.

Finally, a special thanks to the subscribers. 500 people across the county had faith in my promise to complete the series and ordered a copy in advance. Thank you for that. Your names are printed on page 196 and 197.

Bob Ogley

PHOTOGRAPH CREDITS

We are grateful to the following for the use of their photographs. In some cases we have been unable to trace the copyright holder but have made every effort to do so. **Topham Picture Source** 6, 7, 8, 9, 12, 13, 14, 16, 20, 31 (bottom),33 (both), 43, 49, 55, 58, 59, 69, 71, 76, 78, 80, 89, 92, 99, 105, 115, 118, 136, 138, 144 (bottom), 158, 170, 171, 173, 174, 178, 187, 190, 191 (bottom). **Author's collection (Sevenoaks Chronicle)** 15, 24, 30, 38, 39, 40, 41, 45, 61, 68, 74, 77, 81, 87, 94, 97, 108/9, 114, 120, 123, 141, 145, 153, 161, 175, 176, 177 (top), 186. **Medway News** 26, 28, 36, 46, 47, 53, 54, 63, 66, 79, 125, 131, 149, 154, 168, 183, 188, 189. **Kent Messenger** 22, 24, 50, 57,64/ 65, 67, 83, 85, 132, 157, 159, 182. **Kentish Times** 17, 18, 42, 60, 100, 107,117, 128, 130, 139, 140 (bottom), 142, 163, 164, 166, 179, 180. **Folkestone Herald** 72, 73, 75, 98, 110, 111, 116, 146, 148, 154, 162. **Isle of Thanet Gazette** 25, 48, 142, 181. **Kent Fire Brigade Museum** 19, 90. **Courier Newspapers** 11, 69 (bottom) 70, 88, 102, 134/5, 144, 151, 177 (bottom), 191. **Northcliffe Newspapers** 34, 37. **Eurotunnel** 121, 126/7. **Fern Flynn** 4 (both), 10, 27, 122,140, 143, 165, 169. **Peter Brown** 11. **Chris Taylor, Kent County Cricket Club** 21, 23, 45, 137, 167. **Gordon Luck** 32, 51, 113. **Mark Davison** 70. **Terry Tullis** 86. **Tom Morris** 133 (both), 167. **Bill Bonds** 150. **Michael Pett** 160. **Bluewater QA** 185. **Matt Devine** 186. **MNEC QA** 192. **Holly Pelling** 103. **Philip Lane** 84,95. **Mr W.E. Coney** 56. **ATAK** 3.

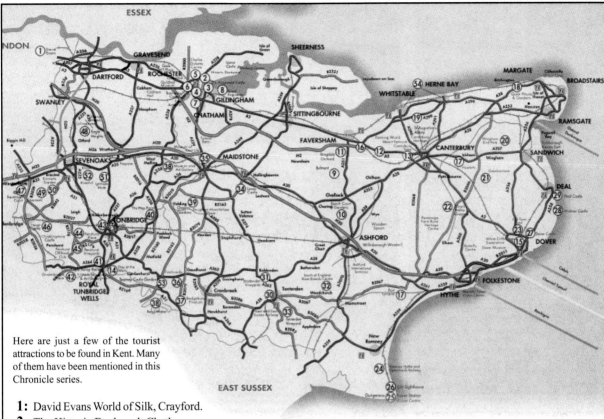

Here are just a few of the tourist attractions to be found in Kent. Many of them have been mentioned in this Chronicle series.

A FEW TOURIST ATTRACTIONS IN KENT

1: David Evans World of Silk, Crayford.
2: The Historic Dockyard, Chatham.
3: Paddle Steamer Kingswear Castle, Historic Dockyard, Chatham.
4: Rochester Castle.
5: The Charles Dickens Centre.
6: The Guidhall Museum, Rochester.
7: Fort Amherst Heritage Park and Caverns, Chatham.
8: Royal Engineers Museum, Gillingham.
9: Belmont, near Faversham.
10: Beech Court gardens, Challock.
11: Brogdale Orchard, Faversham.
12: Mount Ephraim Gardens, Faversham.
13: The Canterbury Tales, Canterbury.
14: A Day of The Wells, Tunbridge Wells.
15: The White Cliffs Experience, Dover.
16: Farming World, Faversham.
17: Howletts and Port Lympne Animal Parks.
18: Quex House and Gardens, Birchington.
19: Canterbury Museums.
20: Wingham Bird Park, Wingham.

21: Goodnestone Park Gardens.
22: Parsonage Farm Rural Heritage Centre, Elham.
23: Dover Old Town Gaol.
24: Romney, Hythe and Dymchurch Railway.
25: Dungeness Power Station.
26: The Old Lighthouse, Dungeness.
27: Dover Castle.
28: Walmer Castle and Gardens.
29: Deal Castle.
30: Kent and East Sussex Railway.
31: Biddenden Vineyards.
32: South of England Rare Breeds Centre.
33: Tenterden Vineyard Park.
34: Leeds Castle.
35: Museum of Kent Life, Cob Tree.
36: Finchcocks Living Museum of Music.

37: Bedgebury Pinetum.
38: Bewl Water.
39: Yalding Organic Gardens.
40: The Hop Farm Country Park, Paddock Wood.
41: Royal Tunbridge Wells.
42: Groombridge Place Gardens.
43: Tonbridge Castle.
44: Penshurst Place and Gardens.
45: Penshurst Vineyards.
46: Hever Castle.
47: Squerryes Court, Westerham.
48: Eagle Heights Bird of Prey. Centre, Eynsford.
49: Chartwell, Westerham.
50: Emmetts Garden, Ide Hill.
51: Ightham Mote.
52: Knole.
53: Scotney Castle Garden.
54: Herne Bay and Whitstable.

*Two of Kent's 16,000 listed buildings, selected in 1975 as houses of special excellence. Above **Finchcocks,** a baroque Georgian mansion famous for Richard Burnett's unique collection of antique keyboard instruments. This museum of musical history stands in its own park two miles west of Goudhurst. Guided tours, demonstrations and recitals are given when the house is open from Easter to late September.*

*Below: **The Cloth Hall**, Biddenden, the home of weavers in the fifteenth century who had come here after persecution on the Continent. The weavers worked in rooms on the first floor lit by large windows beneath seven distinct gables. The Hall has been converted into private homes.*

January 1st: Richard Nixon's aides, Mitchell, Haldeman and Ehrlichman are convicted of trying to cover up Watergate.

January 2nd: Charlie Chaplin, expatriate Englishmen, who was born in South London, has been knighted in the New Year Honours. Arise Sir Charlie.

January 3rd: Charles Kray has been released after spending six years in the long-term wing of Maidstone Prison. His twin brothers Reggie and Ronald are serving 30-year sentences. Charles Kray intends to live with his friends Susan and George Dwyer at Amherst Drive, St Mary Cray.

January 27th: Five bombs exploded in London ending a long truce in the IRA's campaign of bombing and murder.

January 31st: Dr Donald Coggan has been enthroned as Archbishop of Canterbury in a glittering Christian pageant. The royal family was represented by Prince Charles and Princess Anne. Security was tight throughout Canterbury and more than 8,000 people attended the service.

February 4th: Mr Ted Heath is no longer leader of the Conservative Party. He telephoned his father in Broadstairs today with the news that Margaret Thatcher had won the first ballot. Mr Heath senior of Dumpton Gap Road said he 'was shocked'. It is now widely assumed throughout Kent that he will accept a peerage and be known as Lord Heath of Broadstairs.

February 25th: Miners have accepted pay rises of up to 35 per cent.

February: The Stour Centre, built on 20 acres of multi-purpose land between the East and Great Stour at Ashford, has finally opened. It includes a sports stadium, sauna suite, licensed bar, restaurant and snack bar.

Susan's murderer blames the devil

July 13th: **After a seven-day trial at Maidstone, Peter Stout has been jailed for life for the murder of Susan Stevenson at the Great Lines, Chatham, in September last year.**

Susan was hurrying to church when Stout pounced on her, pulled out a knife and rained blow after blow on the defenceless girl.

She dragged herself to the ornamental gardens next to Chatham police station but died later in Medway Accident Centre.

Her death sparked off the biggest murder hunt in the history of the Medway Towns. Stout, of Gillingham, eventually confessed but blamed the devil. "When he thinks I have one of my funny turns he does some extra poking and I give in."

March 1st: John Simpson, aged 26 of Seal Hollow Road, Sevenoaks, has been charged with the murder of 20-year-old Dawn Gregory of Pilgrims Way West, Otford.

March 7th: The body of Lesley Whittle, a young heiress who was kidnapped from her Shropshire home by a man known as the Black Panther, has been found in a 60-foot drain shaft. She was strangled.

March 25th: The mentally deranged Arab Prince Museid today assassinated his uncle, King Faisal of Saudi Arabia.

Rt Hon Eric Varley Minister of Energy opened Kingsnorth Power Station on the Isle of Grain. Costing £113 million it is the only oil and coal fired power station in Britain and is now the biggest in Europe. With an output of 2,000 megawatts, the station can produce sufficient electricity for a city of two million. The power is fed to the National Grid.

April 17th: After a brutal siege of 3½ months Cambodia has fallen under the control of the Communist Khmer Rouge forces.

Twenty-five miles of Kent's Thameside banks are being raised by five feet in readiness for the opening of the £200 million Thames flood barrier in 1979. The work is being carried out by the Southern Water Authority.

April 24th: The number of unemployed in Britain has passed the million mark.

April 31st: With the surrender of Saigon today the war in Vietnam is almost over.

June 6th: Referendum results tonight confirm that British people have voted overwhelmingly to stay in the Common Market with 67.2 per cent in favour.

June 21st: West Indies beat Australia by 17 runs today to win cricket's first World Cup.

July: St Mary's Hall at the King's School, Canterbury, has been opened by the Duchess of Kent.

August 24th: Today is the 100th anniversary of William Webb's historic cross-Channel swim which took him almost 22 hours and made him a hero throughout the land. Webb died in 1883 attempting to swim across the Niagara Falls rapids.

September 29th: Soldiers' local, The Hare and Hounds, Maidstone, was the target for IRA bombers. Thanks to the vigilance of the landlord and police in evacuating the area, no-one was killed. *See page 7.*

September 30th: Muhammad Ali beat Joe Frazier to retain his world heavyweight title.

November 3rd: A North Sea oil pipeline, which runs 110 miles on the seabed to a refinery on the mainland, has been opened by the Queen. Harold Wilson said today that he expects Britain to be self-sufficient in oil by 1980.

December 19th: Chrysler's closure of its components factory, Tilling Stevens in Maidstone, early next year will put more than 400 people out of work, it was announced today.

The £19,000 made by Mike Denness, captain of Kent and England cricket club, during his benefit year is a new county record.

GREAT HITS OF 1975

Sailing
Bye Bye Baby
I Can't Give You Anything

Heath 'beached' after clash with Thatcher

February 13th: Last year Sir Edward Heath's troubled three-and-a-half year reign as Prime Minister ran onto the rocks of an oil crisis and miners' strike. This week, Kent's best-known sailor-politician is well and truly beached after a head-on collision for the leadership of the Tory Party with Margaret Thatcher.

The MP for Finchley, who has lived with her husband Denis at Lamberhurst for nine years, won by 130-119 in the first ballot of Tory MPs and forced Ted Heath to resign. She then went on to become the first woman leader of a British political party by defeating four male rivals.

Mr Heath's supporters, shocked by the election of "an outsider to the mantle of Peel, Disraeli and Churchill" are speaking of her as a stop-gap or temporary aberration which in due course will be corrected.

Mrs Thatcher, aged 49, who has 17-year-old twins Mark and Carol, was ecstatic. "I just beat four chaps", she said. "Now let's get down to work."

Until recently the family lived in The Mount, Lamberhurst, an eight-bedroom centuries old house which snuggles against a small hill and has magnificent views of Goudhurst beyond. The family moved there in 1966 and it served as a successful retreat during holidays and weekends but this year the Thatchers decided to move into a comfortable flat at Scotney Castle.

Her election as Conservative Party leader has left most of her friends and supporters breathless for she is considered both a dissident and an outsider. More extraordinary is the fact that this 'dissident outsider' is a woman.

Yesterday, on the morning after the result had been declared, Mrs Thatcher went round to Mr Heath's house in Wilton Street in an attempt to preserve the spirit and appearance of party unity. No-one knows what was said although there are various, dramatic versions. The meeting was over within seconds.

Many believe the former Prime Minister will now accept a peerage and be known as Lord Heath of Broadstairs and others say he will not join the Shadow Cabinet, even if invited. He will go to the back benches where he will be free to express his personal views. The rift with Margaret Thatcher, say friends, will heal in time.

See page 13

Mrs Thatcher with her twin children, Carol and Mark, seen here when she lived at Farnborough, Kent, before the family moved to Lamberhurst.

The horrors of Moorgate

February 29th: Kent commuters today described the horrors at Moorgate when 33 passengers died in the worst-ever tragedy on the London Underground. Among them was trainee accountant Charles Gale, 23, from Seal who was en route to his city office.

Frank Gaunt, a print designer from Hythe, said the train was whizzing along and then suddenly there was a bang. He found himself sitting on someone else's seat surrounded by a tangle of bodies, choking soot, darkness and complete silence.

The driver, Leslie Newton, apparently accelerated into the blind tunnel when his 8.37 am commuter train from Drayton Park should have been braking. It crashed through sand, over the buffers and embedded itself in a wall.

Mr Gaunt said that many people were pinned to the roof of the carriage by a seat. It had ridden up a wall. "My shoulder was feeling stiff but I managed to free myself and prayed. Then the screaming started."

A doctor on the scene was Mrs Margaret Haig from Ide Hill, Sevenoaks, who crawled among survivors giving them pain-killing gas and injections. "There were bodies up above us and on the side but we ignored them because there was nothing else we could do. Another doctor told me that he had often wondered what hell was like. Now he knew."

Charles Kray released from Maidstone

January 3rd: Charles Kray, pictured here in the centre with his twin brothers, Reggie (left) and Ronnie, has been released after spending six years in the long-term wing of Maidstone Prison. He intends to live with his friends Susan and George Dwyer at Amherst Drive, St Mary Cray, until he is able to buy a new home.

Reggie and Ronnie, who are also in Maidstone Prison, will have a longer wait for their release. The gangland bosses who gained a reputation for violence while also commanding a cult following received life sentences in 1969 for murder. It is believed the brothers still have control of many properties, including pubs, hotels and nightclubs in South London and Kent.

See page 170

Maidstone pub blasted by IRA bombers

September 27th: The IRA bombing campaign on the British mainland moved to Maidstone last night when an explosion outside the Hare and Hounds pub on the Lower Boxley Road rocked the centre of the town and injured two policemen.

The pub, a popular meeting place for servicemen from the Royal Engineers Invicta Barracks, had been deliberately targeted by terrorists who hoped to inflict the kind of carnage caused by recent London and Birmingham pub bombs.

The policemen had been called to the road after a suspicious package was found four feet from the wall of the Hare and Hounds. The landlord, Mr Brian Wooster said: "I realised immediately it was a bomb and cleared the pub of customers. The police arrived and were in the process of evacuating the area when the explosion occurred." He added: "We have a lot of soldiers in the pub and with the recent wave of bombings I knew it must happen locally, sooner or later."

One family who had a lucky escape were Mrs Christine Greenaway and her four children who lived in the house opposite the Hare and Hounds. The two policemen knocked on her door and said: "You've got four minutes to get out." Mrs Greenaway was just preparing to run with her children when an enormous bang threw them across the room. The family escaped serious injury but the house is badly damaged.

Kent police, led by Chief Constable Barry Pain, set up road blocks immediately and put a well-rehearsed emergency plan into operation. All pubs nearby were evacuated and suspicious packages investigated. *See page 32*

The county is losing its stately elms

October 30th: The countryside of Kent is being ravaged by Dutch elm disease. Thousands of these stately trees — in woods and parks, around cricket grounds and alongside river banks — are dying because of a suffocating fungus, spread by beetles, and growing beneath the bark.

The disease, first identified some years ago, has been particularly virulent in the past few months.

In Hythe, it is not so much a rural calamity as an urban disfigurement. Hundreds of magnificent elms planted along the banks of the Royal Military Canal, dug as part of the defences against Napoleon's army, are dead or dying.

According to a report by the Forestry Commission, 6.6 million elms have now been destroyed. The disease started in southern England and appears to be advancing northwards. Some trees are 200 years old.

Local authorities are now working closely alongside conservation groups in a bid to plant replacement trees. The Civic Society in Hythe estimates that 2,000 will be required.

Elizabeth Taylor and her mother Sara. With her brother, Howard she lived with her parents at Little Swallows, Cranbrook.

Happy days in Cranbrook for little Liz Taylor

October 10th: As Elizabeth Taylor and Richard Burton were remarrying today in a remote Botswana village, older people in Cranbrook were recalling the time that "little Liz" lived with her parents in a cottage on the Great Swifts estate, within sight of the famous village windmill.

Mr and Mrs Taylor were offered the cottage by Major Victor Cazalet. They called it Little Swallows and enjoyed several happy years in the village.

One lady who remembers the family well is Mrs May Ealding who worked for the Taylor family and looked after Liz. "She learned to ride in Cranbrook and on occasions we used to hitch the pony to the trap and go shopping in the village. She was a lovely child but very vain."

The family went to America on the outbreak of war and Elizabeth grew into a violet-eyed beauty, making four films by the time she was 12 including

Lassie Come Home and *National Velvet.* She has gone on to make many fine films and won an Oscar for her performance in *Who's Afraid of Virginia Woolf?* (1966).

Today she is celebrated for her glamorous personal life and eight marriages — most notably to Richard Burton in 1964. They were divorced last year after a stormy ten years but, to the delight of villagers in Cranbook, are making another attempt.

Graham Hill with two of his three children, Brigette and Damon.

Kent racing ace Tony Brise dies alongside Graham Hill

November 30th: Graham Hill, twice world motor racing champion and the sport's number one ambassador, died today along with five members of the Lotus Grand Prix team when the light aircraft he was piloting crashed in freezing fog near Elstree Airport yesterday evening.

Among those who died was Tony Brise of Bexley, one of Kent's best-loved and most promising Grand Prix racing drivers who was tipped as a future world champion.

A funeral service for Tony, 24, will be held at St Michael's Church, Wilmington next week. Among the mourners will be his widow Jackie and Bette Hill.

Graham Hill's interest in motor racing began at Brands Hatch in 1953 when he paid six guineas, completed four laps and gave up his free time to work there as an unpaid mechanic.

A year later he joined Colin Chapman and Team Lotus. Hill is the only Formula One champion to have won the other major events, Indianapolis (1966) and Le Mans (1972).

See page 59

Channel Tunnel plan abandoned

January 20th: The concept of a fixed crossing across the Channel, independent of wind or tide, which has been an engineer's dream since the beginning of the 19th century, has foundered yet again.

The scheme, approved by both governments in 1973 for a 32-mile tunnel costing an estimated £468 million, has now been abandoned.

Kent County Council chairman, Mr Robin Leigh-Pemberton, said he was surprised and concerned that the decision was taken without any consultation with the KCC. *See P 82*

July: Work has begun on building the largest on-river flood storage system in Britain at Hayesden, near Tonbridge, in an effort to prevent the kind of disastrous floods which devastated the intensively-farmed flood plain between Tonbridge and Yalding in 1968 and 1974.

The Medway Flood Relief Scheme is unique. The idea is to throttle back flood water in the channel behind a 1,300 metre long barrier, and to release it under control, so that the river level downstream will never rise above "bank-full" condition.

September 22nd: Firemen with turntable ladders rescued several nurses, trapped by fire in their rooms at Oakwood Hospital, Barming, last night. Other nurses, dressed only in night clothes, fled in panic as the blaze spread rapidly through their nurses' home.

The bravery shown by the firemen was extraordinary. Wearing breathing apparatus they fought their way into the blazing building and when the roof collapsed two were seriously injured. More than 100 rooms were badly damaged and many nurses lost all their clothes and belongings.

The Union Windmill, Cranbrook, the finest smock mill in the country. In 1960 it was taken over by Kent County Council which, with assistance from the Society for the Protection of Ancient Buildings, restored it as a working mill. Built by Henry Doubell in 1814 it is the tallest in Kent and the largest in England. It dominates the centre of the 'capital' of the Weald.

75 for 75: The best buildings in Kent

September: Kent's richness in architectural heritage is well known. It has more than 16,000 listed buildings and 250 conservation areas — figures which exceed those of any other county apart from the Greater London Council area. In celebration of European Architectural Heritage Year, the county is holding an exhibition of photographs of 75 buildings of special excellence for 1975. They are:

82 High Street, Dartford (15th century), **Cobham Hall** (16th - 19th), **Cobham College** (14th), **Meopham Windmill** (19th), **Quebec House,** Westerham (16th), **Squerryes Court,** Westerham (17th), **Chevening House** (17th), **Sevenoaks School** (18th), **Knole** (15th), **Archbishop's Palace,** Otford (16th), **Ightham Mote** (14th), **Old Soar,** Plaxtol (14th), **Yotes Court,** Mereworth (17th), **St Lawrence Church,** Mereworth (18th), **Mereworth Castle** (18th).

Hadlow Castle (19th), **Whitbread Hop Farm,** Beltring, **Hever Castle** (14th), **Penshurst Place** (14th), **Somerhill,** Tonbridge (17th), **Groombridge Place** (17th), **The Pantiles,** Tunbridge Wells (17th), **Church of King Charles the Martyr,** Tunbridge Wells (17th), **Finchcocks,** Goudhurst (18th), **Union Windmill,** Cranbrook (19th), **Corn Exchange,** Rochester (18th), **Eastgate House,** Rochester (16th), **The Guildhall,** Rochester (17th), **Restoration House,** Rochester (16th), **Rochester Castle** (12th).

Cathedral Church, Rochester (13th), **Gibraltar Terrace,** Chatham (18th), **Town Hall,** Chatham (19th), **The Quadrangle Storehouse,** Sheerness Dockyard (19th), **The Old Court Hall,** Milton Regis (15th), **80 Abbey Street,** Faversham (15th), **Gillett's Granaries,** Faversham, **The Guildhall,** Faversham (19th), **Lees Court,** Sheldwich (rebuilt after fire in 1910), **Tithe Barn,** Boxley (14th), **All Saints,** Maidstone (14th), **The Archbishop's Palace,** Maidstone (14th), **The Chequers Inn,** Loose, **Estate Cottages,** Linton (19th), **Synyards,** Otham (15th).

Leeds Castle (13th), **Quested Almshouses,** Harrietsham (rebuilt 18th), **Archbishop's Palace,** Charing (14th), **Estate Cottages,** Pluckley (17th), **The Old Cloth Hall,** Biddenden (16th), **Clock Tower, Marine Terrace,** Margate (19th), **Farmhouse and barns,** Sevenscore, Minster-in-Thanet (18th), **Christchurch Cathedral,** Canterbury (from 11th), **The Norman Staircase, King's School,** Canterbury (12th), **Greyfriars,** Canterbury (12th), **Eastbridge Hospital,** Canterbury (12-14th), **St Martin's Church,** Canterbury (14th), **Barns and Oasts, The Manor House,** Littlebourne (18th), **113 and 114 High Street,** Wingham (17th), **Richborough Castle** (3rd).

Manwood Court, Sandwich (16th), **22 High Street,** Sandwich (15th), **The Salutation,** Sandwich (1912), **Chillenden Windmill,** (1868), **St Nicholas Church,** Barfreston (11th), **Betteshanger House** (1886), **13 Middle Street,** Deal (18th), **Deal Castle** (1540), **Dover Castle** (1185), **Roman Pharos Lighthouse,** Dover Castle (1st AD), **Waterloo Crescent,** Dover (1838), **Maison Dieu Hall,** Dover (1221), **Swanton Mill,** near Mersham (17th), **Barns at Westernhanger Manor,** near Stanford (16th), **St Augustine's Church,** Brookland (14th).

'Unless consumption is cut by a half all over Britain, the country will face water rationing until Christmas' — Dennis Howell, Minister of Drought, after the "summer of the century".

January 2nd: It was announced today that the High Court made 1,875 winding-up orders last year, making 1975 the worst year for financial failures in Britain's history.

January 7th: Troops from the Special Air Services have been ordered into South Armagh where 15 Protestants and Catholics have died in sectarian murders in one week.

January 13th: Dame Agatha Christie, Britain's wealthiest author, died today just after completing her latest Poirot story. She was 85 and renowned as Queen of the Detective Story.

January 21st: Two Concorde aircraft took off simultaneously today from London and Paris on their maiden commercial flights.

February 11th: John Curry has won the men's figure skating gold medal at the Innsbruck Winter Olympics with a display of athletic agility.

February 24th: L.S. Lowry, the northern industrial townscape artist, famous for his matchstick characters, died today.

March 16th: Harold Wilson, leader of the Labour Party for 13 years, today resigned as Prime Minister. In a surprise announcement he instructed his press secretary: "Tell lobby correspondents I have a little story that might interest them."

March 19th: Princess Margaret and her husband, the Earl of Snowdon, are to separate after 15 years of marriage.

March 24th: President Isabel Peron has been deposed by Argentina's military leaders in a bloodless coup.

April 5th: James Callaghan, 64, defeated Michael Foot, leader of the left wing, by 176 to 137 in the latest ballot for the job of Britain's Prime Minister.

April 26th: Actor Sid James collapsed and died on stage at Sunderland.

May 1st: Second Division Sunderland has beaten Manchester United 1-0 in the Cup Final.

May 10th: Jeremy Thorpe has resigned from the Liberal Party after claims by a male model, Norman Scott, that they once had a homosexual relationahip.

June 2nd: Lester Piggott today won the Derby at Epsom for a record seventh time.

June 18th: More than 100 are dead and a 1,000 injured after three days of looting, rioting and burning in South Africa's black townships.

July 3rd: The blond long-haired Swede, Bjorn Borg, today became the youngest Wimbledon champion for 45 years by beating Ilie Nastase in the final.

July 4th: In a brilliant military operation Israeli commandos rescued 100 hostages held by pro-Palestinian skyjackers at Entebbe airport today.

Iron railings, cast in Lamberhurst in the early 1700s for St Paul's Cathedral, have been returned to the village and placed outside the village hall. Lamberhurst was once the centre of the Wealden iron-smelting industry, the water to operate the hammers provided by the nearby River Teise. The iron railings stood at St Pauls for more than 200 years and it was a decision by the Dean and Chapter to return them to Lamberhurst.

July 7th: David Steele was today elected leader of the Liberal Party.

July 30th: Richard Ingrams, editor of *Private Eye* is sent to trial on criminal libel charges brought by James Goldsmith.

New wheels and cogs for Big Ben have been cast at the works of MJ Allen in Ashford following the breakdown of Westminster's famous clock

The people of Kent have found many ways of raising money but how about this for a novel idea? Peter Brown, 35, lived in a 135-gallon cider barrel suspended above the village green and raised £1,300 for the All Saints, Biddenden Church Roof Appeal and the building of a sports pavilion and squash courts. For seven days he ate, slept and watched television.

August 1st: In her new book *And The Morrow Is Theirs*, Sue Ryder, wife of wartime fighter pilot Group Captain Leonard Cheshire, says she wants to open a home in Kent, similar to the Cheshire Homes her husband is opening all over the country. Sue, who worked for Special Operations during the war, went to school at Benenden.

Kent's gipsy population is now the largest in the country, but the KCC is still looking for official sites to house the growing number of itinerants. At the moment there are seven which cost the county more than £100,000 per site per year.

August 13th: Winnie Mandela, wife of the jailed African black leader, has been arrested following the recent township riots.

Viv Richards, the West Indian batting sensation from Antigua, today hammered 291 in his team's total of 687-8 against England.

September 9th: Mao Tse Tung, leader of Communist China, died today aged 82.

September 29th: Britain has applied to borrow $3.9 billion from the International Monetary Fund to prop up the pound.

October 24th: Britain's James Hunt has won the Formula One championship from Niki Lauda by a single point.

October 26th: The National Theatre on the South Bank was opened by the Queen today.

November 2nd: Jimmy Carter of Plains, Georgia, is the new President of the United States.

November 29th: The Grant of Arms, recognising Ashford's status as a borough, has been presented by Lord Astor of Hever, Lord Lieutenant of Kent. It was received by the Mayor of Ashford, Cllr Harry Watts.

GREAT HITS OF 1976

Mississippi

Save Your Kisses For Me

1976

Jim Swanton retires — but promises to carry on writing

January: E.W. (Jim) Swanton, well-known in Sandwich, his home town since 1963, has recently retired as the *Daily Telegraph* cricket correspondent after a journalistic career which began in 1927.

One of the most celebrated and prolific members of the press corps and certainly the longest serving, Jim has followed the MCC (and later England) all over the cricketing world, reporting many of the greatest Test matches ever played.

In 1937-38 he had one season with Middlesex and then spent most of the war years as a POW in the Far East, having been captured when Singapore fell.

Jim, who has twice taken his own touring team to the West Indies and once to Malaya, is currently president of Kent Cricket Club, a founder member of I Zingari, a member of the Cricket Society and the MCC. He is a regular BBC broadcaster and has written scores of books about the game.

His latest, *Swanton in Australia,* follows the fortunes of five England tours "down under". On most of these he has been accompanied by his wife Ann, a pianist, painter and former championship golfer, whom he married in 1958.

Jim and Ann Swanton after their wedding in 1958.

Gravesend psychopath charged with five murders

September 12th: An unbridled two-year climax of terror came to an end today when Patrick Mackay, a former Gravesend school caretaker, gardener and odd job man, was sentenced to life imprisonment for the manslaughter of three people. Among his victims was Father Anthony Crean, a retired chaplain, who was brutally stabbed to death in his home at Shorne.

Mackay, who appeared in court charged with five murders, was described as a "cold, psychopathic killer" who was obsessed by Nazi propaganda and the brutalities of the Third Reich.

As a Gravesend schoolboy he was a bully and torturer of pet animals. At the age of 16 he tried to strangle his mother and threatened his sisters. He spent three years in mental wards where he committed violent assaults on nurses and other patients. In 1974 he absconded from a mental hospital and embarked on his rampage of terror.

Father Crean, who had once befriended and tried to help Mackay, was his last victim — killed with a knife and axe in his home near the Rose and Crown pub in Shorne.

Mr Michael Parker QC who defended Mackay at his trial said that in everyday life his client appeared to be normal. He was a classic psychopathic type and admitted the present state of medical science held out no immediate hope for his condition.

The judge said: "You knew what you were doing and you knew it was wrong therefore you are not insane." Mackay was sentenced to life, not for murder, but manslaughter. Two cases were left on file and another five required police investigation.

Kent agrees: there is nothing like a Dame

In Sybil Thorndike and Edith Evans, the county of Kent boasted two of Britain's greatest-ever actress dames — whose commanding performances have held the world of theatre spellbound for most of this century. Sadly, both have died this year Sybil aged 84 and Edith, 88.

Sybil Thorndike's early life was spent in Rochester where her father was a minor canon. She became an accomplished concert pianist but developed chronic cramp and so joined an acting school and switched to the stage.

Soon after her father became Vicar of Aylesford, Sybil toured America where she played no less than 112 different parts, many alongside her less experienced brother Russell.

Returning to England, she joined a repertory company, married Lewis Casson at her father's church and soared to prominence for her performances in Shakespeare, in Greek tragedy and in the plays of George Bernard Shaw. He wrote *St Joan* especially for her; it ran for 244 performances and brought her international fame.

If Sybil was a powerful Joan then Edith Evans was an equally commanding Lady Bracknell in *The Importance of Being Ernest,* which was one of her best-known roles.

Dame Edith began her working career as a milliner and amateur actress. She made her debut on the London stage in 1910 and since 1913, when she turned professional, performed almost without a break. For many years she lived in an Elizabethan manor house at Kilndown, near Goudhurst and died there in October. Villagers knew her as a witty, controversial and very outspoken lady who refused to have her biography written, despite many requests. She drove around in an elegant old Rolls Royce. The funeral service was held at Kilndown Parish Church.

Out of office and out of favour, at least with the new leader of the Conservative Party, Ted Heath has found more time to indulge in his great loves — music, sailing and writing. This week the carpenter's son from Broadstairs, whose three years as Prime Minister coincided with some of the most troubled years of the century, learned that his book, Sailing: A Course Of My Life, *has already sold a staggering 90,000 copies in less than a year and that he is the author of a stunning bestseller.*

Ted is now writing a second book, Music: A Joy For Life *in which he will tell of his excitement at 10 years old when his parents bought him a Bobby Thornton piano which they could ill afford. Here is Mr Heath at the piano (now a Steinway) rehearsing for the Michael Parkinson show in November last year, with Dame Edith Evans, a lady with whom he was not out of favour. She was delighted to hear that advance orders for* Music *were in excess of 42,000 but disappointed that he had no intention yet of writing his political memoirs!*

See page 34

See page 69

November: At the age of 90, Marc Chagall has completed one of the most surprising commissions of his long, illustrious career — the creation of all the stained glass windows in the tiny village church of All Saints, Tudeley, near Tonbridge.

It was the death in 1963 in a sailing accident of 21-year-old Sarah d'Avigdor Goldsmid which led her family and friends to commemorate her name in a lasting and tangible form.

Her father, Sir Henry, a professing Jew like Chagall, commissioned the design of a memorial window. At the dedication in 1967, the great man — pictured here with his family — said he would be happy to "do the church in its entirety". It was his only commission in England.

Inland waterways — a new paradise for Kent

March: The ornithologist has discovered a new paradise; so too have the trout angler, the windsurfer and the sailor — if they don't trip over each other. The giant reservoirs at Bewl Bridge near Lamberhurst and Bough Beech near Edenbridge have, at last, been completed giving Kent the two largest stretches of inland waters in south east England.

With 15 miles of shoreline, well-cleared footpaths and bridleways Bewl Water adds up to 770 acres of water and, when full, the capacity will be 6,900 gallons. Owned by Southern Water the greater part of the reservoir will be used to regulate the level of the River Medway and will serve consumers from the Medway Towns. Water will now reach them from pumping stations and treatment works downstream and much smallers reservoirs on the edges of Rochester and Chatham.

Bough Beech is smaller, containing 2,200 million gallons when full. Although it is well within the Kentish boundaries it is owned by the East Surrey Water Company.

Two vast areas of agricultural land, set in valleys of great natural beauty, were transformed to create these reservoirs. Trees were uprooted, homes demolished — and in some cases moved. Large embankments were built and the area flooded.

Before and during construction the schemes were plagued by controversy but the result is two massive dams that have already become both wildlife sanctuaries and sports centres.

The fly-fisherman can cast his line into waters well stocked with brown and rainbow trout. The dinghy sailor and windsurfer can enjoy the new facilities, but they do need special permits. Nesting birds, passing migrants and the more common species already thrive in this "natural habitat,"

At Bough Beech and Bewl Bridge the Kent Trust for Nature Conservation looks after the new reserves. They are encouraged by both Southern Water and the East Surrey Company who want to be good neighbours.

Two fine old Wealden homes at Bough Beech were dismantled timber by timber and taken to the Downland Open Museum at Singleton where they have been reassembled as exhibits. At Bewl, the 14th century Dunsters Mill House has been resited on a hill after a seven-year battle by the owner Mr Hubert Beale.

In the shade of the old oak tree. This was the scenario for thousands of schoolchildren as the sun shone almost nonstop from May to the summer holiday break. These children are from St John's, Sevenoaks.

Save water, they said: take a bath with a friend

October: This has been a summer to remember. Day after day from May onwards the sun shone down from a cloudless sky and Kent resembled a Mediterranean resort. As rivers and reservoirs dried up and we were told to put a brick in our cistern or bath with a friend to save water it was announced that county had suffered the worst drought since 1727 when records were first kept. For children, outdoor lessons became a way of life.

At Tunbridge Wells the temperature soared to 82F on May 7th, a taste of things to come. In late June the mercury reached or exceeded 90F almost every day for a week — an unprecedented event. During June, the village of Biddenden had no rain at all.

The county became tinder dry. For three months serious blazes stretched firefighters' resources to the limit. Among the worst were those at the amusement arcade, Herne Bay, Giles furniture store in Chatham, Reed Paper Mills at Aylesford, the Napoleonic Fort at Chatham and the Lydd Army Range where exploding ammunition made it a terrifying ordeal for firemen.

The danger was exacerbated by the proximity of high tension electricity wires and the Dungeness Nuclear Power Station. The reactors were switched off and the area evacuated until the fires were brought under control.

As the drought continued into August there were 36 consecutive rainless days in North Kent and the water crisis deepened. In desperation the Government played its trump card and appointed Dennis Howell Minister of Drought. It worked. The persistent block of high pressure broke down and September was one of the wettest ever known.

1976

Lucky Lucan and the tigers of Howletts Zoo

Friends of Lord 'Lucky' Lucan, who was officially named by an inquest jury last year as the killer of his wife's nanny, Sandra Rivett, still believe he is alive, in hiding and the victim of a severe travesty of justice.

Among those in the "magic circle" — as the police call them — is John Aspinall, former proprietor of the Clermont club in Berkeley Square where Lucan gambled and lost thousands of pounds.

Aspinall, who has known Lucan for many years, sold the Clermont for £350,000 in 1972 and bought Howletts, a private zoo near Canterbury. He believes that Lucan is in hiding and innocent, despite his outburst last year when police turned up at Howletts looking for the fugitive earl.

When he was asked if he was proud to be the friend of a man who had allegedly tried to bash his wife to death Aspinall is alleged to have replied: "If she'd been my wife I'd have bashed her to death five years before. Don't come that line with me because who knows into what red hell one's sightly soul will stray under the pressure of a long, dripping attrition of a woman who's always out to reduce you, to whom you are stuck and from whom you've had children."

At the time rumours were circulating that Lucan had committed suicide and Aspinall had disposed of his body by feeding it to his tigers.

Since then Detective Chief Superintendent Roy Ranson and his number two Det Chief Insp David "Buster" Gerring have continued to interview members of the magic circle who closed ranks, many admitting they may well have given Lucan money and help had he begged asylum.

Among Lucan's best friends were Ian and Susan Maxwell Scott, whose home in Uckfield Lucan visited after the murder and Dominick Elwes, another prominent member of Aspinall's Clermont Club.

Elwes, a manic depressive and deeply in debt, committed suicide after the inquest in September last year. John Aspinall spoke in a moving but light-hearted way at his service and upset one member of the congregation who punched Aspinall violently on the nose.

Meanwhile the search for the missing earl goes on. If he returns to Britain he will face a murder trial at the Old Bailey.

Great Train robber lived with friends on the Marsh

February: People on Romney Marsh are set to welcome Great Train Robber, James White, when he is released on parole next month. White, or Bob Lane, as he was then known, had a number of unsuspecting friends while living at Littlestone before his arrest in 1966.

He moved there from a farm at Pett Bottom, near Canterbury, which he had bought with part of his share from the gang's £2.5 million haul.

White, ex-army paratrooper, expert locksmith, master of disguise and holder of countless aliases lived in a ground-floor flat with his wife Sheree and son Stephen. He was caught after a fishing companion recognised a newspaper photograph and tipped off the police.

Lord and Lady Lucan. Police believe she she was the intended victim

'One cannot help wondering how many people have to die before the apparent majority view for the return of capital punishment is recognised and acted upon' — Barry Pain, Chief Constable of Kent.

1977

January 3rd: Roy Jenkins, Home Secretary, has resigned from the Cabinet and from Parliament to become the first British president of the EEC Commission in Brussels.

January 6th: EMI has sacked the Sex Pistols for outrageous behaviour.

January 14th: The Earl of Avon (formerly Sir Anthony Eden) has died aged 79. He had been a heroic worker for world peace and spent the last 20 years in seclusion, suffering from recurring illness.

March 27th: Two jumbo jets collided on the ground in the Canary Islands today killing 574 people. It is the worst tragedy in aviation history.

April 2nd: *Red Rum* today galloped to his third Grand National victory — the first horse to win the famous steeplechase more than twice.

April 25th: A jubilee year duty for Prince Charles was to open Kent County Constabulary's communications and operations centre at its Sutton Road, Maidstone headquarters. Accompanied by the Lord Lieutenant of Kent, Lord Astor, the Prince was introduced to both uniformed and plain clothed officers. He was presented with a souvenir truncheon by Chief Constable Barry Pain.

April 30th: An oil slick of more than 1,000 square miles, which blew out of control from a

Back home: Comedian Bob Hope visits the house at 44 Craigton Road, Eltham, where he was born 73 years ago.

Norwegian rig, is threatening the Scottish east coast.

May 13th: Australian publisher, Kerry Packer, has signed up 35 of the world's best cricketers to play in a series of international contests this autumn.

May 25th: Liverpool today beat the German champions Borussia Moenchengladbach 3-1 in the final of the European Cup.

May 29th: Nigel Short, aged 11, today became the youngest ever player to qualify for a national chess championship.

June 4th: Mr Barry Pain, Chief Constable of Kent, has called for the return of capital punishment. "Crime in Kent is up by 4.8 per cent", he said. "How many people have to die or be seriously injured before the return of capital punishment is recognised and acted upon."

June 6th: Beacons are lit across Kent as the county prepares to celebrate the Queen's Silver Jubilee celebrations.

June 17th: Lady Astor of Hever has launched a new £5 million hovercraft at Ramsgate called *Prince of Wales.*

July 2nd: Kent miners demand £135 for a four-day week despite appeals from NUM president, Joe Gormley for pay restraint.

July 12th: The average price for a house in Kent is now £16,731.

August 16th: The king of Rock 'n Roll, Elvis Presley, was found dead today at Graceland, the Memphis, Tennessee mansion where he has lived for many years. The initial cause of death appears to be a drug overdose. He was 42.

September 26th: Ramsgate's well-known entrepreneur Freddie Laker today launched his cut-price skytrain service to New York. This first walk-on, no frills flight cost £59, cutting the normal air fare to New York by almost £130.

October 28th: Police are searching for a vicious murderer known as "The Yorkshire Ripper".

Patrick Leigh Fermor, a former King's School Canterbury pupil who was expelled for holding hands with a grocer's daughter, and then set out on a 3,000 mile, four year walk from the Hook of Holland to Constantinople, has eventually published a book about the great adventure. It is called *A Time of Gifts* and describes the journey along the Rhine and the Danube, across the Alps and Carpathians and tells of the horrors of burgeoning Nazism.

December 2nd: South African police have been cleared of the death of the country's black consciousness leader, Steve Biko, who was arrested on August 18th and kept naked in leg irons and handcuffs throughout his five-day interrogation.

December 8th: Princess Anne has named her new son Peter Mark Andrew Phillips.

December 10th: The London-based Amnesty International has been awarded this year's Nobel Peace Prize for "securing the ground for freedom".

December 12th: The late Sir Winston Churchill's widow, Baroness Clementine of Chartwell, has died aged 92.

December 25th: British actor and hero of the silent films, Sir Charles Spencer Chaplin, has died aged 88.

GREAT HITS OF 1977

Don't Cry For Me Argentina

When I Need You

Growth of the Rootes empire

Sir Reginald Rootes, who with his brother built up the largest motor car manufacturing and distribution concerns in the country, has died aged 86.

The Rootes empire began with their father's thriving engineering and cycle business at Hawkhurst. The company moved to Maidstone in 1917 and opened a showroom in London.

By 1926 they had taken over Devonshire House, Picadilly where they established the greatest car selling concern in the world.

The Rootes Group as it became took over Humber, Hillman and Commer companies. They acquired Sunbeam, Clement-Talbot and Karrier and were involved in the manufacturer of bombers and armoured cars during the war.

Chrysler UK acquired a majority shareholding in Rootes in 1967, the year Sir Reginald retired.

Chislehurst's prolific play and screenwriter, Ted Willis, was among the personalities at the gala opening of the Churchill Theatre last night. Others included Nicholas Parsons (president of the Churchill Theatre Club), Brian Rix, Roy Castle, Ronnie Barker and Elspeth Gray. They saw the first performance of Willis's new musical — an adaption of an H.G.Wells' story. Willis, who was once a tramp, began his writing career in 1936 and went from strength to strength. He is perhaps best known for the television police series, Dixon of Dock Green, *and is pictured here with some of its souvenirs.*

At last: curtain rises on the Churchill Theatre

July 5th: After nearly 20 years of disappointment, speculation and tragedy, Bromley's great dream of a civic theatre has been realised. Yesterday the curtain rose on the town's multi-million pound Churchill Theatre.

The dream began in 1956 when the old New Theatre faced a threat from commercial development of the site and 42,000 people headed by Sir Laurence Olivier and Sir Michael Redgrave signed a petition calling for it to be saved. The outcome was the establishment of the Bromley Theatre Trust.

In 1961 the project, incorporating a theatre, library and shops, was considered by the old Bromley council. A tender for £1.75 million was accepted — less than half of the final cost of the project.

Since then the plans have been plagued by drainage problems, increased costs, consultant troubles, the three-day working week, unreliable delivery dates for materials, a massive fire which destroyed the New Theatre and, more recently, a freak storm which flooded the building site.

The Churchill Theatre will be formally opened by Prince Charles on July 19th.

See page 163

Seven killed as fire engulfs Dover restaurant

March 28th: Seven people including a fireman died yesterday when fire swept through the Crypt Tavern Restaurant, Dover. One of the biggest tragedies in Kent for many years left seven other firefighters seriously ill in hospital. Doctors said today that acute carbon monoxide poisoning and axphyxia were responsible for both deaths and illness.

The blaze was reported at 2.45 am on Sunday morning when Dover firemen received a call to say that several people were trapped upstairs in the burning building. After attending the scene a major alert was called and within minutes 15 appliances, including pumps, turntable ladders and emergency tenders were in attendance.

As flashovers engulfed the building the conditions inside were appalling but several people suffering from smoke inhalation were carried to safety. Three of the dead, a 19-year-old girl and two children, were found upstairs. Three other bodies brought out were those of the wife and two children of Mr Colin Clay, manager of the restaurant.

At 4 am part of the two-storey section of the building collapsed on top of the fire fighting crews completely burying some of them under tons of rubble. Leading Fireman John Sharp was killed and following the removal of his body from the scene, instructions were given that no more firefighting operations were to be carried out. The building was unsafe.

The coffin bears the body of Leading Fireman John Sharp of Canterbury who died in the Crypt Tavern fire at Dover.

Smouldering for months : now firemen vote for strike action

November 14th: The unthinkable has happened. Just a few months after the Crypt Restaurant tragedy, Kent's firemen along with their colleagues across the country, have gone on strike. Torn between their devotion to the service and discontentment with both pay and conditions the firemen have opted for a national stoppage. The dispute has been smouldering for months.

This week the Royal Engineers stationed at the Invicta Barracks, Maidstone and the Royal Navy's "breathing apparatus and rescue unit" at Chatham have been mobilised. Wartime Green Goddesses have been brought out of mothballs while senior officers have assumed responsibility for fire cover in Kent.

Practically all fire stations, including retained are closed with picket lines manned day and night. Sympathetic members of the public are showering money, food and gifts on the men as they stand outside their stations. Lorry drivers are hooting in support.

Virginia Wade at the All England club during a Wightman Cup game against America's Billie Jean Moffitt-King

Virginia is Wimbledon champion in jubilee year

July 2nd: The former Tunbridge Wells Grammar school-girl, Virginia Wade, 31, has become Britain's most successful tennis player since Fred Perry in the 1930s.

Winner of the US Open in 1968, the Italian championship in 1971 and the Australian in 1972, she has now added the Wimbledon crown. Yesterday in the centenary ladies single final, marked by the presence of the Queen in her jubilee year, Virginia lost the first set to Betty Stove and then rose to victory on the cheers of an ecstatic Centre Court crowd.

Many of her former school friends were at Wimbledon to see her reach the final by beating the reigning champion Chris Evert.

Virginia and her sister went to Tunbridge Wells Grammar School where she spearheaded the school's victory in the Aberdare Cup at Wimbledon. Local people still remember the 17-year-old running down Grove Hill Road to catch the London train for coaching at Queen's Club and how she became England's Number One while a member of the Tunbridge Wells lawn tennis club.

The town is proud of their tennis queen.

The Kent squad at Canterbury. Far right of the front row are four of Kent's finest — Derek Underwood, Asif Iqbal, Alan Knott and Bob Woolmer — who have signed to play in Kerry Packer's World Cricket Series. The TCCB want them to be banned from playing county cricket.

Why Kent may lose its finest cricketers

September: These may have been the golden years of Kent cricket — six trophies won in five years including a shared championship with Middlesex — but players, officials and particularly supporters are not happy. In fact they are experiencing the most topsy-turvy days in the history of the county club.

Mike Denness, the most successful captain since the halcyon days just after the turn of the century is now playing for Essex. He was sacked last year.

Asif Iqbal, after one season in charge and one shared championship pennant, has also lost his job as skipper.

The future of such fine players as Alan Knott, Derek Underwood, Bob Woolmer and Bernard Julien is in considerable doubt . Many county stalwarts are saying they should never play for Kent again.

The reason for all this was broken to the stunned cricketing world in May when England captain Tony Greig revealed that he and several professional players had signed to play in Kerry Packer's World Cricket Series. Among them were the five Kent players.

The sequence of events was startling. In July the International Cricket Conference decided to ban all Packer players from Test Cricket. On August 10th the Test and County Cricket Board agreed on more drastic action — to ban from English county cricket, all those who had signed for Packer. This meant the loss to Kent of its finest players.

The decision by the ICC and the TCCB has been challenged and the two sides will face each other in the High Court in November. The cricket-loving people of Kent await the outcome with bated breath.

All this came after some of the greatest seasons Kent has known. They won the John Player League in 1972, 1973 and last year, when they also won the Benson and Hedges Cup. They won the Gillette Cup in 1974. This year they have shared the championship with Middlesex and are runners-up in the Benson and Hedges.

It is understandable that the mood of the Kent players is swinging between disappointment and elation. For one player, though, there is just elation. Big Norman Graham, the county's 6ft 7in opening bowler has just "declared" benefit takings of £58,000 — a massive sum that matches his size and personality. ***See page 23***

Eddie McHale, a former piper with the Black Watch who lives in Queens Road, Maidstone and runs a children's home, piped children down Dover Street at the start of their silver jubilee party.

Kent celebrates Queen's Silver Jubilee in style

June 18th: Glorious sunshine brought thousands of people out of their homes on Saturday to end a week of celebrations marking the Queen's 25 years on the throne. The festive spirit has been infectious, spreading from town to village to hamlet throughout the county with a chain of bonfires lighting up the night sky as they did when the Spanish Armada approached.

One of the largest events was an all-day sporting festival at Buckmore Park organised by KCC's youth and community service in which teams of 40 young people from each of the 14 divisions in the county competed.

In other parts of the county there were antique fairs, street parties, concerts, special cricket matches, air shows, charity events and swimming galas.

There have also been more lasting memorials, the most notable being the riverside walk at Maidstone which has cost the borough council £70,000. It will link up with the new bridge due to be opened next year. In Sevenoaks an area known as The Shambles is being restored. In Ashford the famous Harper Fountain in Victoria Park is being renovated and cleaned. In Pembury a conservation plan includes the removal of a horse trough from the roadside to the village green.

A spokesman for the South-East Tourist Board said that thousands of foreign visitors, including many from the Commonwealth countries, had arrived in Kent and most historic homes were having a record summer.

January 30th: Mrs Thatcher says Britons fear "being swamped by people of a different culture".

February 20th: Kent has suffered its worst blizzard for many years.

February 15th: Ian Smith and three African leaders have produced a three-year plan aimed at moving Rhodesia over to black rule.

March 2nd: Body snatchers today stole the body of Charlie Chaplin from the Swiss cemetery where he was buried three months ago.

March 15th: The Cambridge boat sank one mile from the finish in today's University Boat Race.

March 24th: A super tanker, the *Amoco Cadiz,* split in two off Brittany today spilling the last of her 220,000 tons of crude oil into the Channel. The worst oil slick ever known is now moving towards the Channel Islands.

April 25th: Birching, which is still practised in the Channel Islands and the Isle of Man, has been outlawed by the European Court.

Eastwell Park House, Ashford has been turned into a luxury hotel.

May 10th: Princess Margaret is seeking a divorce from the Earl of Snowdon.

May 30th: Euopean golfers, including Severiano Ballesteros, will play alongside Britons in the Ryder Cup against the USA.

June 16th: The Pope has banned Prince Michael of Kent from marrying his Catholic financee, Baroness Marie von Reibnitz, in a Catholic Church.

The ancient royal chapel at Leeds Castle has been reconsecrated by the Archbishop of Canterbury after a 400-year gap in worship.

July 26th: The world's first testtube baby was delivered by Caesarean Section in a hospital at Oldham today.

Kent Cricket Club's decision to offer contracts to the "Packer

September: Alan Ealham, the lively Kent cricketer who built his reputation as a match-winning fielder and equally aggressive batsman, has completed his first season as captain of Kent in great style by winning both the county championship and the Benson and Hedges Cup. It has been a remarkable year for both Ealham and his team. Because of the Packer controversy Kent began the season with three players - Asif, Underwood and Woolmer - virtually under notice. Alan Knott didn't play at all but newcomer Paul Downton kept wicket brilliantly throughout the season and Chris Tavare took 48 catches in the slips. At the end of the season Ealham, accompanied by cricket manager Colin Page, was invited to Buckingham Palace to collect the Lord's Taverners Trophy from the Duke of Edinburgh.

players" has led to the resignation from the general committee of David Clark, a former chairman and captain of the club. As President of the MCC and chairman of the ICC he cannot be associated with the decision.

September 18th: President Anwar Sadat of Egypt and Menachem Begin of Israel announced today they had reached agreement on the signing of a peace treaty.

September 30th: Pope John Paul has died after only 33 days in office. It was the shortest papal reign since Stephen II in 752.

The North Downs Way, the long-distance footpath which runs from

Dover to Farnham in Surrey has been officially opened by the Archbishop of Canterbury

October 16th: Cardinal Karol Wojtyla of Poland has become the first non-Italian Pope since 1542.

Hand-sewn cricket ball making in Britain is now confined to just two factories in Kent — Alfred Reader at Teston and Duke and Son at Chiddingstone Causeway. The latter is now in the ownership of Tonbridge Sports Industries which has closed its factory in Park Road, Southborough.

November 4th: Bread is rationed in many Kent shops as a bakers' strike leads to panic buying.

November 30th: Publication of *The Times* and *The Sunday Times* is suspended indefinitely because of industrial dispute.

Princes Charles has received the honorary freedom of the City of Canterbury. Huge crowds gathered for the ceremony.

December 13th: Jeremy Thorpe, former leader of the Liberal Party is accused with three others of conspiracy to murder Norman Scott, former male model. The trial will be held at the Old Bailey.

Kenneth George Ramsden has been charged with the murder of Frances Arnold, aged 29, who was found shot, bound and gagged in her home at Tonbridge in August.

December 17th: Ted Heath MP today conducted the Christmas Carol Concert at the Grand Ballroom in Broadstairs.

December 20th: The IRA has threatened to continue with its Christmas bombing campaign in British cities.

Frank Woolley, the Pride of Kent and one of cricket's greatest allrounders, has died in Canada aged 78.

GREAT HITS OF 1978

*The Rivers of Babylon
Summer Nights*

Not much room on this beach for the hardy winter visitor. Here are the remains of Herne Bay's famous old pier.

Kent's piers destroyed in mighty gale

January 12th: It has been a night of high drama for those living in the coastal towns and villages of East Kent. Hurricane force gusts, in excess of 80 mph, whipped the sea up into such a frenzy that defences capitulated forcing the evacuation of hundreds of people.

The old pier at Margate has gone. A pile of contorted girders and matchwood is floating in the sea with the lifeboat station stranded at the seaward end. Herne Bay's famous old wooden pier has suffered the same fate; scores of boats are damaged beyond repair and a mountain of shingle and debris litters the foreshore right round the Thanet coast. In the Sandown Road snowploughs are today attempting to force a path through the shingle to rescue elderly citizens trapped in their homes.

Nowhere has suffered more than Deal. As the sea water crashed over the defences hundreds of people had to be evacuated, including Mr Len Hunt who heard giant waves crashing against his house at the Marina. The windows collapsed, the door was torn down and the sea swept in battering his furniture.

The greatest drama of the night occurred at the Chequers Inn which stands on the Sandhills at Deal. As the pub became cut off by the rising tide eight customers climbed onto the roof and lit a fire to attract attention. A rescue helicopter from Manston was alerted but the hurricane force winds prevented it from landing. A similar rescue bid by the Royal Marines using a "Gemini" launch also ended in failure. The fire brigade was called but the men were beaten back by the icy flood waters in Golf Road.

As the waters continued to rise and the storm raged the occupants huddled together to keep warm. As dawn broke a local farmer with a tractor-trailer made his way through the deep water and rescued the eight people. They were taken to hospital suffering from shock and exposure.

London teeters on the brink

This week's terrifying tidal surge — the worst since 1953 — nearly caused a major disaster in London as floodwater came within 19 inches of the retaining wall along the Thames embankment. The great flood barrier at Woolwich is nearing completion. It cannot come too soon.

See page 60

The lifeboat station at the far end of Margate Pier is marooned 500 yards out to sea. In the foreground are the twisted girders of a popular friend.

Those in peril on the sea

Kent's famous piers have experienced a love-hate relationship with the weather ever since the first one was built in the early nineteenth century.

That honour went to Herne Bay. Erected in 1831 it was soon in dispute with the tides and quickly fell into disrepair. The new pier — one of the longest and most popular in the country — was introduced in 1873 and a grand pavilion incorporated in 1910.

Margate Pier, built in 1853, was badly damaged in 1877 and again in 1897. Many happy years were to follow but the sea was always too powerful and, in 1976, the authorities declared the pier unsafe and it was closed.

For Herne Bay and Margate this year's tidal surge is the final nail in the coffin.

April 25th: *Torrential rain has been causing havoc all over Kent but nowhere is as bad as the scene in Chamberlain Road, Chatham, where a landslide occurred early on Tuesday morning. Mrs Prudence Brasingham (pictured) said a high wall in Victoria Road behind her home collapsed bringing a garden and greenhouses down with it.*

Six killed in Holly Hill air tragedy

April 30th: Six men were killed when a Piper Lance aircraft crashed into the White Horse Woods on Holly Hill, Snodland, yesterday morning. The men, who were all Dutch, were flying from Amsterdam, Holland to Biggin Hill. Police believe the aircraft hit the trees as it was climbing to avoid the hill.

The last message came as the plane passed over Detling beacon when the pilot radioed Biggin Hill to say he would land in seven minutes.

The mangled wreckage of the Piper has now been taken away for Department of Trade investigations. It has been Medway's worst-ever air disaster.

When Laddie's Spitfire crashed on the ninth at Sandwich

P.B. "Laddie" Lucas, wartime fighter ace, world-class amateur golfer and former MP has published a fascinating autobiography entitled *Five Up* in which he tells of his flying experiences, including the defence of Malta in 1942. Lucas, whose father was secretary and co-founder of the Prince's Club, Sandwich, played for England in the Walker Cup teams of 1936 and 1947. In 1940 his Spitfire was badly damaged over France and Lucas coaxed it home to a crash-landing on his favourite ninth green.

Many famous feature films have been made by Lord Brabourne's Mersham Productions Company, carrying such diverse titles as *Sink The Bismarck (1960), Romeo and Juliet (1966), Up The Junction (1968)* and *Murder On The Orient Express (1974).* This year a new film from the Brabourne stable is the Agatha Christie whodunnit *Death On The Nile,* with Peter Ustinov as Hercule Poirot. Lord Brabourne, who has recently moved to Newhouse in Mersham, is married to Lady Patricia, daughter of Lord Mountbatten of Burma.

The momentous Middle East peace talks between President Sadat of Egypt and Menachem Begin of Israel have moved from Washington to Leeds Castle. This week, amid heavy security, the foreign ministers of Egypt, Israel and the US met to discuss a plan for permanent peace. It is the perfect setting and just what Lady Olive Baillie had envisaged when she established the Leeds Castle Foundation and conference centre.

Lord Avebury, formerly Eric Lubbock, Liberal MP for Orpington, has signed a surety for £5,000 allowing his great friend Jeremy Thorpe to be released from custody. The former leader of the Liberal Party is accused with three other men of conspiracy and incitement to murder Norman Scott, a former male model. He has been committed for trial.

Britain's first light railway which ran from Headcorn to Robertsbridge via Tenterden and was closed in 1954 is on the rails again — thanks to a group of enthusiasts who are still busy restoring many sections of the famous line. The Kent and East Sussex Railway is now owned by 1,200 members of the new operating company who contributed small individual sums and then obtained a mortgage from British Rail to pay for the project. The trains are operated at weekends by volunteers who opened the first 2.5 mile stretch at Tenterden, just over three years ago. It is a delight for the steam enthusiast; among the locos on the line is No 376 Norwegian dating from 1919. This loco was built in Sweden and ended its former days on snow plough duties in the Arctic Circle. One of the stations on the line was called Hell. With this background it has little trouble pulling the Victorian carriages round the notorious sharply curving Tenterden bank and its gradient of one in 50. **See page 71**

Maidstone's new bridge will solve town traffic problems

November 23rd: The Duke of Kent opened Maidstone's £2.5 million St Peter's Bridge today, almost 99 years to the day after the first one had been built on this spot to span the River Medway. He then formally handed it over to Kent County Council and crossed the 61 metre span to see the new riverside walk.

Sir John Howard, chairman of the company which completed the bridge a month ahead of schedule, said his builders had found it difficult working in such a busy town. "Indeed", he said, "we found some of the problems here greater than those we had to cope with on the Humber Bridge — and that is the longest in the world."

The Duke, who arrived in a helicopter of the Queen's Flight, was welcomed by Lord Astor of Hever, Lord Lieutenant of Kent and the Bishop of Maidstone, the Rt Rev Richard Third, who dedicated the bridge. He then dined at County Hall, becoming the first royal visitor to be entertained there.

November 25th: *Gas board officials are investigating explosions which destroyed two homes in Maidstone and Rochester within weeks of each other. In one incident a man died and, in the other, a grandfather and two children had remarkable escapes. The first occurred on November 3rd when Bill Welch, 34, of Charles Street, Maidstone, was buried under tons of rubble following an enormous explosion which destroyed his 19th century terraced home. A next-door neighbour was pulled to safety by fireman but Mr Welch died six days later in the West Kent Hospital.*

The second explosion (see above) occurred yesterday in St Margaret's Street, Rochester. Mr Albert Green was thrown clear by the blast and his grandson Kenny Adams, aged eight, found his own way out, but his grand-daughter, Nicola, 7, was trapped under rubble in her bedroom before being pulled clear by firemen. A spokesman for Segas said: "For explosions of this magnitude there would have been a massive build up of gas."

January 8th: The Khmer Rouge regime in Cambodia has been crushed by Vietnamese forces supported by tanks and fighter planes. Troops have occupied the capital Phnom Penh.

January 16th: The Shah of Iran was driven into exile today by supporters of the Ayatollah Khomeini who has masterminded the downfall of the "Peacock Throne". It is believed that the Shah has flown to Egypt.

February 2nd: Sid Vicious, former member of the group, The Sex Pistols, has died in hospital of a drug overdose.

February 12th: Hundreds of schools in Kent were closed today because of a heating oil shortage caused by the lorry drivers' strike.

February 14th: A peace pact, dubbed the St Valentine's Day Agreement, has been sealed between the Labour Government and the unions. In Parliament James Callaghan has set out long-term plans for reducing inflation. Margaret Thatcher has called it a "boneless wonder".

March 2nd: Referendum results announced today show that devolution is dead. Neither Wales nor Scotland want a mini-parliament.

March 17th: Wales defeated England 27-3 at Cardiff today to clinch the Rugby Union Triple Crown for the fourth successive year and the championship for the second year running. The victory capped a superb decade for Wales.

March 26th: After four major wars and more than 30 years of hostility, Israel and Egypt today signed a peace treaty.

March 28th: The Labour Party has been forced out of office by a single vote. Soon after the Tories won a "no confidence" vote, Mrs Thatcher demanded Parliament's quick dissolution. Mr Callaghan has said: "We shall take our case to the country." *See page 34*

A fascinating book detailing the precise layout of the Lullingstone

May 12th: Miss Anne Roper, the Queen of Romney Marsh, has become the first woman President of the County Society — the Association of Kentish Men and Men of Kent and Fair Maids of Kent. This lively lady is an expert on the history of the Marsh, the driving force behind many projects and a brilliant lecturer on Kentish inns, the Cinque Ports, smuggling, local churches and archaeological studies.

Roman Villa, which was 'rediscovered' in 1949, has been published the by Kent Archaelogical Society. The villa stands on the banks of the River Darent and dates from AD 90, probably at one time as the home of a native farmer.

March 30th: Airey Neave, Tory MP and an aide to Mrs Thatcher, was killed today by a terrorist bomb planted under his car.

April 4th: Zulfikar Ali Bhutto, desposed Premier of Pakistan, has been hanged.

April 24th: A 54-year-old Methodist Bishop, Abel Muzorewa, will become Rhodesia's first black Prime Minister.

Alan Knott and Paul Downton will share the wicket-keeping duties for Kent — Knott for the first half of the season and Downton for the second.

May 12th: Arsenal beat Manchester United 3-2 in the FA Cup Final today.

May 29th: All DC10 airliners in Britain were grounded today following the disaster in Chicago four days ago when the wing of an aircraft was ripped off during takeoff. 273 people died in the worst crash in American history.

May 30th: Nottingham Forest today won the European Cup against Swedish champions Malmo.

June 11th: Marion Morrison, better known as John Wayne or "The Duke", has lost his last battle. The American actor died today of cancer aged 72.

June 18th: The leaders of the world's two most powerful nations, Jimmy Carter and Leonid Brezhnev, today signed an arms limitation treaty.

June 22nd: Jeremy Thorpe's long ordeal ended today when a jury found him not guilty of plotting to murder Norman Scott.

July 15th: The Queen Mother has visited the British Legion Village near Maidstone to open new flats for the elderly. A few weeks ago the Queen opened a new headquarters in Chatham for Lloyds of London.

August 9th: A special area for naturist swimmers has been opened on Brighton beach.

August 14th: The Fastnet international sailing race was hit by savage Atlantic storms today. At least 25 of the 330 yachts between the southern Irish coast and Cornwall were sunk or disabled. Lifeboats, trawlers and

tugs joined with helicopters in a huge rescue in Force 11 hurricane winds. They saved 125 yachtsmen but it is believed that 14 yachtsmen died.

August 15th: Sebastian Coe today ran the 1500 metres in the record time of 3 minutes 32.1 seconds. He now holds three world records.

September: Kent CC, needing to win their last match against Middlesex at Canterbury to become John Player champions, lost by 55 runs.

September 2nd: The "Yorkshire Ripper" today claimed his 12th victim with the brutal murder of a girl student from Bradford.

October 2nd: Rotary International of Great Britain and Ireland (RIBI) has presented Dover with a new lifeboat.

November 9th: Four men have been found guilty of murdering newspaper boy Carl Bridgewater.

November 21st: Sir Anthony Blunt, the Queen's distinguished art adviser, has been named as the "fourth man" in the Burgess, MacLean and Philby affair. He has now been stripped of his knighthood. *See page 34*

November 22nd: Building societies have put the mortgage rate up to a record 15 per cent.

East Kent firemen were airlifted from Lydd to fight a massive blaze on the Swedish cargo ship *MV Birkaland*.

December 7th: Lord Soames has been named as transitional Governor of Rhodesia.

December 10th: Mother Teresa of Calcutta has been awarded the Nobel Peace Prize for her work with the poor of India. She has been described as a "living saint".

GREAT HITS OF 1979

We Don't Talk Anymore
Bright Eyes
Heart of Glass

With the death this year of the lovable, eccentric comedienne, Joyce Grenfell, a curious and remarkable alliance has come to light.

For 22 years Miss Grenfell has been writing to, and receiving letters from, Katharine Moore, the novelist who moved from Sevenoaks to Shoreham in 1960. The two women were the best of friends — but by mutual agreement they never met!

The invisible friendship began in 1957 when Joyce Grenfell made disparaging remarks on the radio about a poem written by the Oxford professor, Walter

Great friends — but they've never met

Raleigh.

Katharine read English at Oxford and, recalling the true worth of her brilliant tutor, she defended him mightily in a long letter to Miss Grenfell who replied immediately.

The 59-year-old writer and the 47-year-old revue artiste, renowned for her quirky monologues on the oddities of human behaviour, began to exchange letters on a regular basis. The two ladies, both from comfortable middle-class families, with so much in

Katharine Moore

common, became firm friends.

Katharine Moore, who was one of Oxford's first women undergraduates, wrote an enchanting children's book in 1936 called *Moog* and, many years later, published *Cordial Relations*, the story of her maiden aunt who was also her nanny. It became a best seller.

Joyce Grenfell established a reputation in revue before the war and, by 1954, was touring the world with her own one-woman two hour show.

January 9th: Memories of the winter of 1947 when blizzard conditions were accompanied by power cuts, rationing and hardship, have been dramatically revived. The winter of 1979 is on course to emulate those grim days.

This week the Isle of Sheppey has been cut off by deep snow drifts. De-icing trains and snowploughs have battled all night to clear the Maidstone to Ashford line and road transport throughout the county is paralysed.

The snow which arrived on December 30th, followed by a surge of bitter air from Scandinavia, has already claimed the life of an elderly man who abandoned his car near Stalisfield Green and went off through deep, powdery snow in search of help.

He was found dead next morning near a telephone box.

Kent grinds to a standstill in this 'winter of discontent'

January 12th: Streets piled with rubbish and dustbins overflowing. Hospitals turning patients away. Food shortages. Bumper to bumper road chaos. Hundreds of workers laid off. Sports fixtures cancelled.

As the lorry drivers' strike takes a stranglehold on industry this is the state of much of Kent today. Nationally it is known as "the winter of discontent".

To add to the growing disruption there has been a two-day rail strike by ASLEF; in fact the only rail service running in the whole of Britain on January 6th was the Romney, Hythe and Dymchurch light railway which was under contract to take students to school at Southlands. Today, ambulancemen and council workers are threatening more disruption.

Union leaders have told James Callaghan, the Prime Minister, they cannot curb many of the widespread and unofficial strikes which have erupted in the past two months in

protest against the five per cent limit on pay rises.

Two hundred workers at Canning Town Glass Works on the Isle of Sheppey have already been laid off. More than 1,500 workers at Kimberly Clark, Larkfield face the same threat. Dockyard pickets, refusing to let out essential supplies of animal feed, have put 170,000 chickens at Harrietsham under the death sentence. 8,000 Kent lorry drivers are backing the TGWU strike call. Kent's docks and all Medway wharves are being picketed. Kent's papermakers are feeling the pinch as there is little indigenous pulp in the UK. Ferries are overloaded.

On top of all this schools have closed at Gravesham, Medway, Swale, Dover, Thanet and Tunbridge Wells.

Kent CBI chairman, Mr Jeremy Leigh-Pemberton, says that the situation is getting so desperate that more closures and short-time working are only a few days away.

Bedgebury murder case: Kent police search for clues

A woman's body, battered beyond recognition and discovered on a remote bridle path at Bedgebury Forest, Goudhurst, is presenting Kent police with the most baffling murder case they've ever known.

The woman was found by three horse riders in the 3,000-acre forest on the afternoon of October 23rd and a post mortem revealed she may have been dead for up to three days. It also revealed that she was six weeks pregnant, had at least one child and had been brutally killed by repeated blows to the head with a blunt instrument.

Although no attempt had been made to hide her body, the murderer left no clues to help identify her or her attacker. More than 100 policemen combed the area for several days. Frogmen searched the lake in the nearby Pinetum but no handbag, shoes or jewellery were found.

Two months after the gruesome discovery, Det Supt Brian Kendall and his murder hunt team are no wiser. "All the time you have an undentified body you have a motiveless murder", he said. "The case is unique but the inquiry will not close."

One theory is that the victim worked on a local farm and may have left at the end of the picking season. More than 700 farms in 24 surrounding parishes have been visited — to no avail. *See page 57.*

Kate Bush — first single, first number one!

Coggan retires

October 8th: On his 70th birthday, Dr Donald Coggan has announced that he will retire at the end of the year as Archbishop of Canterbury. He will be succeeded in January by the Rt Rev Robert Runcie, Bishop of St Albans.

Ladies cricket game washed out

June 13th: Sue Goatman from Hastingsleigh, captain of the England women's cricket team had the disppointment of seeing the one-day international against the West Indies at Mote Park today abandoned without a ball being bowled. Kent's Mary Pilling was also included in the England team.

The teams are hoping for better luck this weekend when when they meet in their first Test Match in this country at Canterbury.

Kate rewrites Brontë to reach number one

The giant recording company EMI is pretty pleased with Dave Gilmour of the pop group Pink Floyd. Recently he recommended they give a contract to Kate Bush, a 20-year-old Kent girl with a unique vocal style.

Having secured the deal, Kate's first single, *Wuthering Heights,* has gone straight to number one and producers at EMI are ecstatic. The Brontë novel, condensed to three minutes, is considered to be one of the most original records ever produced by a UK female singer.

Kate Bush, the talented daughter of a doctor, was born in Plumstead in July 1958 and became a most competent singer and composer. This has been amply proved with her album *The Kick Inside* and her second single *The Man With The Child in His Eyes.* She is certainly no 'one hit wonder'.

Hythe's biennial Venetian Festival held on the Military Canal and watched by thousands of people has been another great success. It is a reminder of the days when the sea was close at hand and brought the town mediaeval prosperity.

IRA bomb kills Lord Mountbatten and two members of the Brabourne family

August 28th: Britain, and especially the county of Kent, is in mourning. The IRA bomb which exploded in the quiet fishing village of Mullaghmore, County Sligo yesterday, killing Earl Mountbatten of Burma, his grandson, Nicholas aged 14 and a 17-year-old boatman, has now claimed the life of the Dowager Lady Brabourne who died in hospital of her injuries.

Lord Mountbatten's daughter, Lady Brabourne and her son Timothy — Nicholas's twin brother — are said to be critical in an intensive care ward. Lord Brabourne is out of intensive care but has both legs and a wrist broken.

"Dickie" Mountbatten was Prince Philip's uncle, the Queen's cousin and mentor to Prince Charles. The Royal Family is said to be in deep shock.

It was mid-morning when Earl Mountbatten and members of his family drove from their Irish home, Classiebawn

Castle, down to the harbour to set out for a day's fishing. Their boat had hardly left the harbour when it was ripped apart by the IRA bomb. The statesman who held a unique position in the British establishment died immediately. So did his grandson.

The IRA have claimed responsibility for what they call "the execution of Lord Louis Mountbatten".

Villagers of Brabourne, Smeeth and Mersham are keeping vigil around their radio or TV sets for the latest news of the survivors, Lady Brabourne and her son Timothy, whom they know so well.

Today they recalled how Lord Brabourne came back from the war, in which he had spent the last years as ADC to Lord Mountbatten in the Far East, to take over a somewhat run-down estate.

The family's great house at Mersham le Hatch had fallen

continued from previous page

into disrepair following the death of his father in Bombay where he was Governor. So the young Lord Brabourne, who succeeded his brother who was killed trying to escape from an Italian POW camp, went to live in the Black House just outside Hatch Park. It was there in 1946 that he took his young bride, Patricia, daughter of Lord Mountbatten.

The Queen, then Princess Elizabeth and third cousin to Mountbatten, stayed with them in their comparatively humble home. The villagers were proud of their connection with the Royal Family.

Seven children were born to the Brabournes and the elder, Norton, is due to marry Penelope Eastwood next month with Prince Charles as his best man. His brothers and sisters are Michael, Joanna, Amanda, Philip and twins Nicholas and Timothy who were caught in the tragedy.

Doctors said today that the next few days will be critical for Lady Brabourne. She has serious chest injuries and may lose the sight of one eye. Timothy had a major operation as soon as he reached hospital which surgeons said was 100 per cent successful. However, he too has serious chest injuries.

Thousands of friends across Kent are praying for them. Lady Brabourne is well-known throughout Kent. She is a JP and Deputy Lieutenant of the county — and takes a great interest in Ashford School at which both her daughters were pupils.

Under a special licence from the Queen, Earl Mountbatten's title and arms pass to Lady Brabourne. She is now Countess Mountbatten and her son Norton, now 31, becomes Lord Romsey, another of Earl Mountbatten's titles.

The funerals of the Dowager Lady Brabourne and Nicholas will be held at Mersham Church on Thursday. Interment will be in the Brabourne vault.

See page 69

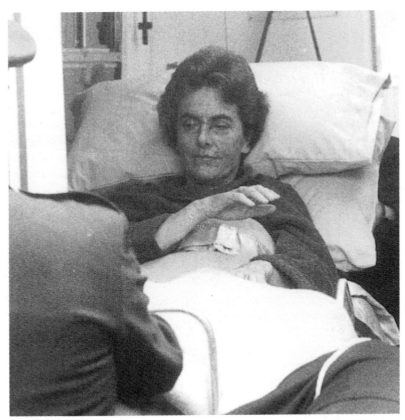

October 2nd: *Lord and Lady Brabourne leave the King Edward VII Hospital for Officers in London five weeks after they were injured in the terrorist bomb. They will convalesce at their home in Mersham.*

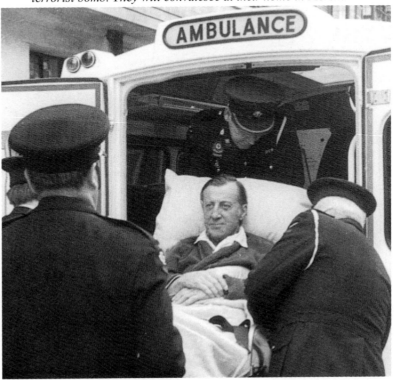

Maggie takes over but there's no job for Ted

May 4th: Margaret Thatcher is Britain's first woman Prime Minister. The triumphant 53-year-old Tory MP for Finchley, quoting from St Francis of Assisi, said yesterday afternoon: "Where there is discord may we bring harmony — where there is despair may we bring hope."

Mrs Thatcher, who has lived in Kent for many years, promised she would transform the British economic and industrial climate. She has a clear mandate to do so for the final tally shows that the Tories have 339 seats with Labour 269 and Liberals 11 — and that represents a difference of two million votes between the major parties.

There is no place for Edward Heath in her new team. She offered him the job of British Ambassador in Washington but he has refused, saying he wants to be close to British politics.

However, a considerable number of Kent MPs have top jobs. John Stanley (Tonbridge and Malling) is the new Minister for Housing. "I can think of no more challenging or worthwhile responsibility or an area where there are more important needs and aspirations to be met," he said.

Ashford's Keith Speed takes over as Under Secretary (Navy) in the Ministry of Defence, a surprise appointment for he was heavily tipped for a Home Office job.

This is a big appointment for the former Royal Navy Reserve lieutenant commander. "Now to quote from Gilbert and Sullivan", he joked, "I am the ruler of the Queen's Navy."

Patrick Mayhew (Tunbridge Wells) is one of the new Parliamentary Under Secretaries and Peter Rees (Dover and Deal) is a Treasury Under Secretary.

All 15 Kent seats are now occupied by Tories, mostly with big majorities. Peggy Fenner (Rochester and Chatham) returns to Westminister with a comfortable 2,688 majority over Bob Bean; newcomer Robert Dunn has taken Dartford from Sydney Irving.

Liberal candidates have taken second place in two constituencies — Maidstone and Folkestone and Hythe. The county's 14 National Front candidates made no significant impact on the poll anywhere.

Mrs Thatcher, clearly in a jubilant mood, said tonight that she "feels an aura of calm". The TUC don't agree. "Keep your hands off the unions", they have warned her. "Persecution begets resistance." *See page 43*

December 18th: From his home in Moscow, Donald Maclean spoke to a Sevenoaks Chronicle *reporter this week about his previous life in Tatsfield and Westerham.*

THE WESTERHAM SPY

December: **The recent news that the Queen's distinguished art adviser, Anthony Blunt, was the "fourth man" in the Burgess, Maclean and Philby defection affair has shocked Buckingham Palace who have stripped Blunt of his knighthood.**

It has also resurrected another previously well-kept secret concerning Donald Maclean who lived at Tatsfield near Westerham until his sudden "disappearance" in June 1951.

Maclean, then aged 38, was head of the American department of the Foreign Office and a diplomat with access to much vital information.

It is now known that he frequently used the dark room at the back of Ernest White's bric-a-brac shop in Westerham to develop photographs of "sensitive" documents. He visited the shop on several occasions. No questions were asked and no-one knew the seriousness of the mission.

Within a few weeks Maclean and Burgess were in Russia and confirmed undercover Soviet spies.

'It is often said that the railway made Ashford. It would also be true to say that, given the production record of its railwaymen, that Ashford made the railway' — local author Vic Mitchell.

January 3rd: More than one quarter of Kent's married women now go out to work and the figure for Britain as a whole is considerably higher. It is the highest of any Common Market country, the jobs mainly being in the service sector.

January 18th: Sir Cecil Beaton, chief photographer of *The Vogue* and royal portrait painter, died at his home in Wiltshire aged 72.

February 13th: Sixpenny pieces will cease to be legal tender after June 30th.

March 4th: Robert Mugabe, aged 52, is Prime Minister of the new state of Zimbabwe.

March 16th: Britain's Alan Minter has won the world middle-weight boxing championship.

March 25th: Britain has decided not to boycott the Olympic Games in Moscow this summer in response to the Sovier invasion of Afghanistan. The Americans will not be sending a team.

March 25th: Robert Runcie, the Bishop of St Albans for the last ten years, has been enthroned as Archbishop of Canterbury in succession to Donald Coggan.

March 27th: An oil platform used as a floating hotel for North Sea rig workers collapsed today with half of the 200 men aboard feared dead.

April 29th: Sir Alfred Hitchcock, who was knighted just four months ago, died today aged 80. Hitchcock directed the first British "talkie" in 1929 and went to Hollywood where he won an Academy Award for *Rebecca*. He was given his first job by the late Sir Michael Balcon who then lived at Henden Manor, Ide Hill.

April 30th: Three gunmen have seized 20 hostages at the Iranian embassy and demand freedom for 91 Arabs in Iran.

May 5th: The SAS made a spectacular assault on the Iranian Embassy in Knightsbridge tonight and rescued the surviving 19

The Saxons came this way

The Saxon Shore Way — a 140-mile long walk from Gravesend round the Kent coast to Hastings — has been opened to the delight of ramblers and all those interested in the maritime history of the county.

This long-distance path offers walkers an unrivalled diversity of scenes, from the wide expanses of the marshland bordering the Thames and Medway Estuary to the white cliffs of Dover, as well as panoramic views over Romney Marsh and the escarpment that marks the ancient coastline between Hythe and Rye.

The Saxon Shore Way links the Roman forts constructed as a defence from Saxon invaders. It crosses the north Kent marshes and runs through the Dicken's villages. Its course takes the pathway alongside the Swale, through Whitstable and Reculver and then the former Wantsum shoreline to Richborough.

hostages. Four of the five gunmen have been killed.

May 10th: Second division West Ham have beaten Arsenal 1-0 in the FA Cup Final.

May 16th: Inflation has risen to 21.8 per cent.

June 4th: BBC musicians strike in protest at the Corporation's plans to axe five orchestras.

June 6th: The Queen Mother took the salute today as the band of the Royal Corps of Transport led the Dunkirk veterans in a march-past at Ramsgate to mark the 40th anniversary of the "great deliverance".

June 12th: Over ten million people in East Africa are threatened by famine. Aid organisations say it is the worst ever known.

Sir Billy Butlin, who opened his first holiday camp in Skegness in 1932, has died aged 80. There are several Butlin hotels in East Kent.

British soccer supporters rioted today in Turin during England's opening match in the European Championship. Play was halted and about 100 youths were later charged. Manager Ron Greenwood spoke of his shame.

June 14th: Unemployment now stands at 1.6 million, the highest since the war. It is still rising.

July 5th: Bjorn Borg, the Swedish tennis ace, today won his fifth successive men's singles title at Wimbledon.

July 24th: Peter Sellers, the brilliant comedian with a gift for mimicry, died today.

August 3rd: Britain's athletes have won four gold medals in the

Olympic Games. The successful four are Allan Wells, Daley Thompson, Steve Ovett and Sebastian Coe.

August 18th: French fishermen have blocked Channel ports in a protest over subsidies. More than 1,500 British holidaymakers are trapped in France.

September 2nd: John Arlott, the most famous of cricket commentators, has retired after describing the last day's play in the Centenary Test Match at Lords.

October 1st: It was announced today that the London *Evening News* which circulates widely in Kent will cease publication at the end of the month.

October 3rd: Council tenants are now allowed to buy their own homes. This follows the passing of the Housing Act.

October 15th: Jim Callaghan has retired as leader of the Labour Party. Michael Foot will be his successor.

October 22nd: Lord Thomson who acquired *The Times* from Lord Astor says the newspaper and its sister *The Sunday Times* will close next year unless sold.

October 23rd: Steven Edwards, 25, a hospital porter, has been jailed for life for the murder of Nika Mina in the William Harvey Hospital, Ashford, on December 16th, 1979.

November 4th: The Republican candidate Ronald Reagan and his running mate George Bush have trounced President Carter and Walter Mondale in the US presidential elections.

December 28th: Southern TV, which has a studio at Dover, has lost its IBA franchise. The new company covering the south will be called TVS.

GREAT HITS OF 1980

Woman in Love

Don't Stand So Close to Me

Graham Sutherland was England's leading painter

February 21st: Graham Sutherland, 76, of The White House, Trottiscliffe, was buried today in the churchyard of the small Kent village where he has lived since 1937. Described by many as "England's leading painter" he specialised in paintings of Welsh scenery which he interpeted in a semi-abstract manner.

An interest in Christian art and symbolism resulted in the great tapestry of *Christ in Glory* above the altar of Coventry Cathedral.

As a vivid portraitist he was well-known for a picture that no longer exists — his strikingly powerful 80th birthday portrait of Winston Churchill which made the great man and his wife very unhappy. Lady Churchill ordered it to be destroyed which Lord Clark the art historian of Saltwood Castle described as "an act unparalleled vandalism".

Sutherland, well-known in Trottiscliffe and surrounding villages, was always elegantly dressed and possessed immense charm. He married Kathleen Frances in 1927 and they were a devoted and inseparable couple until his death on Sunday.

The thin blue line. Policemen put their shoulders into it at Grain.

Police and pickets clash in the Battle of Grain

May 30th: Grain Power Station was turned into a battleground this week as 600 police officers clashed violently with more than 400 pickets.

The dispute concerns the decision to lay off 27 pipe laggers after a pay wrangle and employ "blacklegs" in their place.

Pickets representing two unions arrived from places as far away as Leeds and Liverpool early in the morning. Violence quickly erupted as stones and placards were hurled at coaches taking workers onto the site. Massed police ranks held firm and several arrests were made.

The dispute has finally killed off plans for the biggest oil-fired power station in Europe. It is feared the Grain Power Station is doomed and more than 2,000 jobs will be lost in another vast industrial setback for the beleaguered Medway Towns.

Mr Tim Brinton, MP for Gravesend, has unsuccessfully called for an emergency debate in the House of Commons. ***See page 72***

Charles to marry former Sevenoaks schoolgirl ?

September: Those close to the Royal Family are predicting that Lady Diana Spencer, a former pupil of West Heath School, Sevenoaks, could soon be the wife of Prince Charles. The couple have been seen together on numerous occasions and royal watchers say an "announcement is imminent".

If the couple do marry, Charles will not be bringing his wife to Chevening, the stately home near Sevenoaks. The Prince of Wales took possession of the house in 1974 after the death of Lord Stanhope, who had bequeathed his magnificent house to the nation. Now he has decided that he would prefer to live in the country, away from London and a busy motorway. His rejection of Chevening allows the Prime Minister to nominate a cabinet minister for occupancy.

The photograph (right) of 19-year-old Lady Diana with some of the nursery children in her care has already been syndicated round the world.

She is the daughter of Earl Spencer and, with her two sisters, was a pupil at West Heath a few years ago. It was during a break in her O levels in 1977 that she attended a shoot at Althorp and caught Prince Charles' eye.

News of the couple's romance spread like wildfire round her old school this week. The headmistress, Ruth Rudge, remembered her as a "lovely, lovely girl — but not a model pupil. No girls are".

At West Heath she enjoyed dancing in the gym and practising her already excellent diving. She won cups for games and was one of only a handful of girls to win a cup for service to the school. She was also a

member of the Sevenoaks Voluntary Service Unit and frequently worked with disadvantaged people out of school hours.

Her former schoolfriends remember her best for her terrific dancing. She was good at jiving, rock n' roll, the Charleston and ballet but most of all they envied her for her friendship with

Prince Andrew.

Her older sister, Sarah, now married to Lincolnshire farmer Neil McCorquodale, was one of two girls suspended for three weeks from West Heath for drinking whisky, gin and sherry. She also went out with Prince Charles after leaving school and introduced him to Diana. *See page 43*

Prince Charles is not the only member of the Royal Family in the news. It has just been announced from Buckingham Palace that Her Majesty the Queen Mother is the new Lord Warden of the Cinque Ports, succeeding the late Sir Robert Menzies. The group of ports — Hastings, New Romney, Hythe, Dover, Sandwich, Winchelsea and Rye — retain a ceremonial identity, although their practical function in providing a royal fleet each for the defence of the realm ended long ago. The Queen Mother, who is 80 in August, has already enjoyed a few early birthday celebrations including a party given by the National Trust at Knole, Sevenoaks, on June 25th. It was notable on two counts — the radiance of the principal guest and for the heavy snow that fell!

Motorway route 'will destroy the Valley of Vision'

April: A determined and vociferous battle to prevent a section of the M25 orbital motorway round London being constructed over the North Downs and close to the beautiful Darenth Valley, Shoreham, looks certain now to end in failure.

Mr George Dobry, a Government inspector who last year conducted an 18-week inquiry into the proposed route between Sevenoaks and Swanley, has ruled in favour of the Department of Transport.

Dandag, the Darenth Valley and North Downs Action Group, which protested against the section now says it will appeal and, if necessary, take its case to the High Court. The group argues that the road is unnecessary as the M26 to Wrotham and the M20 onto Swanley will provide a less harmful and less expensive alternative.

The battle began in 1977 when Dandag enrolled environmentalists from all over the country to prevent "this crude, bludgeoning and devastating attack on what is a National Park". Members said the proposed link would desecrate Samuel Palmer's Valley of Vision.

A fighting fund was launched. A painting by Graham Sutherland sold in print form throughout the world and raised thousands of pounds. By March 1978 Dandag had more than 1,000 members and were convinced they could overturn the inquiry result on environmental grounds.

During the inquiry, between September 1978 and March 1979, there were several small skirmishes. One man

continued on page 39

November 22nd: Norman Fowler, Minister of Transport and Mark Wolfson, MP for Sevenoaks on the newly-opened M26 which runs from Wrotham to Sevenoaks. Motorway construction has been a dominant factor in the life of the Sevenoaks and Dartford villages since local residents first realised that the London orbital route (M25) was going right through their district. The route between Godstone and Sevenoaks was opened in November last year by Mr Fowler with the minimum of protest. This was followed by the Chevening interchange and then, this week, by the M26 which caught many by surprise with its lack of access roads to or from the east.

M25 orbital route

continued

chained himself to a pillar in Swanley where the inquiry was held. The opposition claimed that the inquiry was a *fait accompli* and pointed to a bridge close to the A20 at Swanley which had already been erected in readiness for the road from Sevenoaks.

It was all to no avail. Mr Dobry has approved the 8.6 mile route close to the A21. It will follow the line of Polhill, then branch off near Shepherd's Barn Valley and to the West of Lullingstone Park.

Dandag says the decision marks a black day in British planning history, called it a major scandal and immediately appealed against the decision. ***See page 84***

Another tunnel under the Thames

May: When the long-awaited Dartford to Purfleet tunnel was opened in 1963 traffic analysts predicted that two million vehicles a year would use the 4,700 foot long tunnel under the River Thames.

How wrong they were. By the end of the first year that figure had already doubled and, in 1972, a second tunnel was commissioned.

Officially opened this month it has not come a moment too soon, for the Ministry of Transport is predicting up to 65,000 vehicles per day will be using the tunnel. Even that figure is disputed. Motoring organisations say the figure will be nearer 80,000. ***See page 128***

Private enterprise means all change on the buses

October 6th: Olsen Coaches of Strood has become one of the first firms to operate under the 1980 Transport Act, introduced by the Thatcher Government to promote free market forces and private enterprise.

Other Kent firms entering what many predict to be a highly competitive market include Smith's Coaches of Sittingbourne, Swinards of Ashford, Regent of Whitstable, Nu-Venture Coaches of Maidstone and Fuggles of Benenden.

Maidstone and District has introduced an Invictaway network for a group of limited stop services between Medway and London.

More independent commuter services are being introduced throughout the county although most of the operators know that there is an increasing decline in the demand for public transport. In most communities it is now more of a social and political issue.

December 13th: Among those mourning the death of John Lennon who was shot outside his home in New York on Monday morning is Mrs Millie Sutcliffe, mother of the fifth Beatle, who now lives in Dartford Road, Sevenoaks.

Stuart Sutcliffe, who died tragically at the age of 22, was in the band's original line-up and a close friend of John during the early years.

When some of the Beatles were still at school Mrs Sutcliffe's home in Sefton Park, Liverpool, was used for practice sessions and she remembers Paul McCartney singing into a microphone held up by a broomstick. Mrs Sutcliffe said: "Stuart attended the same art college as John and they were great friends until his death. I last saw John after the Beatles' final live concert at the Liverpool Empire. He came to my home and was in a marvellous frame of mind, relaxed, friendly, courteous — absolutely delightful and not at all concerned that the Beatles were disbanding."

Mark Chapman, aged 25, has been charged with the murder of Lennon. Police say he stalked the ex-Beatle for three days before carrying out the shooting.

Ambulancemen extract bodies from the smouldering remains of the Douglas Invader

Daredevil pilot blamed for death crash

September 15th: Seven people were killed on Saturday when an aerobatic stunt at Biggin Hill's 40th anniversary Battle of Britain display went terribly wrong.

A Second World War Douglas Invader bomber, piloted by 41-year-old Don Bullock, crashed into the hillside beyond the airfield after failing to pull out of a barrel roll. On board were four British passengers and two American servicemen.

It has emerged that Captain Bullock, renowned as a daredevil pilot, asked the organisers for an early take-off. He wanted more time to perform a barrel roll in front of 40,000 spectators — a stunt he had performed only once before in the 37-year-old Invader, which was registered in America for survey work only. His request was refused.

Witnesses described how, two minutes into the eight-minute display, the pilot began the fatal roll and then appeared to hesitate. The bomber nose-dived and crashed just yards from a row of houses in Oaklands Road, Biggin Hill.

Friends of Don Bullock explained today that the pilot was upset by the refusal to be allowed extra time for the barrel roll but pointed out that once he was strapped in his plane and the engines were running he was a master of his own destiny. There will be an inquiry and inquest.

'Does the Secretary of State believe that the people of Rochester and Chatham elected me to support a Government that would do this to their dockyard?' — Peggy Fenner MP in the House of Commons.

January 18th: Ten people have died and more than 30 injured by a firebomb thrown into a West Indian party at Deptford.

January 21st: US hostages taken by Iranians who stormed the US Embassy in Teheran have been released in Algiers.

January 25th: Four former cabinet ministers — Roy Jenkins, William Rodgers, David Owen and Shirley Williams— have formed a new radical party designed to change the face of British politics. In what is known as the Limehouse Declaration the breakaway Gang of Four calls for a classless crusade for social justice.

January 27th: Rupert Murdoch will soon be the new owner of *The Times*. He has been allowed to go ahead without the investigation usually required by the Monopolies Commission.

February 18th: In a bid to avoid the kind of head-on clash that brought down the Heath Government, Mrs Thatcher has promised more state money for the coal mines. The plan to close up to 50 pits with the loss of 30,000 jobs has not been amended.

February 24th: The Prince of Wales is to marry the beautiful Lady Diana Spencer. Yesterday he invited the Press to chat to him and his bride-to-be at Buckingham Palace.

March 23rd: Mike Hailwood, winner of nine world motorbike championships and 14 TT titles on the Isle of Man, was killed today in a motorcar accident near his home in Warwickshire. His nine year old daughter also died.

March 26th: In a new book called *Their Trade is Treachery* author Chapman Pincher has claimed that the former head of MI5, Sir Roger Hollis, was in fact a "mole" for the KCB.

March 30th: President Reagan was shot in the chest today in an assassination attempt. He is in hospital in a stable condition.

Peggy Fenner, MP for Rochester and Chatham who was outraged by the decision to close Chatham Dockyard.
See page 46

Alan Ealham who led Kent to the top of the County Championship in 1978 has been sacked as captain of Kent. His place is taken by Asif Iqbal.

April 3rd: Vicountess Monckton of Brenchley was sworn in today as the first woman High Sheriff of Kent. The ceremony took place in the Chapel of St Augustine at Tonbridge School when four of the Vicountess's five children were present, along with 400 guests.The High Sheriff is responsible for the judiciary. She will welcome High Court judges to the county, sit in courts and visit prisons, remand homes and borstals. She lives with her farmer-husband at Harrietsham.

April 4th: The South London streets of Brixton were turned into a battleground tonight as hundreds of youths, black and white, rioted. It was the second successive night of violence.

April 11th: Bobby Sands, a convicted IRA terrorist, close to death after a 42-day hunger strike, has won the South Tyrone and Fermanagh by-election.

April 20th: A ginger-headed youth from South London, Steve Davis, has astounded the snooker world by winning the world title at the age of 23.

May 8th: Ken Livingstone has been elected leader of the Greater London Council.

May 22nd: Peter Sutcliffe, known as the Yorkshire Ripper, was jailed for life today for killing 13 women during a four-year reign of terror.

June 20th: 500 youths have rioted in South London's Peckham.

June 29th: "Tiny" Rowland has been given the go-ahead to buy *The Observer*.

July 13th: In the worst outbreak of civil unrest this century, youths have rioted in Brixton, Bristol and Toxteth and, this weekend, in four other British cities. Right-wing Tory back-benchers blame all the riots on the black community.

August 17th: England have retained the Ashes with another victory against Australia to go 3-1 up in the series.

August 24th: Mark Chapman, aged 25, has been jailed for life for murdering John Lennon.

September 17th: It was announced today that London's Royal Docks are to close which means the end of the capital as a major world port.

October 6th: President Anwar Sadat of Egypt was assassinated today by four armed men.

November 12th: The Church of England's General Synod has voted to admit women to Holy Orders as deacons.

November 18th: England today beat Hungary 1-0 to qualify for the World Cup Finals in 1982.

December: The forgotten British athletes, Harold Abrahams and Eric Liddell, (who was at college in Eltham), are the heroes of a new film released this year called *Chariots of Fire*.

GREAT HITS OF 1981

Under Pressure

Let's Groove

Breaking Away

'This boy is not the murderer' — say villagers

Grave doubts about the validity of the conviction of an 18-year-old youth for the murder of a 79-year-old spinster in Pluckley last year follow a recent television reconstruction of the case.

Gwendoline Marshall was found dead in her garden shed at Enfield Lodge on March 8th 1980. Her hands were tied behind her back and her head had been struck several times with a blunt instrument.

Peter Luckhurst, who knew Miss Marshall and visited her often, at first admitted to the murder but — during the trial in June — said police had put him under pressure. He claimed he had discovered the body but as he had been in trouble with the police for a series of petty thefts, thought it best to walk away.

Pluckley villagers rushed to defend the youth saying the boy and the wealthy, reclusive old lady had a warm regard for each other.

Forensic tests, however, proved the case against Luckhurst to be impregnable and he was sentenced to be detained during Her Majesty's pleasure.

The Defence Committee is now trying to reopen the case by seeking the help of local MPs. They feel that Luckhurst may have been an accomplice but was definitely not the murderer. *See page 127*

Silver City's goodbye to Lydd Airport

October 31st: All efforts to save Ferryfield Airport at Lydd have failed. The one-time home of Silver City Airways which was opened in 1954 as one of the world's busiest airports has closed — and no-one seems to know what the future holds.

The 345-acre site with two runways and a two-storey terminal building has handled thousands of flights and hundreds of tons of cargo. In its heyday there were more than 200 crossings to France each day.

Recently there was a plan to introduce an air, road transport and leisure development at Lydd but the backers pulled out after many talks with Silver City.

At nearby Lympne, where the famous airport closed in 1954, evidence of its wartime usage is limited to the 1942 control tower and a few huts. The post-war airfield is more in evidence where light aircraft still fly. Port Lympne, once the officer's mess, is now part of Howletts Zoo Park and Wildlife Sanctuary.

January 30th: The Who, one of the country's most famous rock bands, were held up at Biggin Hill by fog yesterday en route to a pop concert in their private plane. The boys, who don't seem in the least concerned about their enforced delay, were once well established as the "number three" group behind the Beatles and Rolling Stones in the vanguard of Britain's rock music. The four are Pete Townshend, Roger Daltrey, John Entwistle and drummer Kenny Jones who replaced Keith Moon when he died from a drug overdose.

Diana and her Prince are married

July 29th: Lady Diana Spencer, the former West Heath, Sevenoaks schoolgirl, today married the Prince of Wales watched by more than 700 million TV viewers.

In keeping with tradition the bride was late at St Paul's arriving on the arm of her father Earl Spencer, a former Equerry to the Queen.

After the service the couple rode to Buckingham Palace in a horse-drawn carriage past cheering crowds.

October: "Major Bob" Astles, Idi Amin's former right hand man, has been acquitted of murdering a fisherman but sent back to prison under a Ugandan Detention Order.

The one-time Ashford schoolboy who lived in Mersham and Kingsnorth before joining the Royal Engineers, has been languishing for more than two years in jail.

Astles worked alongside Amin during the Ugandan president's reign of terror but was then accused of killing the fisherman.

The distinguished and controversial playwright, John Osborne, seen here with actress Jill Bennett, has just published a characteristically candid autobiography, A Better Class of Person, *in which he objectively studies his many theatrical milestones.
Osborne, 52, who lives at Christmas Mill, Marsh Green, Edenbridge, achieved immediate fame with his first play* Look Back in Anger *(1956) and with it became the spokesperson for a new generation of English writers, the so-called Angry Young Men. He followed it with an equally brilliant play,* The Entertainer, *a tour de force, for Sir Laurence Olivier starring as Archie Rice. Subsequent successes include* Luther *(1961) and* Inadmissable Evidence *(1964).*

February 4th: **Mrs Thatcher has begun her promised drive to privatise nationalised businesses and two companies, with strong links in Kent, are among the first to experience this "investment revolution".**

Plans to sell off Sealink were announced by Transport Secretary Norman Fowler last year. This week they are joined by British Aerospace, the civil and military aircraft business nationalised in 1977. British Aerospace was created from the merger in 1960 between the Vickers Aircraft Division and two other companies.

Scores of people from North-East Kent worked for the Crayford-based aircraft manufacturer and some still remember the first twin-engined bomber — the Vickers Vimy — which flew from Joyce Green airfield as long ago as 1917. The company's contribution to aviation history later included the Wellington, Spitfire, Viscount and VC10.

Half the shares in British Aerospace will be sold which, the Government hopes, will raise £150 million. Future transfers to the private sector will include British Gas, British Electricity, British Telecommunications and the Trustee Savings Bank. *See page 120*

Archbishop heads appeal to save the windswept Marsh churches

October: An appeal to save the mediaeval churches of Romney Marsh has been launched countrywide following a letter to *The Times* signed by the Most Reverend Robert Runcie, Archbishop of Canterbury, Mr Richard Ingrams, editor of Private Eye and John Piper, the artist.

The Romney Marsh Historic Churches Trust will use all donations to preserve and maintain the fabric of the churches of Brenzett, Brookland, Burmarsh, Dymchurch, East Guldeford, Fairfield, Ivychurch, Lydd, New Romney, Newchurch, Old Romney, St Mary in the Marsh and Snargate.

The windswept churches of the Marsh are among the finest in the country but thousands of pounds are required to prevent them falling into decay and disuse like the churches of Broomhill, Eastbridge, Hope and Midley which are now just ruins and Snave which has been declared redundant.

Parishes in the South Lympne Deanery, which includes those on the other side of the Royal Military Canal, are now united under a single priest.

The great bells of Canterbury

November 16th: The great bell of St Dunstan — named after a man who was Archbishop of Canterbury for 30 years from 959 — has been cleaned, tuned and restored and hung in the Cathedral's new Arundel Tower which had never been supplied with a ring of bells.

Great Dunstan's swinging powerful tone also proclaims a new chapter in the history of Canterbury's bells. During the year a new ring of 14 has been cast for the Oxford Tower and Bell Harry, on top of the Central Tower, has been rehung.

The Cathedral Church of Christ of Canterbury has bells which befit its beauty and status as the Mother Church of England.

At last — The Open returns to Sandwich

May: The Open, the world's oldest international golf championship, will be returning to the Royal St Georges, Sandwich this summer after an absence of 32 years.

Consistently ranked among the leading courses in the world, the links, set among the sand dunes of Sandwich Bay, provide a severe test for even the greatest of golfers. In fact the Royal St George's has hosted the Open Championship on eight occasions but not one winner has managed to be under par after the 72 holes.

It was on these undulating fairways in 1894 that the Open Championship was first played outside Scotland and that was just seven years after the club had been founded. In that year the great J.H.Taylor was the winner with a four-round score of 326.

Founded in 1887 as St George's, the club was accorded the 'Royal' prefix by Edward VII in 1902 and was further honoured when the Prince of Wales accepted the captaincy of the club in 1927-28. Subsequently his brother, later George VI, became an honorary member to continue the royal patronage.

In addition to the Open Championship, the club has hosted the British PGA Championship since 1975, the Walker Cup in 1937 and 1967 and has been the venue for the British Amateur Championship on several occasions.

Winners at the club are a veritable Who's Who of golf — Walter Hagen in the Open in 1922 and 1928, Henry Cotton in 1934, Bobby Locke in 1949 and Nick Faldo in the PGA Championship last year. Tony Jacklin won the Dunlop Masters at the Royal St George's in 1967 when he had the distinction of achieving the first hole in one to be seen live on television.

Favourites for this year's Open Championship are Tom Watson (last year's winner), Jack Nicklaus, Gary Player and Seve Ballesteros. Whoever wins will have to master the undulations of the fairways, the borrows on the greens, the strategically placed bunkers and the prevailing winds.

The players will find many changes to the course as have been required by the Royal and Ancient Championship Committee. New tees on the 1st, 2nd, 4th, 15th and 18th has stretched the course to almost 700 yards. The totally blind drive at the 7th has been eliminated and the condition of the course has never looked so good.

Members of the Royal St George's Golf Club come from all over the world and, in accordance with its constitution, are limited to 675.

See page 142

School chums win England caps

Chris Tavare

Paul Downton

August: Nine years ago Chris Tavare and Paul Downton were members of Sevenoaks School's 1st XI. This year they were playing respectively for Kent and Middlesex, having both been capped by England.

Their extraordinary careers have not quite run parellel. Tavare, 28, three years older than Downton, won a regular place in the Kent team in 1974.

Downton made his mark in 1977 when he was earmarked as a worthy successor to the Packer-contracted Alan Knott and, after only seven championship games, selected for the winter tour of Pakistan and New Zealand.

When Knott resumed his place behind the stumps — for Kent and England — Downton moved to Middlesex. He is certain to take the England job permanently when Knott finally retires.

Two Kent cricketers, Chris Tavare and Graham Dilley played crucial roles in this summer's remarkable Test series against Australia in which England recaptured the Ashes thanks to the heroic exploits of Ian Botham.

In The Third Test at Headingley Dilley scored 56 and shared a remarkable partnership of 111 with Botham (149 not out) for the eighth wicket. The stand turned the tables on Australia and helped transform the near certainty of an innings defeat into a possible victory. That was achieved, thanks to Bob Willis who took 8-43 and bowled the Aussies out for 130.

In the Fourth Test Tavare played an intelligent and careful innings of 50 while Botham blazed away at the other end for his second century of the series. The Somerset all-rounder hit one of the fastest centuries in Test cricket — Tav's was one of the slowest.

Dilley, from Dartford, came to the attention of the Kent staff a few years ago when Kent were playing Pakistani Eaglets. He went up to Alan Knott and asked him the best way to become a

Asif Iqbal, the brilliant 32-year-old Pakistan all-rounder is the new captain of Kent in place of Alan Ealham who was sacked after two successful years in the job.

Graham Dilley

Kent cricketer. "He told me to see Colin Page", said Dilley, "and I got on to a coaching course."

Dilley was then a goldsmith. He is now an international cricketer with a promising career ahead of him.

Chatham hears the terrible truth...

ROYAL DOCKYARD TO CLOSE IN 1984

June 26th: The unthinkable has happened. At 4 pm yesterday, Defence Secretary John Nott announced to an astonished House of Commons: "I regret to have to inform you that the dockyard in Chatham will close in 1984."

Outraged by the news, MP Mrs Peggy Fenner demanded: "Does the Secretary of State believe that the people of Rochester and Chatham elected me to support a Government that would do this to their dockyard?

He needn't. They didn't and I won't. What are his plans in terms of a time factor and how long have we got to fight this diabolical decision?

What are his plans for the 7,000 workforce and their great expertise — 45 per cent of their work dedicated to submarine refitting?

Mr Nott stressed that the famous dockyard and naval base would close in 1984 and that refits of nuclear submarines would be transferred to Devonport and Rosyth. He blamed the high cost of refitting older Leander Class frigates (£70m each) as one of the main reasons for the closure of Chatham. Gillingham MP, Sir Freddy Burden described the announcement as the "most disastrous day I have had in the 30 years I have been an MP".

The great Royal Dockyard at Chatham has been the vanguard of Britain's maritime supremacy for more than four centuries, for it was in 1547 when Henry VIII's fleet came to winter in Jillyngham Water. This supremacy was forged and sustained during the wars against the French and the Dutch in the 17th and 18th centuries.

See page 63

July 1981: A series of protest marches through Chatham followed the news that Chatham Dockyard will close by 1984.

...And so does Ashford

THOUSANDS OF JOBS AT RISK AS RAILWAY WORKS CLOSES

September: The forthcoming closure of Chatham's famous dockyard is not the only grim news facing the unbelieving people of Kent. Ashford's great railway works, built on 185 acres of Kent countryside more than 120 years ago, also faces the axe and up to 950 jobs are at risk

The devastating announcement from British Rail earlier this year that the railway works will be run down and then closed by June 1984 has been met with dogged resistance. This is easily the biggest setback in the history of the town.

Encouraged by union officials storemen have already refused to handle loadings and railwaymen have blacked the movement of materials. Industrial action though may have little effect.

In the last century the railway transformed this once-small market town into a major engineering centre. The carriage and wagon department opened in 1850 and more than 3,000 people were involved in turning out standard designed locomotives. By the 100th anniversary 715 notable engines had been built at Ashford. *See page 56*

'His calm efficiency and professional competence gave the Government the confidence to persist in the face of unpleasant losses...' — Prince Philip on Lord Lewin's vital role in the Falklands War.

January 1st: A new television company which provides south-east England with its own programme for the first time has been established at Maidstone. TV South is turning a field outside Maidstone into a £16 million triple-studio complex. An evening current affairs programme will be called *Coast to Coast.*

January 14th: The Prime Minister's son Mark Thatcher has been found in the Sahara after a frantic two-day search. He went missing on the Paris-Dakar rally.

January 26th: Unemployment in Britain is now above three million for the first time.

February 5th: Laker Airways has collapsed leaving 6,000 passengers stranded.

February 12th: Rupert Murdoch has transferred control of *The Times* and *The Sunday Times* to his company News International.

Cortex runway mines laid at Manston airfield in 1940 during the invasion scare have finally been located and lifted using sophisticated equipment. The famous Spitfire which was a gate guardian for so many years has been restored by the Medway branch of the Royal Aeronautical Society.

February 28th: Alan Knott, Derek Underwood and Bob Woolmer have joined a party of England cricketers to tour South Africa. It is now likely they will be banned from Test cricket and possibly even sacked by Kent.

April 2nd: A single company of Royal Marines guarding Port Stanley has been overwhelmed by Argentine troops intent on claiming sovereignty over the Falkland Islands.

April 5th: A Royal Navy Task Force has set sail for the Falklands in the greatest display of naval strength since Suez.

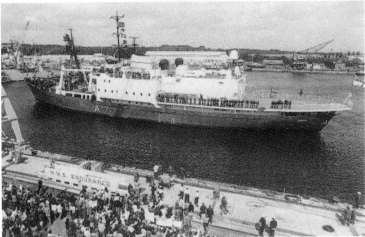

HMS Endurance *returns to Chatham to an ecstatic welcome after her adventures in the South Atlantic. The ice patrol ship was the first on the scene following the capture of the Falkland Islands by Argentinian troops and her crew went to the aid of the Royal Marines.* **See page 52.**

April 7th: Mrs Thatcher announced today the imposition of a 200-mile exclusion zone around the Falklands. The UN has demanded immediate withdrawal of the Argentine invasion force.

April 8th: The rebel cricketers in South Africa have been banned from international cricket for three years.

April 25th: Royal Marine commandos have recaptured South Georgia.

Sabi, the first African elephant to be born in Britain has been delivered at Howletts Zoo Park, near Canterbury.

May 25th: French-built Exocet missiles have hit the *Atlantic Conveyor* and *HMS Coventry* off East Falkland. 24 are feared dead.

May 29th: British Troops have landed on the Falklands. 17 paratroopers have died at Goose Green and two more Royal Navy ships have been sunk.

June 9th: A new coin, the 20p piece, has gone into circulation.

June 14th: British forces are now in control of the Falkland Islands. The known death toll is 255 Britons and 652 Argentinians.

June 21st: Princess Diana gave birth to a boy at St Mary's Hospital, Paddington, today. He will be christened William.

July 7th: Michael Fagan, aged 30, climbed into Buckingham Palace early today and made his way to the Queen's bedroom "for a chat". The Queen woke to find him sitting at the bottom of her bed with a bottle of wine. He asked her for a cigarette.

July 11th: Italy has won the World Cup with a 3-1 victory over West Germany.

August 29th: A 65-year-old American, Ashby Harper, has become the oldest person to swim the English Channel.

August 31st: Israeli troops today drove the Palestine Liberation Organisation out of Beirut. Leader Yassar Arafat said he will continue the struggle and thanked the Lebanese people for the sacrifices they had made.

An 'Arab prince' who arrived in Thanet saying he was interested in buying the ailing Ramsgate ferry port has turned out to be the leader of Thanet council, Derek Dolding, in fancy dress driving a hired American limousine. The 'eastern prince' hoax received worldwide coverage and certainly helped to put Thanet on the map — but Dolding has now been forced to resign over the "fake sheikh" affair.

September 15th: Princess Grace of Monaco has died of head injuries after her car plunged off a mountain road due to brake failure.

December: Stephen Spielberg's latest film success, *ET*, has prompted thousands of British children to request an Extra Terrestrial for Christmas.

December 12th: The proposed siting of 96 US Cruise missiles at Greenham Common brought protests today from 20,000 women who encircled the airbase.

Hythe's impressive tree-planting project, promoted by the Civic Society, continues to be successful. More than 800 have been planted since the great elm disease of 1975.

GREAT HITS OF 1982

Fame
Come on Eileen

An industrial giant is buried

August 27th: Twenty seven years ago the Queen came to Kent to open one of the country's great industrial giants — the BP Kent Oil Refinery on the Isle of Grain. It was the biggest in Europe, it cost £300 million to build and it covered 250 acres. Today, it is obsolete.

This week a small group of workers saw crude oil processed for the last time. They now join the 1,500 people who have lost their jobs.

Grain fell victim mainly because of its size and the Middle East oil crisis of 1979 when prices more than doubled overnight. A recession followed and BP decided to concentrate its work on smaller refineries in other parts of the country.

Grain workers did not give up their jobs without a fight but this week the management were paying tribute to the spirit shown by the men who understood the inevitability of the closure.

May: Work is underway at Reculver on the recovery of Barnes Wallis' famous bouncing bombs. In the early spring of 1943 a series of trials were conducted to see if bombs, dropped from a Lancaster, could skip along the water and explode at a given point. Reculver was the site chosen and the area was sealed off by police. It's a well-known story. The tests were successful and so was the raid by Guy Gibson's 617 Squadron on the Mohne and Eder concrete dams which sent 300 million tons of water sweeping into the Ruhr industrial heartland. Picture shows a US Jolly Green Giant helicopter with two of the practice "bouncing bombs".

Rupert Murdoch sacks editor of *The Times*

March 11th: Following an alleged smear campaign among Tory MP's and charges that he is too critical of the Government's economic line, Harold Evans, editor of *The Times* has been sacked by the new owner, Rupert Murdoch.

Evans, who lives with his second wife Tina Brown at Brasted Chart near Sevenoaks, was appointed editor of Britain's biggest selling quality daily shortly after Murdoch acquired *The Times* in January last year.

The Australian newspaper tycoon — already owner of the *Sun* and *The News of The World* — was spared an investigation by the Monopolies Commission on the insistence of Mrs Thatcher, who had benefited greatly from Murdoch's support during the 1979 election campaign. At the time of the take-over she told the Commons that the delay involved in such an enquiry would risk the permanent closure of *The Times*.

Although Evans, 53, was guaranteed editorial freedom Murdoch hoped he would be supportive of Thatcher, particularly in view of the rise of the new Social Democrat Party and her low standing in the polls.

But Evans, in refusing to tow the Thatcher line, has been accused of being a Labour supporter. Together with charges of overspending and considerable disquiet at changes which Murdoch himself had encouraged, Evans has been told to go. His deputy Charles Douglas-Home will become the new editor.

Evans has not left without a fight. He said: "It is my personal conviction that a news journalist should not engage in active party politics and there is supreme value in the independence of a newspaper."

The former campaigning editor of the *Sunday Times* for 14 years now intends to write a book about his turbulent days with the powerful and unpredictable Rupert Murdoch.

See page 50

Sir Freddie's Skytrain takes a nosedive

February 7th: Freddie Laker's skytrain has been grounded. The lad from Ramsgate who took on the giant state airlines, including British Airways, is now hoping that a late rescue package may revive his great dream of cheap travel for the masses.

There is hope. A merchant bank has suggested it can raise £25 million following the collapse of Laker Airways three days ago and an anonymous businessman, who claims that Sir Freddie is doing more for enterprise in Britain than anyone, has promised £1m. Prince Michael of Kent has offered his backing and so have hundreds of friends from East Kent.

The fleet of wide-bodied jets were run by a staff of 2,000 at Gatwick but, as the recession hit Britain and the dollar rose in value against sterling, Sir Freddie fell into debt.

Then came the shock news that the Skytrains were grounded. A group of banks called in the debts and Laker's planes were corralled in a corner of Gatwick — perhaps never to fly under his livery again.

The pioneer of cheap air travel, who became a hero among thousands, claims he is the victim of a conspiracy as other airlines are offering discounts only on his routes. ***See page 136***

Susan tells of her struggle with words

AS a child Susan Hampshire had great difficulty reading and spelling. The popular blonde star of the hit BBC TV serial *The Forsyte Saga* was one of the 11 per cent of people in Britain suffering from "congenital word blindness" as doctors called it.

Today it is identified as dyslexia and, thanks to a recent *Horizon* documentary which was presented by Susan, thousands of children, once deemed mentally deficient or lazy, now know they have a learning problem — and help is available.

Susan has lived in Kent since she was 17 and says she is infatuated with the county and with the Georgian house in Sandwich she shares with husband Pierre.

Her late mother, who once lived at Eastry, was a woman of rare perception. With patience and understanding she nursed Susan through the years when the sight of words produced nothing but complete confusion.

Despite being such a poor reader she managed to get a job with a repertory company and her career took off. She played Becky Sharp in *Vanity Fair,* the first BBC2 colour series and the showgirl in Terence Rattigan's *The Sleeping Prince.* But it was as Fleur Forsyte she scored her greatest success.

September 28th: *Susan Hampshire, who is now Britain's best-known dyslexic, opens the first Dyslexic Institute's teaching unit in London which will accept children and adults for assessment. With her is fellow sufferer, five-year-old Adam Rickets of Upper Norwood.*

May 29th: *Despite the Falklands War and the fear that his visit might be cancelled, John Paul II has finally stepped into the nave of Canterbury Cathedral and then prayed alongside Archbishop Robert Runcie. He is the first Pope to visit Britain since the breakaway from the Catholic Church at the time of Henry VIII. The two church leaders lit candles for two modern martyrs — a priest who gave his life to save a condemned man at Auschwitz and a Ugandan Archbishop killed by Idi Amin. Later, His Holiness toured the city in a purpose-built taxi, known as the Popemobile!*

Lord Astor dies two years after selling Hever

October: In the space of a few months the county has lost two of its greatest servants, Lord Cornwallis of Linton and Lord Astor of Hever, who were successive Lord Lieutenants of Kent.

Lord Cornwallis, a former Aide de Camp to Field Marshal Haig, chairman of the County Council, president of the County Society, captain of Kent Cricket Club and Pro Chancellor of the University of Kent among many other distinguished offices, was Lord Lieutenant for 28 years.

Gavin Astor inherited *The Times* newspaper from his father and, faced by rising costs, was forced to sell to Lord Thompson in 1966. He was also a man of wide interests

but dominant among them was a long association with the Commonwealth Press Union.

Lord Astor inherited the 13th century moated castle, Italianate gardens and Tudor village at Hever which was created by his grandfather Waldorf at the beginning of the century and it was a cruel blow when rising costs and taxation gave him little alternative but to sell two years ago. The massive Hever estate was divided into separate lots and sold by auction.

Gavin Astor, who died aged 66 is survived by his wife, Lady Irene and two sons, John and Philip.

A moment to savour. Protected by the steel cable, Henry VIII's great flagship is lifted from the seabed.

Heave, ho and up she rises

October 11th: A Bromley-based engineer who lives near Westerham is the designer of the ingenious cradle in which the *Mary Rose* was today lifted from the seabed of the Solent where she has lain for 437 years.

Ron Crocker of Chartfield Farmhouse, Brasted, watched the operation with bated breath as the underwater transfer of the hull to his steel cradle was perfected. He then saw the ship lifted to the surface with infinite slowness. Alongside him was Prince Charles, while millions watched the famous recovery on television.

The cradle carrying the Tudor ship was lifted by *Tog Mor*, a giant floating crane which was loaned, along with the crew, to the Mary Rose Trust by Albert Granville of Knockholt,

chairman of Howard Doris.

When the ship appeared from the water in its cradle it resembled a huge locked box. The total load weighed more than 500 tons — 10 times its weight under water.

The *Mary Rose*, Henry VIII's flagship, capsized and sank in 1545 as she sailed out to do battle with the French. Most of the 700 men aboard lost their lives.

The wreck was first located in the Solent by John Deane of Deptford as long ago as 1846 when a few cannons were recovered. It was then forgotten until recently when the Mary Rose Trust relocated the wreck and lifted scores of Tudor artefacts. These, and the remains of the ship, will be preserved in a museum in Portsmouth.

Marlowe moves

May 22nd: A musical swansong by Mary O'Hara at the The Marlowe Theatre, Canterbury, has been followed by the demolition men who will be preparing the way for a shopping complex on the site.

Inspired by the Festival of Britain, The Marlowe was converted into a theatre from the war-damaged Central Picture House in May 1950 by Hugh Wilson, the city architect.

For 32 years, touring companies have entertained the people of Canterbury with plays, nude revues and celebrity shows. It is planned to build a larger Marlowe Theatre elsewhere in the city.

Kent boys among Task Force heroes

Chatham sailors quickly into the heart of action

June 14th: Families of the Kent boys with the Task Force in the Falkland Islands are jubilant. The Argentinian invaders are flying a white flag over Port Stanley and British forces are in command again after two months of bitter fighting.

Tonight Mrs Thatcher told a cheering House of Commons that victory has been won by an operation which was "boldly planned, bravely executed and brilliantly accomplished".

Sadly, not all the boys who carried the standard for Kent have come through the conflict. Captain David Wood of Gillingham died alongside his commander Lt Col H. Jones in the bitter fighting to recapture Goose Green. He was one of 17 members of the Parachute Regiment killed. Edmund Flanagan, Chief Petty Officer, of Rock Avenue, Gillingham, died on the Atlantic Conveyor and was buried at sea.

Peter Wilkin of Seal, a member of the 45 Commando Unit was injured on *HMS Sir Percival* and paratrooper Lee Fisher of Salisbury Road, Bromley, was left with a 10-inch wound in his left shoulder and is aboard the hospital ship *SS Uganda*. Captain David Hart-Dyke, whose mother lives at The Gatehouse, Lullingstone Castle, suffered facial injuries when his ship, the destroyer *HMS Coventry* was sunk by Argentinian aircraft. Twenty men died when the ship capsized but 200 were rescued.

The Falklands War began on April 2nd when Argentinian troops invaded and captured the island by overwhelming a company of Royal Marines. The Argentine Government insisted that "Los Malvinas" were rightly theirs.

First British ship on the scene was the Chatham-based *HMS Endurance,* an ice patrol ship on survey work in the South Atlantic. Her sailors went to the aid of the Marines in a last-ditch effort to repel the invaders and, armed with sub-machine guns, actually took control of the Town Hall and helped to burn valuable documents while the battle raged outside Government House. When the Island's Governor Mr Rex Hunt surrendered the 10 sailors were taken prisoner along with the Royal Marines.

By then the massive Task Force was on its way. Carriers *HMS Hermes* and *Invincible* led frigates, destroyers and troop carriers to the island with commandos, paratroopers, men from the Special Forces and Harrier jump jets. It was Britain's greatest display of naval strength since Suez.

Among those on board were 200 Royal Engineers from 50 Field Construction Squadron based at Invicta Barracks, Maidstone. Other local lads included Roger Williams from Eynsford, Paul Wooding and John Curtis from Sevenoaks and Chris Bidgood from Cheriton aboard the *Canberra*, three Borough Green boys, Keith Woodhams, Richard Lovelock and Ian Franklin on *Broadsword, Brilliant* and *Courageous* respectively, Peter Roulston from Eynsford on the *Hermes* and Malcolm Shrub from Westerham aboard the *Sir Galahad*.

One Kent couple are particularly relieved — for their son was on *HMS Sheffield*, which was hit by an Exocet missile. It was some time after the disaster that Geoff and Brenda Bates of Brookland heard that 33-year-old Nick, a Lieutenant Commander, had survived the missile attack which killed 30 of his colleagues

The war at sea was followed by the war on land. Soldiers made a two-pronged assault on Port Stanley by "yomping" as the Marines call it across rugged terrain. At Darwin and Goose Green they were outnumbered by three to one in what the Chief of the General Staff described as an "epic battle".

Lieutenant Col Herbert Jones and Gillingham's Captain David Wood died leading a charge on a sub-machine gun post which was holding up their advance. Twelve hours later their 450 men had triumphed leaving the Argentinians with 250 dead and 1,200 taken prisoner.

The end of the fighting came when British troops broke through the last ring of defences round Port Stanley and suddenly white flags began to blossom from places like Tumbledown Mountain, Wireless Ridge and Mount Longton.

The price paid for the victory is high. The Minister of Defence confirmed tonight that the known death toll for the campaign as a whole is 255 Britons and 652 Argentinians.

One Man of Kent who has every reason to be proud of the victory is Lord Lewin, Chief of the Defence Staff and, arguably, the most influential member of Margaret Thatcher's War Cabinet. He provided the link between the politicians in Westminster and the C-in-C Fleet, Admiral Sir John Woodhouse.

Terry Lewin was born in Dover in 1920 and went to Judd School, Tonbridge, before joining the training cruiser *Frobisher* in 1939 and embarking on a distinguished naval career with numerous commands and senior naval posts. In 1977 it was announced that he was to be First Sea Lord and Chief of the Naval Staff.

It was Lord Lewin's decision that a sea blockade of the Falklands — which Mr Nott, the Defence Secretary, had preferred — could never be wholly effective. He argued it would subject the blockading ships to the worst of a South

July 6th: *A full-scale street party was held in honour of 21-year-old paratrooper Ian French of Gillingham when he returned from the Falkland Islands today. Friends and neighbours in Abbey Road rolled out the beer barrels and strung up the bunting while the lad was enjoying an emotional reunion at Brize Norton with his mum Lila and dad Harry.*

Atlantic winter and not achieve the main objective which was the repossession of the Falklands.

Many local communities throughout Kent are preparing to give their lads a hero's welcome when the Task Force returns. At Gillingham a memorial service is being planned at St Mark's Church in honour of David Wood, the 19-year-old paratrooper who was once an outstanding cadet with the town's Air Training Corps.

In other areas, funds are being opened in aid of those who were injured and the Hazlitt Theatre, Maidstone, is putting on a special show to raise money for the families

of those who died. The mayor of Folkestone, Cllr Peter Poole, echoed the feelings of civic leaders throughout Kent when he urged the people of Shepway to send contributions to the South Atlantic Fund.

A Falklands Islands Service will be held in St Paul's Cathedral when Robert Runcie, Archbishop of Canterbury, will remember and pray for the Argentinian dead as well as the British. His planned sermon will not please Mrs Thatcher. The Archbishop has already been an outspoken critic of the uncaring social attitudes he has seen prevail during the early 1980s.

1982

February 3rd: *A runaway articulated lorry hit six cars, two buses and another lorry as it thundered down Maidstone Road, Chatham and through the rush hour traffic today. It eventually tipped over on its side as the driver desperately tried to turn uphill towards Chatham station. Miraculously no-one was killed but a father and his baby son were thrown out of the back of their car as it was crushed by the juggernaut. They are both in hospital with head injuries.*

January 7th: Australia have won the Test series against England to regain the Ashes.

January 17th: Television viewers can now tune in at breakfast time as early morning programmes are introduced.

January 31st: From today it is compulsory to wear a seat belt in the front seat of a car.

A chamber containing human bones has been discovered at St Nicholas at Wade church by a man replacing light bulbs! Apparently his ladder placed on the tiled floor of the church sank under his weight and a great hole exposed the chamber. The vicar was called and found between 15 to 20 skeletons, several hundred years old. They have been examined, reinterred and the burial chamber filled in.

February 1st: The Thames Barrier was lifted for the first time today following a flood alert.

February 10th: East Kent ground to a halt today under 14 inches of snow. Bus services from Folkestone and Dover have been supended and children sent home from school.

February 15th: The Metro is now the fastest-selling car in Kent.

February 28th: Kent miners are striking in protest at proposed pit closures.   *See pages 72 & 73*

April 1st: Hundreds of CND supporters from Kent were among those who formed a 14-mile human chain at Greenham and Aldermaston today.

Harold Evans, former editor of *The Times* and *The Sunday Times,* has written his own inside story of life at the heart of these great newspapers. His book is called *Good Times, Bad Times.*

April 11th: The film *Ghandi* has won eight Oscars — a record for a British film.

England batsman, Chris Tavare of Sevenoaks, has been chosen as captain of Kent in succession to Asif Iqbal.

*The Right Hon Robin Leigh-Pemberton, the former Grenadier Guardsman, farmer, barrister and banker who last year succeeded Lord Astor of Hever as Lord Lieutenant of Kent has been given a little more responsibility — Governor of the Bank of England! A JP and one-time chairman of the Kent County Council, Robin Leigh-Pemberton lives with his wife, Rosemary at Torry Hill, a 2,000-acre family estate among the North Downs near Sittingbourne. The couple have five sons. He is also chairman of the National Westminster Bank and actively involved in numerous Kent organisations including the Playing Fields Association, Agricultural Society, Canterbury and Rochester Cathedral Trusts, Kent Association of Youth Clubs and Kent Cricket Club. He is also Pro-Chancellor of the University of Kent.
One of Mr Leigh-Pemberton's first duties in his dual role has been to open the new offices of the* Sevenoaks Chronicle.

Gillingham barber Gerry Harley has beaten his own world record by shaving 987 men in one hour and raising thousands of pounds for muscular dystrophy.

April 22nd: A £1 coin has come into circulation.

April 25th: It is believed that *The Sunday Time*s has paid £1 million for 60 volumes of diaries written by Adolf Hitler. It is being described as the most remarkable historical find of the century.

May 21st: Brighton has drawn 2-2 with Manchester United in the FA Cup Final.

June 11th: Geoffrey Howe has become Foreign Secretary and will take over the occupancy of Chevening House, Chevening, the former home of Prince Charles.

June 18th: Tory backbencher Bernard Weatherill has been chosen to succeed George Thomas as Speaker of the House of Commons.

July over England was the warmest since records were first devised. On the 16th Gillingham recorded 91F.

August 14th: Steve Cram, in the 1500 metres and Daley Thompson in the decathlon, have won gold medals for England in the Olympic Games.

October 2nd: Neil Kinnock, 41-year-old Welshman, has become Labour's new leader by an overwhelming majority.

October 15th: Trade and Industry Secretary Cecil Parkinson has resigned from the cabinet over his extra-marital relationship with Sara Keays.

October 24th: Dennis Nilsen has confessed to 15 or 16 murders.

December 8th: The Duchess of Kent today opened Ashford's new £4 million Civic Centre in Tannery Lane.

GREAT HITS OF 1983

Uptown Girl
Karma Chameleon

55

1983

Families shattered by railway redundancies

The people of Ashford are having great difficulty in coming to terms with the rapid run-down of the Rail Works — for each week comes news of another shattering redundancy notice. Scores of families are now affected; many of the menfolk have given a lifetime of service.

Ashford Rail Works at Newtown were established in 1847 and the great steam locomotives built, until the switch from steam to diesel and then to electricity ended the need for many of the heavy skills

Even in the difficult years after the war Ashford boasted 156 apprentices in various trades and its own team of more than 100 ambulancemen. All sporting facilities were catered for including football, cricket, bowls and tennis.

Photograph shows some of the senior staff saying goodbye to Loco 737 (No 11 "D" Class) which was built at Ashford in 1901, prior to it's deposit in the National Railway Museum in 1960. **See page 104**

£25m bullion haul from Brinks Mat warehouse

November 26th: The Great Train Robbers in Maidstone Prison must be green with envy, or perhaps even admiration. Today, at Heathrow Airport, a highly-organised gang carried out Britain's biggest robbery when they stole gold bars worth £25 million from the Brinks Mat security warehouse.

The raid was planned to the finest detail. The six men broke through a formidable array of alarms, held up six guards inside and took an hour loading the three-ton haul onto a lorry.

As Kent harbours some of the country's most wanted criminals the county police have been alerted. They are watching the Channel ports carefully for it is believed that the gang may already be melting down the gold and preparing to smuggle it out of the country. **See page 76**

February 15th: Standpipes and water bowsers have been brought out of mothballs and water companies across Kent are appealing for consumers to use less water as water workers throughout the country strike for the first time.

While the people of Kent fear their taps will run dry, white collar workers are doing their best to keep the water flowing — but they can't repair burst mains.

The Buckland area of Dover and Coxheath, near Maidstone, are two areas where water has been brought in by tankers. In other places householders have been queuing in the snow for bucketfulls of water from standpipes. It has been another winter of discontent.

Aspinall tells of pact with tiger keeper

Casino millionaire John Aspinall who owns Howletts Zoo Park at Bekesbourne near Canterbury and Port Lympne Zoo near Hythe has appeared at Canterbury Crown Court charged in connection with the death last year of Brian Stocks, head keeper at Howletts, who had been mauled by a tigress. The jury decided that Mr Aspinall could not be blamed after hearing that the keepers loved their work and accepted the risks that went with it. Mr Aspinall told the court he had made a pact with Brian Stocks which said that no animal would be destroyed if either man were killed. **See page 106**

Another woman found dead at Bedgebury beauty spot

June 12th: After 12 months of exhaustive inquiries involving more than 50 detectives, extensive house-to-house questioning and the distribution of 10,000 handbills appealing for help, Kent police are no nearer to finding the killer of 46-year-old Jean Brook.

The mother of three was found battered to death in Bedgebury Forest near Goudhurst last June — a mile from the spot where an unidentified pregnant woman met her death in 1979.

As the two murder mysteries deepen, detectives are keeping open their incident room at Cranbrook. Det Supt Brian Kendall, leading the hunt for the killer (or killers), said there had been a good response from the public but they were still looking for the vital clues that could lead to an arrest.

Mrs Brook drove a motor spares delivery van and was on the "Cranbrook run" on the day she died. It is believed she was alone as she stopped in the forest for a picnic lunch spreading a blanket behind her van. Some hours later a woodcutter, who lived nearby, noticed the van had not been driven away and raised the alarm. Mrs Brook's body was found by police 50 yards away.

May: Princess Diana's concern for the elderly and disabled was clearly evident on her first official visit to Kent this month. More than 300 people turned out to welcome her to Canterbury where she opened the warden-assisted flats at Cranmer House, London Road. Diana, as patron of the pre-Playgroup's Association, also met about 80 children and their leaders. Later she visited the Cathedral and opened a lift for the disabled.

Lord Clark's son disputes sale of Turner painting

December: **Colin Clark, the younger son of Kenneth Clark, who died in May at his home Saltwood Castle, has started a High Court action to stop the sale of a Turner painting, *Seascape Folkestone.***

Mr Clark claims the painting had been left to him in his father's will and the executors, who include his elder brother Alan, are acting unfairly. The painting, apparently, is worth several million pounds.

Lord Clark was a wealthy art historian who will be best remembered for his epic and witty TV series *Civilisation* (1969). In his younger days he was director of the National Gallery and, in addition to his many books on art, author of a lively two-part autobiography completed in 1974.

Lord Clark, who was 80, championed Henry Moore and Graham Sutherland. He moved to Saltwood after the war.

His eldest son Alan, a barrister and military historian, has been MP for Plymouth Sutton since 1974 and is currently Under Secretary of State for Employment.

Colin, who has a twin sister Colette, worked as a personal assistant to Laurence Olivier and Vivien Leigh and later directed documentaries.

He said recently he has lived a life in the shadow of his father and brother, who has benefited greatly from his father's estate. *See page 139*

The best of Henry Moore at Folkestone

July 1st: Henry Moore, the sculptor with an international reputation, is to hold an exhibition of his famous work at the New Metropole Arts Centre, Folkestone, from tomorrow. He said that it was while living in a cottage at Kingston before the war that he seized the opportunity to make sculpture and nature enhance each other.

Moore and his wife moved to Kent in 1931 to be near his sister Betty. They bought a cottage at Barfreston and later moved into a bigger one at Kingston.

It was here that Moore, now 84, was first able to work on a large scale against an open landscape. "I feel that the sky and nature are the best setting for my sculpture", he said. "They are asymmetrical, unlike an architectural background with its verticals and horizontals. In a natural setting the background to a sculpture changes if you move only a very small distance."

Henry Moore's most characteristic works are reclining, semi-abstract figures, often made up of separate parts. His best-known works are more directly figurative, including the famous *Madonna and Child*, sculpted in 1944.

The Moores remained in Kent until after Dunkirk when the area was declared a restricted zone. He was friendly with Lord Clark of Saltwood who was president of the New Metropole Arts Centre until his death.

The exhibition, open until August 28th, will also feature 32 drawings. As Moore has been described as the greatest artist since Turner this is another coup for the Metropole.

Labour "dead and buried" as jubilant Tories sweep the board

June 10th: The Tories are back in power tonight with a landslide general election victory. As predicted, they have taken every seat in Kent.

The overall Conservative majority of 144 is the biggest since Labour's victory in 1945.

Once again it has been a personal triumph for Mrs Thatcher who has invited two Kent MPs to join the Cabinet. John Stanley (Tonbridge) becomes Armed Forces Minister and Patrick Mayhew QC (Tunbridge Wells) has been appointed Solicitor General and knighted.

From his home in Kilndown today, Sir Patrick said his new job was "full of variety and interest as one of the principal legal advisers to the Government".

In most Kent seats the Liberal/SDP Alliance is runner up with Labour now almost wiped out as an electoral force in the county.

Two significant results were at Chatham where Peggy Fenner held on to a 9,000-plus majority despite the impending closure of Chatham Dockyard and the subsequent upheaval and at Ashford where Keith Speed's majority was almost 14,000.

At Maidstone John Wells gained a majority of more than 7,000 even though boundary changes had transferred about 27,000 to the new Mid-Kent constituency. Here, the first MP is Andrew Rowe.

Although the Labour party is in disarray, their spokesman Gordon Carey said: "We will bounce back one day. I would say that many of our votes are on loan to the Alliance."

Peter Blaine, Alliance candidate at Tunbridge Wells, disagreed. "Social changes are causing Labour to be in long-term decline. That trend is bound to continue. We are now established as the clear opposition party."

Family of seven die in massive explosion

November 7th: It is now known that seven members of an Asian family, who were killed when equipment and solvents exploded below their flat in Arthur Street, Gravesend, were engaged in an illicit shoe-making business.

The tragedy occurred yesterday (Sunday) and so powerful was the explosion that the two-storey building completely collapsed and flames quickly spread to neighbouring properties.

Firemen were confronted by an appalling sight when they arrived on the scene. Several people were inside the building but it was impossible to enter because of the intense heat of the inferno. Immediately in front was a blazing minibus and, trapped underneath, a man who had jumped, on fire, from a window.

Eight appliances attended and, as bystanders helped to release the man from under the vehicle, jets were directed to the back and front of the building. A turntable ladder was also requested and in the most hazardous conditions firemen entered the still-blazing remains. Three firemen received burns and were taken to hospital. The victims were eventually found dead under the smouldering debris — one man, three women and three small children. The man released from under the mini-bus died later in hospital.

Police have discovered that the building, formerly a public house, was being used illegally at basement/ground floor level for the manufacture of shoes and involved the use of inflammable adhesives and solvents.

November 3rd: Damon Hill, the 23-year-old son of twice-world motor racing champion, the late Graham Hill, with his mother Bette at Brands Hatch. On Sunday (November 6th) Damon will race a 140-mph Argo JM 14 single-seater in the first of five Formula Ford races for the BBC Grandstand Trophy which aims to spotlight the talents of rising young British racing drivers. The question everyone at Brands Hatch is asking — "will Damon take after his dad and one day win the world Formula One championship?" **See page 161**

Folkestone to Venice on the Orient Express

❋ Shipping magnate and owner of Sea Link, James Sherwood, has now spent more than £11 million restoring the world-famous Orient Express.

The Orient Express was inaugurated in 1883 and ran between Paris and Istanbul, providing first class service for more than 70 years.

In its centenary year the Pullman carriages have been carefully renovated and, this week, celebrity passengers were invited to make the inaugural journey (1983-style) from London to Folkestone and then on to Venice.

For future passengers the train ride will cost £700.

❋ A £300 million cross-Channel electricity converter station , currently being built in Church Lane, Aldington, will go onto full stream in 1986 and only one or two men will be required to operate it.

The idea of the station is to take AC electricity out of the national grid at off-peak periods and sell it to France. It will travel under the Channel from East Cliffe, Folkestone, to a French converter station.

❋ The Medway Queen, heroine of the Dunkirk evacuation, has sank off St Mary's Wharf, Chatham, putting the steamer's restoration project in jeopardy. The damage is estimated at £20,000.

❋ Former BBC radio commentator, Michael Standing, whose voice was known to millions, has died at his home in Trottiscliffe aged 74.

Mr Standing was a pre-war national celebrity and was responsible for the first Test Match commentaries. As a BBC war correspondent he reported on the D-Day landings

May 8th: The giant Thames Flood Barrier, built by the GLC at a cost of £460 million, was opened by the Queen at Woolwich today.

As she pushed the button in the control room the giant gates inched up to stand against the tide and play a vital role in defending London from the sea.

Thousands of people were present to see the "royal touch" and appreciate the technology which went into the largest movable flood barrier in the world.

The barrier will be lifted whenever there is a danger that London will be flooded. Tidal waters have frequently lapped against the parapets of the Thames Embankment and, on occasions, surged through the streets. Notoriously, in 1928 and 1953, London was on the brink of a major calamity.

January 2nd: Kent's lakes and rivers are being contaminated by acid rain but not as seriously as those in Scotland and Cumbria, according to an environmental report today.

February 10th: Harold Macmillan has accepted a hereditary earldom on his 90th birthday. For many years he has refused a peerage.

February 14th: Jane Torville and Christopher Dean today won the Olympic Gold for ice skating in Sarajevo. They were accompanied by the rhythms of Ravel's Bolero.

February 29th: John Francombe has become only the second jockey in National Hunt racing history to ride 1,000 winners in hurdles and steeplechases.

March 15th: A pay offer of 5.2 per cent and a programme of pit closures has led to a nationwide miners' strike with only 21 of Britain's 174 mines working normally.

March 21st: Brenda Dean, leader of SOGAT '82, has become the first woman to head a major union.

April 6th: Zola Budd, the 17-year-old South African distance runner, will be eligible to run for Britain in the Los Angeles Olympic Games. She has been given a British passport.

April 23rd: A new disease known as AIDS has been discovered. US Health Secretary Margaret Heckler said a blood test will be available in six months and a vaccine in two years.

May 8th: The Thames Flood Barrier has been officially opened.

May 4th: Diana Fluck, better known as Diana Dors, died today aged 53, less than a fortnight after opening a drive-in cinema near Maidstone.

May 19th: Sir John Betjeman, Britain's most popular poet, died today not long after being incapacitated by a stroke.

Double joy. Christopher Cowdrey, the 26-year-old son of Colin Cowdrey, has been chosen to tour with England and elected Kent captain in place of Chris Tavare. See page 67

May 29th: Eric Morecambe, 58-year-old comedian, died of a heart attack today during a charity show at Tewkesbury Theatre. The Morecambe and Wise Show attracted television audiences of 20 million in the 1970s.

June 7th: 120 striking miners were arrested today during a mass lobby outside Parliament.

Princess Alexandra opened the new £20 million Maidstone Hospital.

June 22nd: Richard Branson's new Virgin Atlantic Flight left Gatwick for New York today for a cost of £99 single.

July 12th: Robert Maxwell has bought the *Mirror* newspaper

group for £113 million.

July 28th: The 23rd Olympic Games opened in Los Angeles.

Tony Pawson, the former Kent cricketer and amateur international footballer, has added to his sporting achievements — by becoming the world's fly-fishing champion.

August 2nd: Ten-day old Hollie Roffey from Springwood Drive, Godington Park Ashford has made medical history by becoming the youngest person to be given a new heart.

August 8th: Tessa Sanderson, Sebastian Coe and Daley Thompson have won gold medals for England at Los Angeles.

August: During the past few weeks three more famous Englishmen have died — Richard Burton who was twice married to Elizabeth Taylor, James Mason, one of the most underestimated British actors and novelist J.B. Priestley.

September 16th: A second son, Henry Charles Albert David, has been born to Prince Charles and Princess Diana.

October 19th: Kent and England all-rounder Bob Woolmer has retired from playing cricket and will take up a full-time coaching appointment in South Africa.

October 31st: Mrs Indira Ghandi, Prime Minister of India, was shot down and killed today by one of her Sikh bodyguards.

November 6th: President Reagan defeated his Democratic opponent Walter Mondale by a big majority in the US presidential elections.

November 12th: Chancellor Nigel Lawson says that the £1 note will be gradually phased out. No more are to be printed.

November 19th: A further 2,300 miners have returned to work bringing the total of working miners to around 62,000.

December 10th: Desmond Tutu, the Anglican Bishop of Johannesburg, has won the Nobel Peace Prize for his non-violent struggle against apartheid.

December 14th: Britain's top rock stars, led by Bob Geldof of the Boomtown Rats, have come together to help the starving refugees of Ethiopia. Their song *Do They Know It's Christmas* has topped the charts and is set to raise millions of pounds. *See page 80*

GREAT HITS OF 1984

I Just Called To Say I Love You

Do They Know It's Christmas?

See James Bond from the comfort of your car

April 22nd: Blonde actress Diana Dors, who is suffering from cancer, today opened Britain's first drive-in cinema at Allington near Maidstone — her husband Alan Lake helping to cut the red ribbon.

Drive-in cinemas are incredibly popular in America but because of the vagaries of the British weather the concept has always been considered a non-starter in this country— until now.

The Drive-in Movie Show UK Ltd has set up a large screen in the car park of the Kent garden centre. The opening night film, *Never Say Never,* stars Sean Connery as James Bond and has attracted scores of customers who pay £4.60p per car. The car park can accommodate 150 cars.

Meals will be served on trays by roller-skating waitresses and waiters. There are no shortage of experts in this field as five international roller skaters live in the Maidstone area.

May 4th: Diana Dors died today from cancer of the stomach and lymph glands. To the admiration of thousands of adoring fans the incredibly brave Diana continued to appear on chat shows and make public appearances knowing that death was near.

Mystery parcel bomb kills Ightham housewife

June 6th: An unnamed Englishman who lives in Spain is wanted by Kent police for questioning in connection with the murder of Ightham housewife Barbara Harrold who died of heart failure after opening a parcel bomb in the kitchen of her home, Old Cottage.

It was on May 21st that Mrs Harrold, aged 53, received a parcel tied with a red ribbon. It was addressed to her personally. As she pulled the wrapping apart a huge explosion rocked the house and blew out the windows. A detonator embedded itself in the ceiling and Mrs Harrold, severely injured with a hand blown off, lay on the kitchen floor.

The victim was taken to Canterbury Hospital where she died six days later and police identified the weapon as a pipe-bomb favoured by terrorist groups. It was designed to maim horribly or even kill.

In their enquiries police have discovered that the parcel was posted from Roseacre sub-post office in Bearsted by a man whom they believe was staying with his relatives in Maidstone. The murder team know the suspect had bought the Harrolds' former holiday home at Denia in Spain and that there had been some acrimony over the purchase deal. "Hate mail" had been frequently received by the Harrolds.

Through the Home Office and with the help of Interpol and the Spanish police Kent police hope the suspect can be charged with the illegal possession of firearms and extradited. **See page 69**

Gunned down by a madman

Two-year-old Jodie Woodward is fighting for her life after being gunned down by the next-door neighbour on a housing estate at Walderslade near Chatham.

According to eyewitnesses Rod Davie burst into the Woodward's home yesterday with a gun "looking for his wife". Jodie was alone in the house with her mum Cheryl.

In blind anger Davie fired the weapon at the toddler who took the full force in the face. She suffered appalling facial injuries. The man then killed himself.

Jodie has lost an eye and may suffer damage to the brain.

Chatham Dockyard was a symbol of Britain's maritime supremacy

Date: The great royal dockyard at Chatham, where for more than four centuries Britain's maritime supremacy was forged and sustained, has finally closed. Yesterday (Friday) two Royal Marine drummers led the last detachment of sailors out of the gates of HMS Pembroke as the Royal Navy said farewell to the Medway Towns.

It was three years ago that Defence Secretary John Nott announced the closure of the Dockyard. People in the Medway Towns were stunned but despite that, the yardmen — now threatened with the dole queue — continued with the refit of *HMS Hermione* and two nuclear submarines.

The Falklands War provided a brief respite. Men were diverted away from *Hermione* to prepare other ships for service. The refit then continued and gradually Chatham emptied of warships until only the Leander class frigate remained.

The White Ensign which has fluttered over thousands of ships in the royal dockyard may never fly here again. The giant basins are empty.

On Friday the last officers and men, resident at HMS Pembroke, were led out of Alexandra Gate by Cmdr "Robbie" Wilson who locked up and then handed over the last ensign to Gillingham mayor, Cllr Lionel Dollery.

Among the sailors who marched from the base were veterans from Gillingham's Pembroke House who had memories of naval life through two world wars. They heard Cmdr Wilson say that it was a very, very sad day for the Navy. "The red bricks of HMS Pembroke have been a comforting sight for servicemen and their families during all the conflicts of the last 80 years."

Cmdr Wilson was presented with a silver facsimile of the key which locked the gates as a tribute from his men. He then climbed into a brewery dray with Medway's civic leaders which took them to a naval farewell celebration at the Royal Marine pub outside the base.

See page 64 and 65

The white ensign is lowered for the last time. The Medway Towns' long association with the great royal dockyard, founded by Queen Elizabeth I during the threat from the Spanish Armada, is finally over.

CHATHAM DOCKYARD: THE STORY IN BRIEF

1547: Henry VIII's fleet winters in Jillyngham Water.

1581: First dry dock built at Chatham. Enlarged by the Stuarts to become the main naval station in the kingdom.

1667: English fleet in the Medway surprised and humiliated by the Dutch.

1758: Fortifications known as the Chatham Lanes built. Strengthened during the Napoleonic Wars.

1765: Chatham's most famous ship the *Victory* is built of stout Kentish oak and launched.

1805: *Victory*, now 40 years old, achieves glory at Trafalgar. Nelson's body returns to Kent in a barrel of alcohol.

1816: Charles Dickens moves to Chatham with his father, a navy pay officer. Now a garrison town.

1914: Three Chatham-based cruisers sunk by one U-Boat with the loss of 1,500 lives — many of them local men.

1939: Cruisers *Ajax* and *Achilles* from Chatham fight the pocket battleship *Graf Spee* in the Battle of the River Plate.

1939-1945: Chatham-built ships fight at Jutland and submarines sink German warships.

1966: Chatham enters the nuclear age with the advent of the reactor-powered submarine.

1982: Chatham-refitted ships win last battle honours in the Falklands War.

A museum, perhaps, or deterioration

What is the future now for Chatham Dockyard? What is to be done with the huge waterfront stores whose bricks bear graffiti carved by generations of sailors? What will happen to the sail and colour lofts built by Napoleonic prisoners of war?

It is known that the Government's Property Services Agency will look after the buildings until English Estates formally takes control in April and applies for listed status.

The ideal solution, promoted by numerous organisations, would be to turn the whole site into a museum so that the many thousands who used to flock to the traditional Navy Days can return to visit exhibitions, displays, working ropery and flagloft.

There are fears, however, that Government departments will pass the buck and the buildings will deteriorate.

Chatham Dockyard in its heyday. Here are three miles of naval dockyards built on 500 acres, including many relics from Dickens' times, lines of multiple stores, a workplace for many thousands of people and centuries of nautical history. For much of the 19th century this was the largest industrial centre in Kent, whose prosperity was swelled by cement, engineering and numerous other activities. Its closure brings to an end a chapter of British Naval history.

1984

Queen security dilemma as IRA bomb blasts Brighton hotel

October 19th: Security for the visit of the Queen and Prince Philip to Maidstone next week will be tightened considerably following the bombing of the Grand Hotel, Brighton.

The IRA device was intended to assassinate most of the British cabinet during the Conservative Party conference on October 12th. Three people were killed and Mrs Thatcher narrowly escaped death.

Since the tragedy, politicians have emphasised that total security in a democratic society is impossible. Sir Patrick Mayhew, MP for Tunbridge Wells, said: "Security for the Queen's visit will be a matter for the Chief Constable, but everybody realises there is no means by which total security can be imposed."

These are tense days and the royal visit will present Kent police with a major dilemma. The Queen will arrive via the A20 and be taken into the Crown Courts. That will be followed by a processional drive through the town to Session House Square. The route will be heavily policed.

Those who died in the Brighton bombing included one MP, Sir Anthony Berry, and the wife of the government chief whip John Wakeham. More than 30 people were pulled, badly injured, from the rubble including the Employment Secretary Norman Tebbit and his wife.

None of Kent's MPs were hurt in the blast. Patrick Mayhew and his wife Jean were on the third floor and made their way to safety via a smoke filled corridor. Mid Kent MP Andrew Rowe had walked past the hotel just a few hours before the bomb went off.

The aftermath of Sunday's tragedy in Cobham. Minutes before the incident the car park of the Ship had been packed with customers' cars.

Air race pilots collide over village

August 24th: Two light aircraft crashed into each other above the village of Cobham during the annual Rochester Air Show on Sunday, killing both pilots.

One of the planes, a four-seater Piper Cherokee, fell into the car park of the Ship Inn, skidded across the main road and pushed a car into the wall of a house. The second, a two-seater Bolkow, attempted an emergency landing but hit power cables and crashed into a cornfield.

There were lucky escapes for scores of people in Cobham, including those on the village cricket pitch who found themselves dodging falling debris.

The pilots were competing in the Kent Messenger Air Race which is staged every year by the Royal Aero Club.

Chris Cowdrey takes the helm for Kent

October: Five years ago certain cricket commentators were suggesting that Kent's "Packer players" should never represent the county again — a view repeated when Underwood, Knott and Woolmer joined the rebel South African tour last year.

The players have not only survived but played a crucial role in helping the county to reach the Nat-West final in two successive seasons — 1983 and 1984. In each case Kent lost — in the gathering gloom of a September Saturday.

There is little doubt that Chris Tavare's two seasons as captain coincided with a definite improvement in results so it came as a shock to many supporters when the England player was sacked after the second Lords defeat. He has been replaced by Chris Cowdrey.

In the past few years controversy has never been far away from the Kent dressing room but nor has individual success. Since 1981, Underwood, Knott, Woolmer, Tavare and Dilley have represented England. This year Richard Ellison made a successful England debut and the county's West Indian all-rounder, Eldine Baptiste, was chosen for his country. Finally, Cowdrey has clinched his place in the England party to tour India this winter.

During 1984 Underwood proved he is still the best left-arm bowler in the country — but he will remember the season for a remarkable innings against Sussex at Hastings in a game which produced Kent's first tie for 10 years.

Coming in as night watchman Underwood scored 111 — his maiden century in first class cricket. He shared a big partnership with Kent's new overseas signing Terry Alderman, who also took nine wickets in the game

Kent's senior circuit judge, John Streeter, accompanies The Queen to the new Law Courts on the riverside at Maidstone

Queen opens new law courts

October 30th: The Queen and Prince Philip today opened Kent's £14 million law courts on Maidstone's riverside.

Robed borough councillors formed a procession from the Town Hall to the new courts following two open carriages which carried the mayor Cllr Michael Nightingale, MP Sir John Wells and the chairman of Kent County Council, Cllr Ron Powling.

The carriages were pulled by Whitbread shire horses who winter in Paddock Wood.

Later the Queen enjoyed a tour of the Medway Towns, visiting the Molly Wisdom Hospice, Rochester's Corn Exchange, Chatham Dockyard and Gillingham Business Park.

Earlier in the year the Queen Mother also visited the Medway Towns in her role as patron of the Arethusa Venture Centre in Lower Upnor which offers fun breaks for underprivileged young people from city centres.

A parcel bomb, an air crash, a hovercraft disaster and now a motorway tragedy on a misty December morning. A horrible year for the county.

M25 carnage in morning fog

December 12th: The notoriously misty stretch of the M25 through the Holmesdale Valley, between Sevenoaks and Godstone, was the scene yesterday (Tuesday) of one of the worst accidents in motorway history. 22 vehicles were swallowed in a bank of fog from which nine people never emerged.

It was six o'clock in the morning and traffic, travelling clockwise near the Surrey/Kent border, was encountering patchy fog in the dips and hollows where the M25 follows the southern edge of the North Downs.

Suddenly, without warning juggernauts, vans and cars became victims of the most ghastly pile-up.

Within seconds vehicles were reduced to balls of twisted metal as they ran into one another. To add to the appalling carnage fire broke out immediately and those, unable to escape from their cars, were burned to death.

The crash occurred at a place where there are no exits for 18 miles and police, ambulancemen and firemen were hampered in their attempts to reach the injured and dying by the sheer volume of traffic on the M25.

By nine o'clock the fog had cleared and the fires were out leaving a charred and twisted heap of vehicles most with the paint burnt off by the ferocity of the blaze.

'Some 60,000 men have voluntarily left the mining industry. Not one of them has been made redundant against his will. We have the same coal production today as we had in 1983' — Ian MacGregor.

January 4th: P & O has sold its Channel car ferry fleet to Townsend Thorensen (European Ferries).

January 10th: Britain's traffic problems will soon be a thing of the past — according to Clive Sinclair. The electronics genius has unveiled a battery and pedal-powered tricycle called the C5. It will cost £399.

February 5th: The Archbishop of Canterbury's special representative, Terry Waite, has secured the freedom of four Britons held hostage in Libya.

February 25th: Just half the country's miners are still on strike. 3,807 are now back at work.

March 3rd: The NUM decision to call off its year-long strike has been greeted with scenes of fury in Kent where miners have voted to continue the dispute. Mrs Thatcher is claiming a "famous victory".

March 11th: The House of Fraser, owners of Harrods, is now in the ownership of the Egyptian Al Fayed brothers.

March 12th: Mikhail Gorbachev, aged 54, has been appointed head of the Soviet Communist Party.

Keith Raymond Cottingham, who was arrested by Kent police in Spain in connection with the death of Barbara Harrold, has been released after spending a few months in custody. Extradition requirements are being negotiated with the Spanish Government.

March 28th: The great artist Marc Chagall died in Paris today aged 97. One of his last commissions was to design the stained glass windows in All Saints Church, Tudeley, near Tonbridge. They were dedicated this year.

April 11th: An 18-month old boy has become the first Briton to die of Aids.

April 30th: The Venerable Wilfred Wood, aged 49, Archdeacon of Southwark since 1982, is the first

January 1st: Countess Mountbatten of Burma, who was badly injured by the terrorist bomb which killed her father in 1979, has been appointed Vice Lord-Lieutenant of Kent. The title has been approved by the Queen who, a month ago, attended the wedding in Ashford of the Countess's daughter, Joanna. She is seen here with one Mountbatten rose.

black priest to become an Anglican bishop in Britain. He takes over as Bishop of Croydon.

May 11th: Forty soccer fans died today when fire swept through the wooden stand of Bradford City football ground. Many deaths were caused by crushing and trampling.

A special Act of Parliament has had to be passed to allow Alan Monk of Ashford to marry his own mother-in-law. Alan's former wife Jeanette was a bridesmaid and became his stepdaughter!

May 16th: Home Secretary Leon Brittan today announced new police and court powers to combat violence on picket lines.

May 30th: Rampaging Liverpool fans are being blamed for the tragedy at Heysel Stadium, Brussels last night. A wall collapsed as the British fans charged the Juventus team supporters leaving 41 dead and at least 350 injured.

June 23rd: An Indian Boeing 747 crashed into the sea off Ireland this morning killing all 323 on board. It is believed that Sikh extremists are responsible.

July 2nd: The Church of England has approved the ordination of women deacons.

July 27th: In the British Open Golf Championship at the Royal St George's, Sandwich, this

week Sandy Lyle became the first British Open winner since Tony Jacklin, 16 years ago.

August 26th: Zola Budd today set a new world record for the 5,000 metres in an invitation race at Crystal Palace. A few weeks ago Steve Cram took a second off Sebastian's Coe's world record in the Dream Mile at Oslo.

September 15th: Europe's golfers have recaptured the Ryder Cup from the United States.

September 17th: Laura Ashley, whose fashion empire began in a converted mill near Westerham, died today after a fall at her home. She was 60 and head of a multi-million pound international business employing 4,000 people.

October 7th: A London policeman, Pc Keith Blakelock, was hacked to death tonight as several hundred black youths rioted after the death of a black woman during a police search of her flat.

A teachers' dispute in which the NUT and the NASUWT have staged a series of three-day strikes, has dragged on for most of the year with neither Government or unions willing to give way.

December 29th: Rupert Murdoch has ordered his new plant at Wapping to be fully operational by early next year.

The much acclaimed film script *My Beautiful Launderette* was written by Bromley-born Hanif Kureishi. He also wrote *Outskirts* which was earlier performed at The Royal Court and *Buddha of Surburbia*.

Jodie Woodward, the two-year-old who was gunned down by a man who then killed himself at Chatham last year, has recovered from her injuries after a series of painful operations. She has lost an eye but there is no brain damage.

GREAT HITS OF 1985

The Power Of Love
I Know Him So Well

January has been the coldest month in Kent since the infamous winter of 1963 when snow lay on the ground for almost three months. This week a reading of 3F (-16C) was recorded at Jubilee Corner, Ashford and many of the villages on the North Downs are cut off by deep snow. Pegwell Bay is frozen for almost half a mile out to sea.

Paul Way helps Europe to win Ryder Cup

September 15th: Tonbridge golfer Paul Way, 22, played a brave and vital role for the victorious European Ryder Cup team this week. In a thrilling finish at The Belfry the United States were beaten by five points — their first defeat in the Ryder Cup for 28 years.

Way, who practiced at the West Malling and Neville golf courses, won three of the matches in which he played, including the Sunday singles against Ray Floyd.

For several days before the match Paul was advised by some members of the golfing press to pull out of the team because of a loss of form.

His father Dennis disagreed. "Paul has the temperament for the big occasion", he said. He certainly proved it.

Four die in hovercraft tragedy

April 1st: Rescuers yesterday called off their search for two passengers who were swept into the sea off Dover last Saturday after the *Princess Margaret* hovercraft was thrown against a breakwater by a Force Seven wind. Two others who died have already been identified.

Coastguards believe their is no hope of finding a 15-year-old French boy or a 13-year- old girl.

Nine other people are still detained with injuries which include extensive bruising, severe lacerations and the effects of swallowing fuel oil.

The Department of Transport will examine the wreck today.

Jean Rook — her outspoken style has made her famous.

Fleet Street's 'first lady' assaulted by masked raiders at Edenbridge home

February 3rd: The *Daily Express* columnist Jean Rook — known as "the first bitch of Fleet Street" — is believed to be the highest paid female journalist in newspaper history. The price of fame, however, can be painful.

Two days ago, masked raiders broke into her home at Edenbridge, dragged her down the stairs by her hair and assaulted both her and her husband, Geoffrey Nash. They were then tied up together while the raiders ransacked the house.

The couple are devastated. Apart from losing many valuables, including all Jean's jewellery, the robbers stole personal items which cannot be replaced.

Jean Rook has never really kept her address a secret, telling readers on many occasions how she loves to come home from London "to salvation" in Edenbridge where she has a Victorian loo, a large red telephone box in the garden, a penny farthing in the shed and a four-poster bed. She has also boasted about her expensive tastes — an XJ6 in the garage, a son at Eton and clothes in the wardrobe from the finest couturiers.

Through her column Jean Rook, 54, has been giving practical advice to her readers ever since she left the *Daily Sketch* where she was fashion editor. Recently she told the Queen to pluck her eyebrows and the Archbishop of Canterbury to "stop bleating".

Express readers love her attacks on the establishment (and the church) and the venom which she freely distributes in a warm-hearted tongue-in-cheek way. Thousands have written to wish her a speedy recovery.

The end of the (Eridge) line?

July 6th: The five-mile route which links Tunbridge Wells West station with Eridge closed today — despite a pending High Court case challenging British Rail's decision.

The Eridge Line Action Group which has secured the judicial review says that by closing the line British Rail is showing utter disregard of public interest.

This week parish councils and hundreds of individuals promised to help fund the action group's High Court case. A spokesman said: "If ELAG compels the Minister to reconsider his ruling British Rail will incur needless expense in closing then re-opening the line."

The last train on the Eridge line was driven by 63-year-old Roy Coomber who retires next month after 45 years' service at Tunbridge Wells West as a fireman and driver.

If the High Court case fails a move will be made to launch an Eridge line preservation society.

See page 165

Kent miners show defiance to the end

June: Two years ago Arthur Scargill, President of the National Union of Miners, discovered a Government plan to close more than half the country's coal mines by the end of the 1980s. Among them were the Kent pits at Tilmanstone and Snowdown.

With a few days he had made the first moves in a battle that was intended to bring the Government to its knees. "This totally undemocratic Thatcher Government", Scargill told his delegates, "can easily push through whatever law it chooses. We can watch social destruction and repression on a truly horrific scale and wait for the inevitable holocaust. Or we can fight back."

Within weeks miners across the country were striking against the programme of closures and the Coal Board's "miserly" 5.2% pay offer.

Kent, having devised the policy of picketing power stations in 1972 and 1974 which led to the three-day week and the downfall of the Heath Government, had hoped a similar strategy might work again. In the East Kent mining community "solidarity" was the keyword.

The miners argued that their livelihoods were under threat. Years earlier, Terry Harrison, secretary of the Betteshanger branch of the NUM had warned that the colliery was losing up to £100,000 a week because of the then steel strike. He said the future was serious for the pit which employed more than 1,000 miners and was the largest in Kent.

Similar concerns came from the smaller Snowdown and Tilmanstone collieries. The National Coal Board confirmed at the time that stock piling was taking place but they had no idea where the figures came from and there were no plans to close the pits.

Scargill, however, was proved right. With a 141-seat majority Mrs

Betteshanger miners after a meeting in their Welfare Club at Mill Hill, Deal.

Thatcher was determined to stop the drain on taxpayers money being poured into the pits at the rate of £875 million in the current year. She mobilised her forces. Mr Ian MacGregor, chairman of the National Coal Board, had the job of stopping Scargill. He said: "If we are to stop the rot and waste and inefficiency, then the irresistible force must meet the immovable object."

After the most bitter confrontation, authoratively viewed as the greatest constitutional crisis faced by the Thatcher Government, the action has failed.

Unlike the earlier disputes this was a manipulated strike taken without a ballot and it lost the miners vital public support. Additionally, Mrs Thatcher introduced new industrial relations legislation making the mass picketing of power stations illegal.

Even more critical to the miners' cause was the fact that the three biggest generating stations in the South — Kingsnorth, Grain and Littlebrook, all in north Kent, were capable of burning coal or oil and linked by a protected pipeline.

Pickets and police clash at Tilmanstone. One of the many ugly scenes as the long strike continued.

The miners, failing to accept the inevitable, refused to give in. There were ugly clashes between police and pickets at Tilmanstone, a long sit-down at the coal face at Betteshanger and wives and children displayed a loyalty that was simply quite moving. As money for food ran out, mass feeding centres were established in Dover and Deal.

From the miners strike headquarters at Magness House, Mill Hill, Deal the wives formed an action committee to raise cash and ease the burden. They started with a simple jumble sale.

As the months rolled on Britain did not come to a standstill as the miners expected. Huge stockpiles of coal had not been depleted and, as far as the Kent miners were concerned, the biggest blow came last September when a huge Soviet tanker pulled into the Kingsnorth terminal and unloaded thousands of gallons of strike-breaking fuel oil.

It was then that miners began to lose heart and some, faced with a huge backlog of mortgage payments, drifted back to work. Now police had to protect them at the pits with paramilitary style operations.

The end came on March 11th this year when the NUM voted to return to work. The militant Kent branch, however, voted against a settlement and were the last to return to their pits.

Many were served with immediate redundancy notices for Snowdown never reopened and Tilmanstone is due to close this month. Betteshanger, the oldest pit of all, is still in production but uncertainty about the future is taking its toll on the workforce.

So 18 months of anger and bitter confrontation has ended. Ian MacGregor blames public apathy. "Over the years", he said, "it had allowed unions to presume they were immune to the fundamentals of British law, that they could use intimidatory mobs rather than a few men to picket, for example." He praised the police who protected the power stations and he praised the managers of the country's electrical supply who performed miracles.

But the miners also had their heroes and heroines; the wives, for example and the stubborn Jack Collins, Kent NUM secretary, who led his men bravely from the front knowing all the time that he was dying of leukaemia.

Since taking the coveted title of Young Musician of the Year in 1984, Emma Johnson, the brilliant clarinettist from Petts Wood, has become an international soloist, appearing at various prestigious centres throughout the country. Emma was a pupil at Sevenoaks School. She beat 470 contestants to take the title and the £500 prize money and millions saw her play Crussell's clarinet concerto. She is on course to enjoy a stunning career of what she enjoys most — making music.

Michael Howard and his model wife

As a top photographic model Sandra Paul was one of the best-known faces of the sixties. Today, her famous smile is seen in an entirely new role — as the political hostess of one of the Government's rising stars, Michael Howard, MP for Folkestone and Hythe.

Newly-appointed as a junior minister at the Department of Trade, Howard has been marked out as a high-flyer since his election to Parliament two years ago.

Sandra, a beautiful blonde of 45 and the mother of Howard's two children, Nicholas and Larissa, made her break into modelling when she was booked to do a photographic session with Norman Parkinson in 1958. She appeared in Vogue magazine and her career took off.

From the age of 18 until her 30s Sandra travelled the world on photographic assignments. "In those days there were no such things as tight budgets", she said. "It was a smaller profession, quite cosy, one big happy family really."

Sandra, who has a 23-year-old son by a former marriage, met Michael Howard at a Red Cross function in Hampshire. "We talked about books", she said. "A week later I received a certain book from Michael asking me what I thought about it. We've been together ever since."

Howard, who was born in Llanelli, is a former President of the Cambridge Union (1962) and friendly with four former students all tipped to become Cabinet members — Peter Lilley, Norman Lamont, Kenneth Clarke and John Gummer. Opponents describe them as the Cambridge mafia.

He has a legal mind of formidable skill and has been at the front rank of his generation at the Bar since he took silk in 1982. *See page 168*

Myra Hindley may soon be released

May 2nd: Medway's parole review committee has recommended the release of the notorious murderer Myra Hindley from Cookham Wood prison in Rochester.

The committee of five chaired by Mrs Daphne MacDonald, former mayor, made the decision after studying reports on Hindley's attitude, character and behaviour.

It is only part of the review procedure. The Home Secretary will be responsible for the final decision. *See page 83*

October 4th: In the wake of the great industrial crisis which has hit the power industry, Grain — the largest oil-fired power station in Europe — opened its doors to the public this week in a public relations exercise that attracted more than 20,000 people.

The station, which cost £600 million to build and employs 400 people, was keen to show how electricity is generated and the work of the Central Electricity Generating Board in caring for the environment. The turbine hall and boiler house is ¼ mile long.

April 19th: Two new bypasses costing £5 million were opened today. One takes traffic away from the centre of Walderslade and the other eases delays on the busy A229 over Blue Bell Hill.

December 10th: Princess Diana, patron of the National Rubella Council, visited the William Harvey Hospital, Ashford, to meet the women who had been vaccinated against German measles.

Kenneth Noye acquitted for the murder of undercover detective

November 1985: Kenneth Noye, a man with £3.2 million in offshore accounts and the mastermind behind the laundering of the Brinks Mat gold bullion, has been acquitted of the murder of Detective Constable John Fordham earlier this year.

Fordham, 45, an officer with C11, the specialist surveillance branch of the Flying Squad, was stabbed to death by Noye in the grounds of Hollywood Cottage, West Kingsdown.

In defence Noye explained that he had been alerted by his barking dogs and went into his garden. "Suddenly a masked man loomed up in front of me. I could see two eye holes. I just froze in horror. I thought it was my lot. I was going to be a dead man."

Noye, who was holding a knife, immediately began to stab the man as hard as he could. The blade cut through five layers of clothing, a camouflage suit, a waterproof suit, a jumper, sweatshirt and vest. Two blows penetrated the heart.

The Central Criminal Court had already heard that C11 had accumulated enough information about Kenneth Noye and his laundering operation to arrest him.

On the evening of January 26th, Fordham and Detective Constable Neil Murphy were detailed to enter the grounds of Hollywood Cottage. Noye was known to be inside the house with Barry Reader, who was the principal courier in the Brinks Mat raid. Their wives were with them.

At 6.45 Fordham radioed to his colleagues outside the gates that hostile dogs had approached him and Murphy. Later he reported that a man with a torch had come out of the house and was calling the dogs. At this stage Murphy had retreated towards the gates hoping to draw the dogs after him. He was unsuccessful.

At 6.37 Murphy heard a man shout: "Show us your ID then and I'll blow your head off." He called his colleagues and police entered the grounds in numbers. Fordham was gasping "he's done me, he's stabbed me".

Noye was arrested and Reader who had run off was picked up later. A search of Hollywood Cottage uncovered 11 bars of gold and £69,000 of cash.

The jury acquitted Noye on the grounds that he was defending himself from an apparently dangerous trespasser. ***See page 139***

Ken Noye — alerted by his dogs.

John Fordham — stabbed twice.

The search continues for Brinks Mat gold

Scotland Yard have uncovered full details of Kenneth Noye's role in the Brinks Mat robbery of November 1983. It was his job to re-smelt the 6,800 gold ingots valued at £26 million, remove the identification marks and dispose of it in small parcels on the legitimate gold market.

The laundering operation was conducted from Hollywood Cottage but the re-smelting took place in a converted coachhouse in the West

Country. It was so successful that the Bank of England were unaware of the considerable amounts of money passing hands.

Four men have already been tried for the robbery — the biggest ever in Britain. Two were jailed for 25 years and one for six. The fourth man was acquitted. Noye and his courier, Barry Richards, will stand trial for their part in the raid next year.

Kenneth Noye has lived in South

London and Kent for years. He has been described as a printer, property dealer and builder. At the age of 35 he is a multi-millionaire.

Noye built Hollywood Cottage which, in fact, is a large 10-bedroom mansion standing in 20 acres of grounds. The swimming pool is empty but built into it are secret storage compartments.

So far little of the Brinks Mat gold has been retrieved.

Kenneth Noye's wife Brenda outside Hollywood Cottage, West Kingsdown. Eleven gold bars and £69,000 in cash were found in the house but the secret storage compartments in the swimming pool were empty.

Developers respond to the shopping boom

Shopping malls, pedestrian precincts, multi-storey car parks and vast town centre complexes, housing the top retail outlets, are springing up all over Kent.

The county's largest shopping centres are the Pentagon, Chatham which is already celebrating its tenth successful year, the Stoneborough at Maidstone, the Broadway at Bexleyheath and the out-of-town centre at Hempstead Valley. Housewives love them; with central heating, air conditioning, ventilation, automatic lifts, escalators and bright lights everywhere, shopping is a luxury.

Chatham's Pentagon opened in 1975 on a 4.5 acre construction site in the historic heart of the town. 2,500 piles had to be sunk to carry the giant structure which now houses seven large stores and 80 individual shops.

The Broadway at Bexleyheath, which dominates the skyline from all approaches, was opened by the Duke of Edinburgh in 1984 and draws customers from all the south-east London boroughs. Hempstead Valley, opened in 1978, welcomes customers from the Medway Towns.

Most towns now have their own complex with a multi-storey car park attached such as the St George's Centre at Gravesend and The Priory at Dartford. It has meant years and years of town hall arguments with the clear message that progress is more important than sentimentality. The Angel Football Ground, Tonbridge — once the headquarters of Kent Cricket Club — is a good example. Despite objections the playing area is being turned into a car park encircled by two giant stores, smaller shops and a leisure centre. It will open next year.

As more and more developers get the nod, constructors are expected to move to other sites and in a few years, The Glades at Bromley, the Royal Victoria Place at Tunbridge Wells and Tufton Centre, Ashford will be household names. One town is having more difficulty than most. Despite a succession of plans and costly professional advice no decision has yet been made over the proposed Bligh's Meadow Centre at Sevenoaks. The most vociferous opponents to the scheme are the townsfolk themselves.

After an absence of 10 years from the TV screens, heart-throb British singer-turned-actor Adam Faith recently made a welcome return by playing the lead role in a delightful BBC play, Just Another Little Blues Song. *Adam, who has had to learn how to play the saxophone, also has a new home in an isolated spot on the Pilgrims Way near Westerham — an area which he simply adores. Adam Faith, stage name of Terry Nelhams, is now 45. He was one of Britain's leading pop stars in the early 60 s, having topped the charts with both his first two singles,* Poor Me *and* What Do You Want. *He followed that with a string of 60 hits and such films as* Yesterday's Hero, McVicar, Foxes *and* Stardust. *He achieved his greatest television success as a sharp cockney character in the central role of the TV series* Budgie. *He is pictured here with his saxophone and co-star Dawn Archibald.*

April 20th: *Motorists on the A2 at Cobham escaped serious injury when a section of a 200-ton bridge fell on the road at 8.30 am today. Miraculously, scores of drivers managed to pull up as the bridge came crashing down after being struck by a digger on the back of a lorry. One car stopped a few yards short of the reinforced concrete as it hit the road. A police spokesman said: "It's amazing there wasn't a mass fatality (sic). I dread to think what would have happened if there had been a coach underneath." The lorry driver from Longfield was taken to hospital suffering from severe shock.*

A 21-year-old football mad North Kent building worker, who was born in Woolwich and grew up on the Honor Oak council estate in Brockley, has been offered a trial by Crystal Palace after being rejected by Brighton. Ian Wright, who has two sons from two different relationships, experienced several brushes with the law during his tempestuous days in south-east London, including a five-day sentence in Chelmsford prison. He has one real ambition; to play centre forward for England.

Tom Thumb's revival

A Civic Restoration Award has been given to The Tom Thumb theatre which is situated on the Eastern Esplanade at Cliftonville and boasts the smallest stage in the world (seven feet by 10 feet). The Theatre was built as a coach house in 1896 but has been derelict for many years. Lesley Parr-Byrne a former theatrical agent and her daughter Sarah have now seen its potential as a tiny Victorian theatre, conveying the atmosphere of those far-off music hall days.

A Room with a View

A film adaptation of E.M. Forster's famous novel, *A Room with a View,* has won three Academy Awards at the Oscar ceremony.

Produced and directed by Ismail Merchant and James Ivory, much of the film was made in the grounds of Foxwold, a large house at Brasted Chart , near Westerham, where a small lake was restored for a controversial nude scene.

Julian Sands, Helena Bonham-Carter, Maggie Smith, Denholm Elliott and Simon Callow head a superb cast, whose characters breach more and more of the social restraints of the day.

Forster, who lived in Tunbridge Wells before the turn of the century, was a champion of freedom and tolerance and frequently exposed the weaknesses of the English middle classes.

Bob Geldof raises more millions for famine relief

July 7th: Last Christmas Bob Geldof brought together Britain's rock superstars to help the starving millions in Ethiopia and the Sudan. This week he has done it again on an international scale.

Following the *Band Aid* single, *Do They Know It's Christmas*, which raised tens of thousands of pounds, he has arranged simultaneous concerts in London and America to create *Live Aid* — the biggest rock jamboree the world has ever seen.

Bob Geldof who lives with his girlfriend Paula Yates at Davington Priory, near Faversham, persuaded the elite of the rock world to perform at Wembley Stadium and the JFK Stadium, Philadelphia.

More than one and a half billion people in 160 countries watched the concerts live on television. David Bowie, Mick Jagger, Queen and Dire Straits were among those who turned out for free and helped raise a staggering £40 million.

Geldof, who is now better known as the king of Live Aid than a lead singer with the Boomtown Rats, is having difficulty finding time to restore his ancient Priory. The last Benedictine nuns left 450 years ago and it fell into total disrepair.

In the meantime raising millions for Africa's famine-stricken poor is taking up most of his time. MPs in Sweden and the UK have proposed the singer for a Nobel Peace Prize. ***See page 84***

'Stick to one partner or use condoms. Drug users, never share needles. Don't die of ignorance' — Part of the slogan for the £20 million Aids campaign launched this year.

January 2nd: England's cricket tour of Bangladesh has been cancelled followed a row over ties with South Africa.

January 15th: Mikhail Gorbachev wants to eliminate all nuclear arms by the turn of the century.

January 24th: Michael Heseltine and Leon Brittan have resigned from the cabinet over Westland Helicopters.

January 28th: The entire crew of the American space shuttle, *Challenger*, was killed today when it exploded seconds after lift-off.

February 12th: Mrs Thatcher and President Mitterand today signed the Channel Tunnel Treaty in Canterbury.

February 25th: Ferdinand Marcos, President of the Phillipines for 20 years, has been finally toppled from power.

March 31st: The Labour-controlled Greater London Council has been abolished as unnecessary and wasteful. Powers will now pass to the borough councils.

April 15th: United States bombers, flying from British bases, have attacked terrorist targets in Libya. Mrs Thatcher faces fierce criticism.

April 18th: Guinness has won the battle for control of the Distillers Group.

April 24th: The Duchess of Windsor died today in Paris aged 89. It was almost 50 years ago that her husband King Edward VIII gave up his throne to marry her.

April 30th: The Number Four nuclear reactor at Chernobyl Power Station in the Ukraine exploded today. According to Soviet TV, two people have been killed and the area evacuated. Other reactors have been closed.

June 23rd: Patrick Magee is given eight life sentences for the Brighton bombing and other terrorist offences. He will now

June 9th: Prince Charles is pictured with Lord de Lisle during his visit to Penshurst Place today. The house and gardens have been in the ownership of the Sidney family since the 16th century; the great soldier and poet Sir Philip Sidney was a favourite of Elizabeth I. Lord de Lisle, who won the VC in the second world war and was briefly an MP and cabinet minister, spent nearly five years as Governor General of Australia. The wonderful 14th century great hall is the core of Penshurst Place.

remain in prison perhaps for the rest of his life.

June 29th: Argentina beat West Germany today by 3-2 in the final of the World Cup in Mexico. England lost to the eventual winners in the quarter final which included Diego Maradona's notorious "hand of God" goal.

July 21st: Twenty per cent of children are now born outside marriage, according to a report published today.

July 23rd: Prince Andrew and Sarah Ferguson, the Duke and Duchess of York, were married in Westminster Abbey today.

July 30th: Divers who have found the wreck of the *Titanic* on the sea bed say it sank when the rivets popped out of place — not because of an enormous gash in the hull.

September 24th: Following the flotation of the Trustee Savings Bank, an estimated four million have applied for shares.

Radio Kent's new £1.5 million studios at Sun Pier, Chatham, have been opened by Princess Alexandra. She was shown around by station manager Mike Marsh.

October 26th: Jeffrey Archer resigned today as deputy chairman of the Conservative Party over allegations of an affair with a prostitute.

November 21st: The Government today launched a "Safe Sex" campaign to help combat the growing menace of Aids.

November 22nd: At the age of 20 Mike Tyson is the world's WBC new heavyweight champion. He beat Trevor Berbick today in less than two rounds.

November 30th: Mr Terry Waite. the Archbishop of Canterbury's special representative, has secured the release of Mr David Jacobson, an American, held hostage for 18 months.

December 1st: The Guinness takeover of Distillers is to be investigated by the Department of Trade following allegations of misconduct.

December 29th: Harold Macmillan, the first Earl of Stockton, Prime Minister from 1957 to 1963 and MP for Bromley 1945 to 1964, has died at the age of 92. As one of the political giants of the century he will always be known for his Wind of Change speech and the slogan *"You've Never Had It So Good"*.

Among Hollywood idols to die this year are James Cagney, the best-loved bad guy of gangster movies and Cary Grant who starred alongside all the leading ladies of the movie industry. Grant, who married five times, was 82. Cagney was 86.

GREAT HITS OF 1986

I Want to Wake Up With You
Every Loser Wins
Don't Leave Me This Way

Channel Tunnel gets go-ahead: work will start next year

The concept of a fixed crossing, independent of wind and tide, between Dover and Calais has been an engineer's dream since the beginning of the 19th century when a serious proposal was put forward in a brief period of peace during the Napoleonic wars.

A French engineer named Albert Mathieu-Favier was the mastermind behind that 1802 plan. He envisaged that passengers would travel in horse-drawn coaches in an undersea tunnel ventilated by huge iron chimneys. The resumption of war between Britain and France meant an end to M Mathieu-Favier's scheme.

The first proper agreement between the two countries was signed in 1875, after 20 years of preparatory work by many including, at the start, Isambard Kingdom Brunel and Robert Stephenson — and later another Frenchman, M.J.A. Thome de Gamond who presented his scheme at the Great Exhibition in Paris. His tunnel would have run via an artificial island on the Varne Bank in mid-Channel.

In 1876 a Channel Tunnel Company was formed. A tunnel boring machine was designed by military engineers Frederick Beaumont and Thomas English and work began at Sangatte, near Calais and Shakespeare Cliff. Shafts were sunk, headings driven obliquely under the sea and a "submarine railway" bored more than a mile out. All to no avail. In 1882 tunnelling was ordered to stop by the Board of Trade who feared a French invasion was a distinct possibility.

A new Channel Tunnel Railway

January 21st: There really is going to be a Channel Tunnel. Yesterday, in Lille, Mrs Thatcher and President Mitterand confirmed the project would go ahead and that work should begin next year. Four consortia have been bidding for the contract and one, led by Trafalgar House, submitted an ambitious scheme which would have allowed motorists to drive to France, partly through a tunnel and partly across an enormous bridge.

In the end the job went to The Channel Tunnel Group who propose an all-rail tunnel; with vehicles being loaded onto special trains at Cheriton near Folkestone. The contract is known as the "fixed-link franchise" and includes a commitment to look at the possibility of building another tunnel, a drive-through tunnel for cars, by the year 2000.

Mrs Thatcher said yesterday: "Let me assure you we have looked with the greatest possible care at the effects the link will have on the environment. Also the construction process will attract many jobs, and when it's open, the tunnel should prove to be the magnet for Kent."

Kent, however, is bracing itself for a fight. People are worried about terrorism and rabies, about the effects on the ferry industry and the loss of England's island status. Above all they are worried the development will scar or destroy many acres of beautiful countryside.

An Anglo-French construction and operating company will be financed initially by banks in many countries. The Tunnel will be 31 miles long. There will be four trains an hour in each direction with through services from London to Brussel and Paris. Fares will be about £50 per car. The Channel Tunnel Treaty will be signed in Canterbury next month.

There is one consolation for campaigners worried about the environmental implications for the Garden of England. British Rail and the Government have made it clear that a new rail link between London and the coast will not be needed. Existing lines can cope. See page 126

Existing railway lines can cope with the traffic

Bill was drawn up in 1907 after many years of campaigning by Sir Edward Watkin, Chairman of the South Eastern Railway Company. This time objections came from the War Office who said that Britain would no longer be protected by the sea and the world's greatest navy.

The scheme was resurrected in the 1920s but did not progress beyond trial borings. It was not until 1973 that the two Governments approved a 32-mile link costing an estimated £468 million. The announcement was accompanied by the usual fear of invasion plus worries about the likelihood of rabies, the sacrifice of many acres of heritage coast and the damage to Kent by traffic straying off the existing motorways. 250 metres of tunnel were bored but the scheme foundered again ...until this week!

Princess Anne on Glowing Promise, *trained by Barry Hills, leads the field at Folkestone.*

The future of racing at Folkestone

November 4th: Princess Anne, who represented Britain at the 1976 Olympics in Montreal, is perhaps better known as an excellent three-day eventer. But yesterday she took the saddle at Folkestone in the Leeds Amateur Rider Stakes over 1.5 miles — and came a commendable third.

The Princess Royal, who arrived and left by helicopter, also learned that Folkestone Racecourse is undergoing major improvements. Work will begin later this year on building 57 stables and a new judges' tower, alongside the modern Tattersall's Stand which is to include entering boxes, restaurant and an enlarged Tote area.

Today the course — the only venue for flat racing in Kent — is owned by Folkestone Racecourse PLC and has come a long way since its future was under threat 20 years ago.

Folkestone racecourse is 90 years old. The original course was founded in 1896 under the chairmanship of Lord Hardinge of Penshurst when 210 acres of land were purchased and a lease acquired for a further 310 acres. Three courses were laid out and nearby Westenhanger House converted into a clubhouse. The first meeting was in 1898 under National Hunt Rules.

At the beginning of the century the racecourse went into liquidation and a new company was formed to run the business. It proved to be so popular that the directors of South East Railways provided free travel for horses with lads and built a new station with unloading bays for horse boxes. Race day trains ran from London in one and a half hours at 4s return third class.

Myra Hindley talks of 2 more murders

November: Britain's most notorious female murderer, Myra Hindley, who is serving life in Cookham Wood, Rochester for her part in the Moors murders, has finally broken her long silence and confessed that she and Ian Brady committed other murders

From her prison cell she said this week that the bodies of two children are buried somewhere on Saddleworth Moor but she cannot remember the exact spot. Police will search the area immediately and may take Hindley with them.

The couple were convicted in 1966 for murdering a teenager and two children and photographing them in their dying moments.

In a few years time Hindley may be considered for parole. Her future then will be in the hands of the Home Secretary.

The opening of the Swanley to Sevenoaks link of the M25 — known as the "missing link" — completes London's orbital motorway south of the Thames. This, the most sensitive route of all and the subject of both an inquiry and High Court battle, is part of a £950 million Government investment for the largest orbital motorway in the world. Contractors had to excavate 2.8 million cubic metres of earth and chalk to make structural embankments and lessen the environmental impact of the scheme. Several bridges have been built including the Polhill bridleway bridge in which an archway captures views of the valley below the escarpment. It is estimated that up to 70,000 vehicles a day will use the new section.

July 24th: Famine aid hero Bob Geldof of Davington Priory, Faversham has been already been given the Freedom of Swale and received an Honorary Degree from the Chancellor of the University of Kent, Jo Grimond.

Today came the sweetest award of all — an Honorary Knighthood from the Queen. The Irish singer, who was the inspiration behind Band Aid and Live Aid, travelled to Buckingham Palace with his girlfriend, Paula Yates.

Millionaire saves Brands Hatch

May 23rd: Months of speculation about the future of Brands Hatch is finally over. Computer millionaire John Foulston has bought the Grand Prix circuit for £5.25 million ensuring that motor racing will continue there "for his lifetime".

A motor racing enthusiast and former amateur driver, Mr Foulston had to pay almost double the original price to fight off fierce competition from supermarket groups who wanted Brands, Oulton Park and Snetterton circuits for development.

The circuit's managing director John Webb is delighted and so are the 106 employees who heard the news broadcast over the tannoy during Sunday's race meeting.

Brands Hatch began in the 1930s as a grass track for motorcycles. In 1964 it became the location of the British Grand Prix, a position it has retained on alternate years. This year's winner was Nigel Mansell in a Williams. *See page 104*

Aldington's Press Baron takes his seat in the Lords

June 19th: Bill Deedes gave up his 13-hour working day as editor of the *Daily Telegraph* earlier this year. At 72, and just as energetic and clear-thinking as ever, he was keen to continue as an independent freelance journalist. It meant no more getting home at midnight after catching the 10.30 pm from London and driving to his home in Aldington.

Today, the former MP for Ashford who successfully fought nine general elections campaigns, has a new job and a new title. He is Baron William Deedes of Aldington and will soon be taking up his seat in the House of Lords.

The Old Harrovian, holder of the Military Cross, ex-Cabinet minister, who delighted *Telegraph* readers with his Peterborough column, was made a life peer in the Queen's birthday honours list.

Before joining the *Telegraph* he worked for the now defunct *Morning Post* and saw service as a war correspondent in Abyssinia in 1935. Among his colleagues was Evelyn Waugh who turned the experiences of the press corps into the hilarious novel, *Scoop*.

During his 24 years as MP, Bill was Parliamentary Under Secretary for the Home Office from 1955 to 1957.

He is married to Hilary and the couple have two sons (one deceased) and three daughters. His eldest son Jeremy is currently managing editor for the Eddie Shah hi-tech colour daily, *Today*.

Bill Deedes lived at Saltwood Castle and Sandling Park before moving to a roomy Victorian house at Aldington. In this photograph (taken a few years later) he is seen with Jonathan Holborow, editor of The Mail on Sunday *who also lives in the village.*

The words flow from Wye's remarkable writing team

December: The remarkable husband and wife writing team of Michael and Mollie Hardwick continues to be prolific. Michael's latest book — he has written more than 100 — is called *The Complete Guide to Sherlock Holmes* which has already sold more than 50,000 copies.

Mollie's output is no less abundant. She has produced at least one historical romance every year since 1954 alongside scores of biographies and television scripts, including, last year, *Juliet Bravo*.

The couple were colleagues with the BBC as scriptwriters and producers. After their marriage in 1961 they moved to Great Mongeham, near Deal and then to Church Street, Wye, where they share the same study and write more than 75,000 words each, each week.

Some years ago Michael dared to complete *The Mystery of Edwin Drood* for Charles Dickens. He's also written a Sherlock Holmes novel, abridged all Trollope's Palliser novels and published such popular books as *The Great Fire Of London* and *The Discovery of Japan*.

Perhaps he is best known for his ITV television series, *Upstairs Downstairs,* which has spawned nine books — *Mr Bellamy's Story, Mr Hudson's Diaries, Upstairs Downstairs Omnibus* and numerous others in collaboration with his wife.

Julie Tullis went to sleep in her tent on K2 and never woke up again.

Julie Tullis dies on K2 - her 'special mountain'

August 22nd: Julie Tullis, Britain's greatest woman mountaineer, died in her sleep after being trapped in a snowstorm on K2 — her "most special" mountain in the Himalayas.

Julie, who lived at Groombridge with husband Terry, was among seven climbers who perished during their descent after conquering the 28,250 foot peak, second highest mountain in the world and by far the hardest.

Mrs Tullis, with Briton, Alan Rouse, took part in an unsuccessful climb of K2 last month. They then joined a mixed party of Britons, Austrians and Poles for one more try.

Seven died on the way down. One of the survivors was Kurt Liemberger with whom Julie collaborated in making thrilling films. He said: "She went to sleep in her tent and never woke up again."

She was in superb physical condition but that was not sufficient to withstand the biting wind, cold and lack of food and oxygen as the party waited many days for the weather to clear. The team were last in contact with base on August 4th. After that anxiety began to mount.

Julie, 47, was a climbing instructor at Harrison Rocks near Tunbridge Wells and, with her husband, had helped to develop the Bowles Outdoor Pursuits Centre.

The couple lived in a converted chicken house on the site then moved to Groombridge where they bought Saxby's Stores and added a tearoom which became a centre for climbers.

In Julie's autobiography, which is due out next month, she writes: "Of all the mountains K2 is the most special to me." Her family have decided to leave her body on the mountain. ***See page 141***

'The first thing on everybody's mind as soon as they got out was helping others to escape. Time didn't mean a thing' — Stephen Homewood, assistant purser aboard the *Herald of Free Enterprise*.

January 9th: Guinness chief executive Ernest Saunders has resigned over the DTI inquiry which followed the Distillers' takeover.

January 12th: Prince Edward has resigned from the Royal Marines.

January 29th: Soviet leader Mikhail Gorbachev has called for greater democracy in the Soviet Communist Party.

February 2nd: Members of the Special Branch today raided the BBC offices in Glasgow and removed vanloads of material allegedly gathered for the controversial programme on *Britain's Secret Society.*

February 11th: Cynthia Payne is cleared by an Old Bailey jury of running a brothel.

February 26th: Michael Checkland is appointed director-general of the BBC in succession to Alisdair Milne who has resigned.

The Church of England General Synod today gave the go-ahead for the ordination of women.

March 6th: More than 200 cross-Channel passengers are feared dead after a car ferry, The *Herald of Free Enterprise,* capsized off Zeebrugge.

March 19th: Winston Silcott has been jailed for life for the murder of Pc Blakelock during riots at Tottenham.

April 1st: MPs today voted against the restoration of hanging.

April 7th: The *Herald of Free Enterprise* is refloated. A memorial service is to be held in Canterbury.

May 2nd: The traditional red telephone box is to disappear under British Telecom's modernisation plans. They have been landmarks since the 1930s.

It is 50 years since the nuns, expelled from Bavaria by the Nazis, bought Minster Abbey — thus bringing it back into the hands

*Caron Keating, daughter of Gloria Hunniford, who lives in Sevenoaks, plants a new sapling to replace one of the six famous oaks destroyed in the great October storm. **See page 93.***

of the Benedictines who founded the monastery over 800 years ago. To mark the milestone the nuns plan to build a new chapel.
See page 92

May 16th: Coventry City beat Tottenham Hotspur 3-2 in the FA Cup Final.

June 8th: Princess Anne has been given the title Princess Royal.

June 28th: Nick Faldo, 29 and Laura Davies, 23, have won their respective Open championships — Faldo by a single stroke at Muirfield.

June 30th: Rupert Murdoch has purchased *Today* newspaper from

the Lonrho group.

July 1st: Police have discovered the body of one of the missing victims of Moors murderers, Brady and Hindley.

July 12th: Nigel Mansell today won the British Grand Prix.

August 4th: Moors murderer Ian Brady claimed today he committed five more killings.

August 20th: A gunman Michael Ryan, aged 27, shot dead 14 people and left 15 wounded in, or near, the town of Hungerford today. He later turned the gun upon himself.

The East Kent Light Railway linking the collieries has been finally closed by British Rail. The track has not been lifted as it has been acquired by the EKLR Society with the aim of purchasing the line as a working museum railway.

September 27th: The European team has retained the Ryder Cup after a day of almost unbearable tension at Muirfield Village, Ohio.

October 8th: The Director of Public Prosecutions will now decide whether charges should be made following the inquiry into the Zeebrugge disaster.

October 19th: Thousands of homes in Kent are still without electricity three days after the Great Storm.

October 19th: The London Stock Exchange crashed today following an almost unprecedented tidal wave of selling. Fifty billion pounds was wiped off the value of publicly-owned companies making it almost double the drop of the Great Crash of October 1929.

November 8th: An IRA bomb which exploded in a disused school killed 11 people today and injured 63 during the annual Remembrance Day parade in the town of Enniskillen.

November 17th: The Government is to introduce a community charge or "poll tax" in April 1990.

November 19th: An inferno at King's Cross underground station which started on a wooden escalator killed 30 people tonight. Surgeons said the injuries included some of the worst flash burns they had ever seen.

December 31st: Several heroes of Zeebrugge have been honoured by the Queen in the New Year's Honours list.

GREAT HITS OF 1987

Never Gonna Give You Up

I wanna Dance With

Somebody (Who Loves Me)

John Stanley MP for Tonbridge and Malling has been touring his constituency with the army distributing food parcels. At the police headquarters in Maidstone an RAF Chinook helicopter air-lifted an Army Land Rover to a stricken village near Rochester. In some places conditions have been described as "unbelievable".

Kent paralysed — it's like Siberia out there

January 14th: The M2 motorway has been blocked for almost a week, villages on the Downs isolated and transport in the county paralysed following the heaviest snowfall since the infamous winter of 1963.

The bitter weather arrived from Scandinavia on Saturday (January 10th). Penetrating frost was followed by a blizzard which raged all day on Sunday. By Monday the temperature had dropped to -13C making it the coldest day since 1867.

The Medway villages bore the brunt of the snow showers which followed. Ferocious easterly winds blew the snow into huge drifts and visibility was reduced to just a few feet as clouds of ice crystals were blasted off the fields.

Today the RAF and Army are helping villagers cut off by mountainous snow drifts. Green Goddesses have been brought out to help the county's fire brigade. Parts of Kent have a level snow depth of 29 inches. Villages on the Isles of Grain and Sheppey are cut off, Hastingsleigh, Elmstead and Bodsham are impassable. One resident told the *Kentish Express*: "It's just like Siberia. If we go out we find ourselves walking on the tops of hedges."

Radio Kent have set up a "snow line" with regular bulletins to help those in distress. It has been invaluable especially for those stranded in their cars on the A20. At Lenham the Army rescued motorists entombed in six feet of snow.

Terry Waite kidnapped in Beirut

February 2nd: Terry Waite, the special representative of the Archbishop of Canterbury, who has done so much to negotiate the release of western hostages, is reported to be "under arrest" in Beirut.

All week prayers have been said in the Cathedral as fears were expressed about his safety. News bulletins today confirm the worst. Waite was seized on January 21st as he left his seafront hotel in West Beirut to visit hostages held by supporters of the Hezbollah, the militant followers of Ayatollah Khomeini.

Terry Waite is known to be a conscientious and meticulous negotiator who secured the release of an American held hostage for 18 months in Beirut. It was then revealed that Oliver North, a member of President Reagan's national security council, had set up an "arms-for-hostage" deal with the Iranians using Waite as an innocent pawn.

The CIA plot, or Irangate, as it was known may have seriously damaged Waite's standing in the Middle East, certainly among those who follow the Ayatollah.

Terry Waite is pictured (above left) with the Archbishop of Canterbury, the Right Rev Robert Runcie, his wife Frances, daughter Ruth and son Mark. ***See page 128***

Triple crossing for Philip Rush

Ever since Captain Matthew Webb became the first man to swim across the Straits of Dover in August 1875 a whole host of extraordinary records have proliferated.

In 1979 an American girl, Penny Dean, achieved the fastest time by either sex with 7 hr 40 min. In 1983 a girl of 12, Samantha Druce, swam the Channel in 15 hr 27 min. A British swimmer Michael Read achieved a total of 31 crossings between 1969 and 1984 — six of them in one year.

This year has seen another great achievement. Philip Rush of New Zealand crossed from England to France, back to England and again to France in one continuous swim.

This fastest-ever triple crossing took 28 hr 21 min.

See page 160

Ferry capsizes: 200 feared dead

March 6th: In the worst peacetime shipping tragedy since the sinking of the *Titanic* more than 200 cross-channel passengers were feared dead tonight after a car ferry capsized in the bitterly cold waters off the Belgian port of Zeebrugge.

The *Herald of Free Enterprise,* owned by Townsend Thoresen, rolled and sank a mile out to sea. Reports suggest that the bow doors were still open as she sailed enabling water to pour onto the car deck.

The ferry was bound for Dover when she rolled on to her side leaving one third of the hull still above the water. It happened so swiftly that there was no time to send an SOS and scores of passengers were trapped in the submerged section.

Rescuers in the form of Dutch and Belgian ships and helicopters were soon on the scene with divers. They were greeted by the appalling sight of an 8,000-ton roll-on roll-off ferry lying on her side while frantic passengers were trying to scramble through windows and onto the starboard deck.

The divers climbed through the side of the ship and went immediately into the submerged section to try to locate trapped passengers. They found bodies, some still huddled together, floating in the water. Other dead bodies were on the bridge and in cabins.

Many people from Kent are among those feared dead.

They include four members of one family — Carol Delafield, 43, her husband Brian, 47, her son by her first marriage, Andrew Fox, aged 11 and her stepdaughter Sharon, aged 17. They lived at Boxley Road, Maidstone and were on a day trip to Belgium.

Also missing is Lita Harris, aged 34, of Carnation Crescent, West Malling. Her boyfriend Nick Kember and friends Dean and Julie Scoble survived the disaster. Nick said: "We were in the lounge when the sea came crashing in. I tried to hold onto Lita but the water just took me away. Our side of the boat went down in 10 seconds flat and when I emerged I grabbed a table and held on. Around me were people in the water screaming."

Almost one third of the 84 *Herald of Free Enterprise* crew come from Shepway and seven of these are missing, presumed dead. They include Glen Butler of Chilham Road, Folkestone, Barry Allan, of Morehall Avenue, Cheriton, Daniel Burthe of Ashley Avenue, Cheriton, Stanley Darby of Canterbury Road, Hawkinge, Steve Ewell of Garden Road, Folkestone, David Santer of Holland Avenue, Cheriton and John Warwick of Enbrook Road, Sandgate.

Alongside the tragedy are many stories of heroic deeds. Assistant purser Stephen Homewood toiled for six hours in the cold and dark to save the lives of passengers and crewmen. Mr Homewood of Canterbury Road, Folkestone,

(continued from page 90)

said: "The first things on everybody's mind as soon as they got out was helping others to escape. Time didn't mean a thing."

Another hero is the boatswain, Terry Ayling, who was one of the first to make it out of the vessel. Together with three colleagues he hauled the badly injured Captain David Lewry and Chief Officer Sable to safety.

Mr Ayling of Marler Road, Cheriton, was on the starboard side of the ferry when she capsized. He said: "She went over to about 45 degrees. It reminded me of a horror film. The port side was like a 40-foot well and when we broke one of the portholes all we could hear was pushing, screaming and crying. One baby was still strapped in his pushchair when we pulled him out."

Another who is safe and sound at her Eastfields home in Folkestone is Mrs Jenny Leslie. a stewardess who was actually serving a customer carrying a baby in the perfumery when suddenly the boat began to sway. The mother disappeared but Mrs Leslie grabbed the baby, tucked him in her skirt and knotted him in so she could use her free hands to stay above the water which was coming in fast.

David Tracey, a 24-year-old steward was another who was "washed away on a wall of water" and survived. "People were eating", he said, "when the ferry capsized. They expected it to right itself but it didn't."

"Plates of glass were breaking and the head waiter Mick Skippen tried to calm everybody. He was doing a good job but the windows broke and a wall of water swept in."

Mr Tracey was washed into the galley. It took him 20 minutes to smash a window and climb into the TV lounge. He climbed cupboards and shelves in the pitch dark and later discovered he had been one of the few survivors from the restaurant.

Hundreds of volunteers from the Samaritans, Red Cross and Salvation Army in Kent shared the massive burden in providing practical help for relatives and friends who converged on Dover for news of their loved ones. Close relatives were taken to Enterprise House Dover, the headquarters of Townsend Thorensen, where the grief was almost too much to bear.

Kent Fire Brigade played a major part in the rescue operation. Within hours of the news reaching HQ 50 men, five tons of equipment and ten appliances were leaving from RAF Manston in a Hercules. On arrival a fire fighting party went on board the stricken ship and the brigade's thermal imaging cameras were used. At first light a brigade command support unit and more men and equipment went by ferry to Calais and drove to Zeebrugge.

Townsend Thoresen employs 5,000 people in Dover. The *Herald of Free Enterprise* was built in 1980 and is one of a trio of sister ships on the Dover to Calais route.

TV viewers see the Herald lifted

April 6th: One month after she rolled over and sank in the cold waters off Zeebrugge, the *Herald of Free Enterprise* has been lifted from the seabed and towed back to the Belgian port. The skilful operation, performed by salvage tugs, was seen by more than 400 journalists and dozens of television crews from around the world.

Among those watching was the editor of the Belgium newspaper *Het Volk*, Mr Fred Vandenbussche who said that a day of human endeavour was followed by a day of human grief.

"The lifting of the *Herald*", he said, "was as tense as a Hitchcock film — and the first hours were the most absorbing when something could have gone dangerously wrong."

"The ferry was sitting two metres deep on the sea bed. Tons more sand and salt had got in and this was the X Factor that threatens every salvage operation."

Nine hours later the *Herald* was sitting upright in 18 metres of water. The technical success, however, was marred by the sight of the stricken vessel. All port side windows were broken and, caught up with the salt, mud and debris, were the bodies of many victims. Seven British and 12 Belgian divers had the gruesome responsibility of removing 63 bodies from the upper decks.

Before the massive steel graveyard could be floated back to Zeebrugge water had to be pumped out and the bow doors closed. The *Herald*, accompanied by the tugs and a silent flotilla, was then handed over to its owners Townsend Thorensen.

Divers now had the repugnant task of searching the lower decks and open spaces. Two days after the ferry had been lifted they bought out 111 more bodies and a temporary morgue was set up at the marine base.

Also on the ferry were 1,100 tons of cargo including cars, wagons and trucks.

The inquest into the *Herald of Free Enterprise* disaster will be held in October, followed by a full inquiry. If a verdict of unlawful killing is returned then the Director of Public Prosecution will have to decide whether or not charges should be made.

See page 98

1987

Midnight blaze wrecks Minster Abbey chapel

August 28th: In a dramatic midnight blaze the chapel of the historic Minster Abbey was completely gutted on Friday. And while the building was still smouldering Mother Prioress Concordia went into the Chapel to retrieve the consecrated bread.

The inferno followed a violent electric storm over Minster village which caused a power cut. It is is believed a candle set a shelf alight and within minutes the Chapel and the gift shop were burning furiously.

The Mother Prioress said the Abbey, which was founded by Benedictines over 800 years ago, suffered no damage but the guest house nearby was scorched by the heat.

The nuns had already planned to build a new permanent chapel and will launch an appeal for about £100,000.

I won't be long on the back benches, says Ann

June 12th: In another historic general election the Tories have surged back to power in the most emphatic way. Mrs Thatcher becomes the first Prime Minister this century to secure a third consecutive term of office and she is backed by a massive parliamentary majority.

In Kent the Conservatives swept the board with a majority of more than 10,000 in every seat except Dover, Folkestone, Gravesham and Medway.

They helped to secure a final election scoreboard of — Tories 375 seats, Labour 229, Alliance 22 and Others 24.

There was particular satisfaction for Tonbridge and Malling MP, John Stanley, the former Armed Services Minister who was returned with ease and promoted to Number Two in the Northern Ireland office.

Mr Stanley had earlier been the victim of a stinging attack by the *Guardian* newspaper who described him as a "humourless rightwing workaholic". They also said his religious views as a "Protestant evangelical influenced by an unorthodox belief in reincarnation" would cause problems in his new job.

Also delighted with the result are Kent's two new MPs Jacques Arnold of Gravesham and Ann Widdecombe of Maidstone who won her seat with an increased Tory majority. The next day she paid an unofficial visit to the House of Commons in order to find her way around. "I got lost in the Lords", she said, "and decided that I just had to walk around until the red carpet gave way to green and then I would know I was back in the Commons."

Ann said she does not intend to be long on the back benches. "I am very ambitious. I aim to get as far as possible as quickly as possible. When I make my maiden speech I will do it in style." *See page 138*

Kent lashed by storm of the century

October 16th: A furious storm driven by hurricane-force winds hit Kent in the early hours of this morning and left a swathe of damage and destruction that, in places, is quite unbelievable. Millions of giant trees, some more than 250 years old, litter country roads, caravans have been reduced to matchwood and greenhouses lie in shattered heaps. Much of the county has no electricity or telephone.

It was a night that no-one will ever forget. The winds arrived without warning in the small hours and roared through the county grabbing everything in their path. Electricity pylons tumbled like skittles, sending high voltage cables writhing and arcing through the night like lightning. Cars were crushed, communications crippled and the landscape changed for ever. The cost of the damage across southern England is estimated at £300 million and 17 people are believed to have died.

There had been nothing unusual about the weather forecast. Storm winds were reported to be sweeping across the Atlantic but they were going to miss Britain. Just after midnight trees began to go down on the Channel Islands. At 2.30 am a man was killed in Sussex as a chimney pot tumbled and an hour later high voltage power lines in Kent were "tripping". The wind speed now measured more than 100 mph.

In Folkestone, the cross-Channel ferry *Hengist* broke her port moorings one by one. Each mooring was replaced by the crew but as water continued to sweep over the ship the master decided to start the engines and put to sea. The sea, however, was rolling violently and the engines tripped. The propellers were lifted out of the water and the *Hengist*, in complete darkness, rode the waves for several hours with the captain, Sid Bridgewater and his crew fearing she would soon turn turtle. At 5 am she was blown onto the Warren where she remains, firmly beached.

Another ship at sea was the 8,000 ton Sealink vessel *St Christopher*. With passengers and vehicles on board she lay all night off Dover while 40 foot waves crashed against the hull. Three lorries toppled over and slid to and fro crushing many cars. The ship finally docked at 2pm this afternoon.

The drama was not confined to those at sea. A caravan park on top of the cliffs at Capel was demolished, the roof of a swimming pool was lifted off in Hythe, giant waves flooded the promenade at Sandgate and at Port Lympne, zookeepers mounted a round-the-clock vigil to comfort the animals and prevent escape.

One animal did escape at Howletts Zoo. Xiang, a seven-year-old clouded leopard, walked out of her cage and is now roaming free in the countryside.

Woodlands suffered badly. At Chilham Castle a 300 yard double avenue of 150 year old limes came down. Not one tree survived. At Bedgebury Forest, Goudhurst, 5,500 acres of woodland, the equivalent of 10 years of harvesting, are lying on the ground. Right across the county great trees in full leaf caught the wind. After many days of heavy rain the ground was sodden so the roots were not restrained and almost every species toppled like ninepins.

The heavily wooded area around the towns of Sevenoaks and Westerham suffered badly. Six of the seven famous oak trees, planted in 1902 on the Vine Cricket Ground to commemorate the coronation of Edward VII, toppled over. At Knole Park, hundreds of ancient trees which had withstood gales for 400 years or more failed to resist the power of these winds and Lord Sackville, owner of the great deer park, is devastated. The Toys Hill woodland, at nearly 800 feet the highest in Kent, suffered 90 per cent destruction. In fact the conditions this afternoon are so bad that Mark Wolfson, MP for Sevenoaks, has persuaded the Government to declare a state of emergency and send soldiers with heavy lifting gear into the countryside.

The hurricane-force wind bulldozed its relentless course across every National Trust garden in the county. Scotney, Emmetts, Sissinghurst, Ightham Mote and Chartwell lost hardwood trees and many other valuable species — centuries of careful management ruined in just two hours.

Today the Meteorological Office is under fire from both press and public for its failure to predict the hurricane. "We could have got it better", said a spokesman.

November 1st: Most of the lights are on again in Kent and telephone lines have been reconnected after days of hectic activity. Helicopters were brought in to detect the faults and engineers and linesmen drafted in from all over England. They were backed up by soldiers from the Royal Engineers and the Gurkha Rifle Regiment, who brought their famous jungle fighting qualities to the more remote areas of Kent. In many areas it was more than a fortnight before householders could dispense with Tilly lamps and makeshift meals cooked over an open fire.

Insurers say there has been nothing to compare with the cost of the 1987 storm in Britain in modern times. They estimate that that approximately one insured household in six in south-east England suffered substantial damage. More than a million claims have been received and they are still coming in.

The Meteorological Office, in apologising for "getting it wrong", say a storm of this ferocity is unlikely to occur again for at least 250 years. ***See page 97***

Above: The remains of a greenhouse at Grigg Lane, Headcorn. Left: Broken limbs and open skies at Knole Park, Sevenoaks.

A JCB eats its way across Hosey Common, near Westerham dwarfed by the fallen trees on either side.

'Leaking flask' puts Tonbridge on nuclear alert

September 10th: The town of Tonbridge was on full scale alert yesterday after a British Rail employee discovered liquid seeping from a flask containing spent nuclear fuel rods. The flask was on a train en route to Sellafield from Dungeness Power Station.

A nuclear alert was immediately put into operation by Southern Region who terminated all trains at Sevenoaks to the dismay of 5,000 Kent-bound businessmen and women. Police and the fire brigade descended on the residential areas around the west goods yard. Carrying geiger counters they imposed instant exclusion zones and warned people to be wary but not to panic.

Officials of the Central Electricity Generating Board who tested the leaking liquid have now confirmed that lubricating oil was seeping from the wagon carrying the sealed flask. A spokesman said today that the whole thing was a complete non-event and the mass panic which ensued would not have occurred if BR had adopted the correct procedure of informing CEGB first.

The incident, however, is certain to resurrect concern over the route of the nuclear waste trains. Because of this the CEGB plans to hold a public relations exercise in which a 140-ton diesel locomotive will ram a nuclear flask at 100 mph to prove that it can remain intact.

Terror grips bed-sit land as police seek man who murdered two girls

December 16th: In June this year, 24-year-old Wendy Knell was found brutally murdered in her bedsit flat at Guildford Road, Tunbridge Wells. Yesterday, the body of Caroline Pierce, 20, also of Tunbridge Wells, was found, partly submerged in a dyke near the village of St Mary-in-the-Marsh. Police believe the two murders may be linked and have launched a massive hunt for the killer.

Although there is no definite evidence to suggest one man killed both girls there are chilling similarities in each case. Both victims, Caroline and Wendy, lived alone in bedsit accommodation and died from head wounds following sexual assault. Both were in their 20s and managed a shop and restaurant respectively that were 400 yards distant from one another.

A fever of terror has gripped Tunbridge Wells since the gruesome discovery of the two girls, particularly in the Camden Road area where they lived and worked, for nobody knows if the killer, or killers, will strike again.

Women are refusing to go out at night alone and those once living alone in flats or 'digs' are doubling up with friends or going home to their parents. The police are especially vigilant.

Wendy Knell was the manageress of Supersnaps in Camden Road. A set of keys containing a "woman of the year" tag has gone missing along with a small amount of cash. Caroline Pierce also lost her keys. The tag in this case was Buster Brown's, the American-style restaurant she ran in Camden Road.

Police say that the discovery of the keys will be vital to their ongoing investigations. Already more than 100 detectives are involved in the case and interviews are taking place at the rate of hundreds a day.

Detective Chief Inspector Dave Stevens said his team had already spoken to those who knew the girls well. Caroline, a former pupil of Tunbridge Wells Girls' Grammar School, went missing three weeks ago and his worst fears were confirmed when her body was discovered on Romney Marsh.

He is hoping that there might be someone somewhere who might have seen somebody acting suspiciously when her body was dumped in a drainage ditch.

See page 102

Cathy's 'miracle' recovery

December 31st: A 10-year-old girl from Minster, near Canterbury, is recovering at home from a frenzied knife attack near her home earlier this year.

Cathy Humphrey was stabbed six times and doctors at the Kent and Canterbury feared she wouldn't pull through and her mother was warned not to hold out hope.

After four days on a ventilator Cathy was able to breathe without help and moved out of intensive care. A month later, against all expectations, she was discharged and sent home.

Her recovery has been described as a miracle. Wellwishers from all over the country have sent her presents, flowers and money and her mother, grateful for the generosity of people she had never met, is setting up a fund to buy a new life ventilator for the Kent and Canterbury hospital.

See page 97

'A head surfaced, "Hello Mary." It was Phil Wells! His arm was over a piece of flotsam. "Are you OK?"
"I'm fine" — Mary Campion from Beckenham on her ordeal in the sea after the *Jupiter* sank.

February 3rd: Nurses from hospitals in Kent were among the hundreds who marched on Parliament today to demand more money for the NHS.

February 4th: More than 1,500 lorries are blocking the roads to Dover as seamen continued their strike today, bringing chaos to ferry ports. Only French and Belgian-owned ferries are operating. Sealink and P & O have won injunctions against the National Union of Seamen and the union's funds could be seized.

February 5th: People throughout Kent put charity before dignity today by wearing red noses in aid of Comic Relief, a campaign to combat famine in Africa.

Cathy Humphrey, still recovering from her stab wounds, has presented a £12,000 ventilator to the Kent and Canterbury Hospital.

February 15th: P & O European Ferries have announced that 2,300 striking Dover seamen are to be sacked.

February 19th: A British skier has become the darling of the Winter Olympics at Calgary — even though he finished last. Eddie Edwards, nicknamed "the Eagle", stole the show in the breathtaking ski jump.

March 7th: Three members of an IRA "active service unit" were gunned down by British soldiers in Gibraltar today.

March 10th: The Prince of Wales and his skiing party were caught in an avalanche today near Klosters in Switzerland. Major Hugh Lindsay, a former equerry to the Queen, has been killed.

The Duke and Duchess of Kent visited the Sevenoaks area as a guest of the trust fund *Trees For The Future* which is raising money to repair woodland damaged by the 1987 storm. The couple planted a tree at Valence School for the Handicapped, Westerham and accepted a cheque to the fund for £12,000 from the publishers of the best-selling book *In The Wake of the Hurricane*.

October 16th: The seven oak saplings, planted on Sevenoaks Vine last year to replace the six giant oak trees which fell in the hurricane, have been vandalised. They were discovered snapped in half this week by people attending a small ceremony to bury a capsule containing memorabilia of the great storm. Sevenoaks Town Council is now planning to plant seven mature oaks. They will be at least ten feet high and protected by a grille and Securicor guard.

March 19th: A West Belfast lynch mob killed two British soldiers today after they drove at high speed into an IRA funeral cortege.

March 29th: A skyscraper is to be built in London's docklands. It will be the biggest in Britain.

A 27-year-old London bus driver, Kelvin Chapman, has been jailed for 14 years for the abduction and attempted murder of 10-year-old Cathy Humphrey of Minster. Cathy was viciously stabbed sx times and left to die. Her recovery was described as a miracle.

May 6th: Graeme Hick, the Worcestershire batsman today scored 406 not out, the highest innings in England this century.

May 10th: South African athlete Zola Budd has returned home after a great controversy about her eligibility to run for England.

May 20th: Many Kent publicans, are delighted that the new Licensing Act has been given royal assent. From the summer, pubs will be able to remain open from 11 am to 11pm during weekdays.

June 11th: More than 80,000 people today celebrated Nelson Mandela's 70th birthday at Wembley Stadium.

July 5th: The Church of England Synod has voted to go ahead with plans for the ordination of women.

July 6th: A massive explosion on the Piper Alpha oil rig in the North Sea has killed 150 workers.

July 28th: A former Royal Marine commando, Paddy Ashdown, has been elected leader of the Social and Liberal Democrats.

August 8th: Iran and Iraq have agreed to sign a truce after eight years of war.

August 10th: The disease that has killed thousands of seals along the north-west coast of Europe has now reached the Kent coast. One young victim, a pup, was rescued from Ramsgate harbour and is making a slow but steady recovery. Thousands though are dying from a mystery virus.

September 16th: Hundreds of thousands of people in the Caribbean have been made homeless by Hurricane Gilbert, the worst storm the Western world has seen this century.

September 30th: Olympic world record holder Ben Johnson has been stripped of his 100 metres gold medal after being found guilty of using drugs.

October 31st: Mrs Thatcher's decision to freeze child benefit for a second year has prompted Neil Kinnock to call her "a cheat".

November 8th: George Bush is the new American President. He won a comfortable victory today over his Democratic opponent Michael Dukakis.

December 12th: A packed commuter train today rammed into the back of another at Clapham Junction. 36 people are feared dead.

December 22nd: A Pan American jumbo jet today exploded in the skies above the Scottish town of Lockerbie killing all 259 passengers on board and 11 on the ground.

GREAT HITS OF 1988

The Only Way is Up

I Should be So Lucky

Zeebrugge hero, Stephen Homewood.

Zeebrugge hero awarded Queen's Gallantry Medal

January 1st: The hero of the Zeebrugge tragedy, assistant purser Stephen Homewood, has been awarded the Queen's Gallantry Medal in the New Year Honours list. Homewood, 35, who still suffers from the after-effects of Britain's worst shipping disaster since the *Titanic*, stayed on board for more than six hours after the ferry capsized to rescue people.

Stephen, who lives at Folkestone, is one of four men of the *Herald* crew to be named in the Honours List. Another is the ferry's former head waiter Michael Skippen who was in the restaurant trying to calm everybody down when the water rushed in.

A different kind of trauma faces seven other members of the *Herald* crew. Manslaughter charges have been brought against them and Townsend Thoresen, the ferry company which owned the *Herald of Free Enterprise*. Scores of survivors will give evidence at the Old Bailey and endure once again the memory of that night when the ferry sank a mile off the Belgian port of Zeebrugge.

The case is fairly straightforward. Why were the ferry's bow doors left open? After the cars and lorries had been loaded and before the ship sailed for Dover the normal procedure would be to close the doors — sealing the gap through which the vehicles had driven. It is a task usually carried out by the deck store keeper and watched over by the chief officer who is normally in charge of loading the ship.

Already an inquest at Dover Town Hall has returned a verdict of unlawful killing on the 187 victims and an official inquiry which followed, accused Townsend Thoresen of "sloppiness from top to bottom" and demanded that the directors should be changed. The trial will follow.

See page 115

Ultimatum to seamen: 'work or get the sack'

It's been another winter of discontent. In early February 2,000 ferry workers at Dover went on strike over proposed new manning levels. With full support from the National Union of Seamen, the P&O fleet at Dover sailed to a halt.

The company, desperate to cut costs to compete with the future threat from the Channel Tunnel, eventually issued an ultimatum: "Go back to work or we'll sack the lot of you." Hundreds surrendered but the scene was set for bitter exchanges on the picket line as coachloads of "scabs" were driven to work past crowds of jeering strikers.

Sealink mounted a sympathy strike and, by May, Dover was in chaos. Furious lorry drivers, angry at the long delays, blockaded the entire port for four days. The strike, however, fizzled out — defeated by the Tories' new industrial relations legislation.

Trouble at the seaport was followed by trouble at the airport as Gatwick was hit by an epidemic of flight delays due to a series of strikes by air traffic controllers on the Continent.

Thousands of families from the South-East endured a nightmare wait of two days in the cramped confines of the departure lounge living on £5 food vouchers and sleeping on baggage trolleys.

An uncomfortable winter too for postmen and their customers. A dispute in the south-east triggered a national strike over regional bonus payments, mailboxes were sealed and a backlog of ten million letters built up while the dispute lasted.

January: Torrential rain caused widespread flooding this month. All over Kent rivers have burst their banks and at Yalding, where the rivers Medway, Teise and Beult meet, caravans and hopfields have been under water and homes cut off.

Anglican churchgoers through Kent have been paying tribute to the Rt Rev Dr David Say on his retirement as the 104th Bishop of Rochester. His place will be taken by the Rt Rev Anthony Turnbull who becomes patron of 76 livings of the Archdeaconries of Rochester, Tonbridge and Bromley.

David Say, who lives at Wye, is an imposing figure who stands well over seven feet high when wearing his mitre. Chairman of the committee on State Aid for Churches in Use, pro-Chancellor of the University of Kent and President of the Friends of Kent Churches, he has been Bishop of Rochester since 1964.

Anthony Turnbull, who has been chief secretary of the Church Army and archdeacon of Rochester since 1984, is married with one son and two daughters. He is fond of cricket and, like his predecessor, enjoys walking.

The Princess of Wales was a guest at the wedding of her cousin Edward Berry to Joanna Leschalles, 29, of Cranbrook, youngest daughter of the former High Sheriff of Kent, Anthony Leschalles. The five page boys at St Dunstan's Church, Cranbrook included the young Princes William and Harry.

There has been great concern this summer over water pollution particularly in seaside towns where water companies have been urged to invest in more treatment works. To prove that the sea at Dungeness is free of health hazards, MP Michael Howard drank a glass of water discharged into the Channel from the nuclear power station.

Hypnotist helps Liz Hobbs to make a fighting recovery

Elizabeth Hobbs, the former world water ski champion, proudly holds the MBE presented to her for achieving the highest honours in her sport.

In 1982 Liz, who lives at Seasalter near Whitstable, won the World, European and British Ladies speed record — 75.6 mph on Lake Windermere. Two years later, in Australia, she became world water ski champion for the second time and announced she was aiming for a hat trick.

Tragically, she suffered a horrifying crash which left her with a broken sternum and serious injuries to her neck, ribs and lung. With the help of Canterbury hypnotist Kathryn Garstin she made an astonishing recovery and was able to train again.

Liz Hobbs is a member of the Whitstable Water Ski Club along with Peter and Jackie, her mother and father. Peter drives the boat which tows her.

How Neptune is helping to save our coastline

Enterprise Neptune, a campaign to save Britain's coastline which was launched by the National Trust in the form of an appeal in 1965, has acquired many national landmarks including Langdon Cliffs, given by Dover Town Council this year.

The National Trust want as many unspoilt areas of coastline for permanent preservation and public access following concerns about the exploitation of our shores after the Second World War.

The growth in car ownership and leisure time has led to cars parks, access roads, obtrusive groups of caravans and mobile homes being sited in sensitive areas. And there is nowhere more sensitive than the White Cliffs of Dover.

Post-war planning legislation has added to the problem; permanent development of bungalows, power stations and oil refineries springing up over what had been miles of rolling, open cliffland.

A recent survey of the whole coastline of England, Wales and Northern Ireland showed that of 4,960 kilometres of coast, roughly one-third has been developed, and another one-third is either not of sufficient merit or already in safe hands. This leaves 1,450 kilometres of coastline to save — an area that is being lost through development at an estimated 10 kilometres a year. The battle continues.

Beckenham schoolgirls on disaster cruise

October 21st: Sixteen Beckenham schoolgirls, one boy and 15 teachers escaped serious injury yesterday when their Greek cruise liner collided with an Italian freighter off the Mediterannean coast of Piracus.

The girls from Cator Park School were among 391 schoolchildren, 84 adults and 110 crew and had been on board the *Jupiter* for just 15 minutes when the collision occurred. It took 40 minutes for the ship to reach a list of 80 degrees and then sink vertically, stern first, in 270 feet of water.

It is now known that a teacher and child from another school were drowned along with two crew members.

Mary Campion, leader of the Beckenham party, said the children reacted with great courage. "Terrified, they hung from railings with a sheer incline of deck and an oil-covered night sea below them. Selflessly they still noticed other passengers in distress and encouraged fear-paralysed friends into movement. They used their initiative and saved lives."

Thanks to the skill of the Piraeus seamen who held the rescue boats in position until the last possible moment and to the dexterity of the passengers, most of whom could swim, all but four were saved. The evacuation did not begin until the Jupiter's list reached 80 degrees and then the evacuation chain moved at speed.

There were many deeds of bravery. Edward Lodge, a profoundly deaf Beckenham parent, pulled children to safety from the water. Laura Gill, aged 14, helped to rescue

A bird's eye view of the Jupiter. Aboard were more than 500 children, teachers and crew.

a child from another school and teacher Philip Wells who was still suffering from the effects of a stroke was saved by 16-year-old Rick Elmes.

The organiser of the trip, Schools Abroad, have pledged to repay the fee of all those on board and the *Jupiter* plans an additional £200 each. The Beckenham children will be reunited with their parents on Saturday.

Edward Lodge (back row) with some of the Beckenham girls who survived the Jupiter nightmare. They are Maria Lodge, Lorraine Veasey, Karyl Nisbett, Sairah Alam, Amanda Kershaw, Susan Briton, Maria Servier and Chloe Warrington. Everyone of them had a harrowing story to tell.

So did Mary Campion, leader of the party, who found herself wedged against the stairs and, above her, hanging on to the perimeter rail a line of children moving hand over hand to where the crew were waiting. There were no lifeboats because the speed at which Jupiter was sinking had prevented them from being lowered. The ship had now reached a list of 80 degrees and there were still 40 people on board — 10 from Cator School.

Mrs Campion said: "Time seemed frozen with an inner silence.......holding on to a rail I sank with the ship. Warm water covered my ankles, then it was up to my waist.....I swam off at speed. Glancing behind I saw the Jupiter — a pointed arch with reddish overtones hung against the sky. It seemed to wait, hestitating, before sliding below the sea."

Mrs Campion swam and swam. The sea was calm, warm and empty but soon she came across colleagues hanging onto pieces of flotsam. They were eventually picked up by a pilot boat, taken to shore and reunited with some of their children. At this stage Mrs Campion had no idea what had become of her girls still on board when the Jupiter sank. She later learned all had dived or fallen into the sea and all had been picked up.

September 19th: Six hundred Tonbridge School pupils were evacuated on Saturday morning (Sept 17th) as fire swept through the Edwardian chapel and threatened the main building. The cause is believed to be an electrical fault connected with work on the roof. The alarm was raised by a schoolboy who noticed smoke coming from the roof. When the first firemen arrived the building was burning from end to end. Only an hour earlier school pupils had attended a service in the chapel given by language teacher Bill Burns who made reference in his address to "tongues of fire".
The chapel was destroyed along with stained glass windows commemorating the school's dead of three wars and a fine English oak Burns organ.

More murder inquiries for busy police

November 20th: The widow of Derek Brann, a Folkestone taxicab driver, who was stabbed to death and dumped on the A20 near Sellindge, has made an emotional appeal on television for help in tracking down the killer of her husband.

Mr Brann disappeared on November 6th and his heavily bloodstained taxicab was found abandoned in Folkestone. It took two weeks for police to find his body after a helicopter search of the area.

A reward has been offered but police cannot yet even establish a motive for such a brutal killing. They are conducting a mass fingerprinting exercise in the Folkestone area.

The importance of fingerprint techniques and other areas of forensic science has been clearly proved in two other murder inquiries. Recently brought to justice are the killers of Paddy Kirwan, an invalid, found dead in his home at Dale Street, Chatham and Cicily Landless who was murdered in her home at Swanley. In each case the perpetrators of these hideous crimes left behind a set of fingerprints.

Kent police are no nearer finding the killer or killers of the two Tunbridge Wells girls, Caroline Pierce and Wendy Knell who died last year. Up to 100 detectives are still involved in the hunt and thousands of people have been interviewed. They include Stuart Durkin, recently jailed for a separate knife attack and rape of a woman in Tunbridge Wells. This is Durkin's second time behind bars — in 1983 he was imprisoned in Sweden for murdering his wife. Durkin, of Mount Ephraim, Tunbridge Wells, was questioned at length over the bedsit murders but no charges were brought.

**'I am sick. Sick with anger, sick with sorrow but also sick with determination to carry on' —
Lieut-Col John Ware, Royal Marines Director of Music after the IRA bomb tragedy at Deal.**

January 7th: Michinomiya Hirohito, Emperor of Japan since 1927, died today aged 82. His son, Crown Prince Akihito, automatically suceeds to the Chrysanthemum Throne.

January 8th: A British Midland Boeing 737 crashed onto an embankment on the M1 motorway today killing 52 passengers and crew. 65 escaped.

January 20th: George Bush today became the 20th President of the United States.

February 5th: Rupert Murdoch's £25 million Sky TV satellite network was launched today. It doubles the number of channels available in Britain.

February 15th: Ayatollah Khomeini of Iran has ordered the execution of the British author Salman Rushdie for blaspheming Islam in his book *Satanic Verses*.

February 25th: The heavyweight boxing title fight between Frank Bruno and Mike Tyson ended in the fifth round when the referee stopped the fight and declared Tyson the winner.

February 26th: More than 15,000 people, mainly from Kent, have taken part in a protest at plans to build a high-speed rail link to the Channel Tunnel.

Gary Mason from Walderslade has won the British heavyweight boxing title. Mason, who runs a jewellery shop in Gillingham called Punch 'n Jewellery knocked out former champion Hughroy Currie in the fourth round.

April 15th: Ninety-five people were crushed to death today and 170 were injured during the FA Cup semi-final match between Liverpool and Nottingham Forest at Hillsborough in Sheffield. It is believed the disaster was caused when a policeman ordered a gate to be opened to accommodate more fans.

May 5th: Mrs Thatcher today celebrated her 10th year as Prime Minister. Most writers agree she

The long hot summer took a heavy toll on the River Darent. Here, at Horton Kirby a dry river bed leaves the rubbish (and the fish) completely stranded.

has been a strong leader who has radically changed the nation. On other issues there is no consensus.

May 19th: Inflation has risen to eight per cent in Britain.

May 20th: Liverpool, who had considered quitting the competition after the Hillsborough disaster, today won the FA Cup by beating Merseyside rivals Everton 3-2 in extra time.

June 9th: Several hundred people are thought to have been killed in Beijing's Tiananmen Square today when the Chinese People's Liberation Army fired indiscriminately.

June 28th: There was chaos in London today as a second national one-day rail strike coincided with a virtual shutdown of the Underground.

July 11th: London theatres dimmed their lights tonight in

tribute to Lord Olivier who died in his sleep aged 82.

July 8th: A Bill privatising the water industry has been passed by the House of Lords.

July 22nd: More than 100,000 consumers in south-east London and Kent have been without water as supplies have dried up in the intense heat. Restrictions on the use of water have been introduced as weather experts forecast no respite from the heat.

July 25th: Foreign Secretary Geoffrey Howe, whose house at Chevening goes with the job, has been replaced by John Major, the Chief Secretary to the Treasury. Mrs Thatcher has offered Howe the position of Home Secretary but he has refused.

August 20th: It is feared that 26 people have drowned in the Thames following a collision between a pleasure boat, the

Marchioness and a dredger *Bowbelle*. About 150 people were enjoying a party on the pleasure boat when the collision occurred near Blackfriars Bridge.

Kent peer Lord Aldington has been awarded £1.5 million in libel damages following allegations that he had knowingly sent 70,000 Cossacks to their death in Russia while helping to organise repatriation of refugees after the Second World War.

August 31st: Princess Anne and Mark Phillips have announced their intention to separate.

October 26th: Nigel Lawson, the Chancellor of the Exchequer, resigned tonight throwing the Government into further turmoil. Mrs Thatcher has asked John Major, her recently appointed Foreign Secretary, to replace Mr Lawson.

November 8th: Army and RAF ambulances were out on the streets of London today as the ambulance workers' dispute escalated. The decision to send in the troops follows the suspension of 2,500 crew members who are working to rule in a national campaign for better pay and conditions.

November 10th: The Berlin Wall — the symbol of a divided world since August 1961— has been destroyed, at least symbolically. Thousands poured through checkpoints today as East Germans were declared free to leave their country.

December 3rd: Mikhail Gorbachev and George Bush have hailed the start of a new era in superpower relations and the official end of the Cold War. It follows news that the Communist Government in Czechoslovakia has collapsed and the Rumanian dictator Nicolae Ceausescu and his wife of Rumania have been executed.

GREAT HITS OF 1989

Ride On Time

Too Many Broken Hearts

103

Boomtown Ashford will be gateway to the East

When the great railway works at Ashford closed putting many people out of work the future for this once-booming Kent town was grim. That is now in the past. Ashford has been chosen as the site for a huge new international rail terminal for passengers bound for the continent via the Channel Tunnel.

When the tunnel opens it is anticipated that 1.8 million passengers will use the terminal each year. Parking space will be provided for 5,000 cars.

Eurotunnel, the Anglo-French group which is building the tunnel, has earmarked Ashford as the site for an inland clearing depot for customs checking of all road freight. The two developments will create thousands of temporary construction jobs and up to 1,200 permanent jobs beyond that.

Ashford's good fortune has infuriated rival local authorities in Kent. Around 12,000 people are employed in Kent by cross-Channel ferry services which local seamen now fear could be wiped out altogether. Mr James Sherwood of Sealink has already warned that all 2,500 of his men could lose their jobs and Dover be turned into a ghost town.

The Channel Tunnel rail link means that Ashford is now identified as Kent's major economic growth centre. Thousands of square metres of new office space will be required together with more than 2,000 new homes. A new village will be built and places like High Halden, Charing, Hothfield and Mersham will be expanded. There are plans for a new business park modelled on the popular Cambridge Science Park.

Ashford is enjoying boom town conditions which other towns can only dream about. *See page 176*

Police accused of fiddling crime figures

The newly appointed Chief Constable of Kent, Paul Condon, has faced many problems in his meteoric rise to the top but the recent controversy facing him and his senior officers is without precedent. A number of his policemen have been "cooking" the crime figures.

Allegations that Kent detectives were persuading prisoners to confess to crimes they hadn't committed in order to boost the clear-up rate were actually made three years ago by a Chatham Pc, Ron Walker.

At first no-one really took him seriously but eventually successive investigations were launched by two other forces and the Police Complaints Authority. Pc Walker was proved right.

The Chief Constable, deciding on a lenient course of action, has sacked one detective and disciplined nearly 30 others. Pc Walker said the punishments are a joke.

Kentish wine comes of age

September: **Kent is on course to celebrate a vintage year — and not only for its hops which are ripening nicely. As the sun continues to shine the county's vineyard owners are confident of a bountiful harvest.**

Since the late 60s vineyards have sprung up all over Kent and today there are almost a dozen centres producing quality wine and, more important, competing well with their French and German rivals across the Channel.

The best-known vineyards are at Lamberhurst, Biddenden, Tenterden and Penshurst with smaller wineries at Ash, Elham, Headcorn, Leeds and Staple. It's a high risk business as the Kentish soil and climatic conditions make wine growing a constant tussle and there is little incentive in the way of Government subsidy. But this year grapes are at the peak of perfection several weeks earlier than usual.

Kentish wine has come of age.

NICOLA TAKES OVER BRANDS

With the tragic death of John Foulston in a racing accident, his daughter Nicola, aged 21, has inherited a business that is losing around £30,000 a year — Brands Hatch.

Foulston bought the Kent Grand Prix circuit and three other racing courses in 1986 with a mission to make them profitable. As a businessman he had built up a £40 million computer company and was not short of ideas. Nicola, who takes over as chief executive, has a staff of 140 at Brands.

She plans to get more spectators through the gates and more people interested in motorsports. She is aware that racing is expensive and inaccessible to the public but is willing to learn the hard way. *See page 166*

Superstar David Essex related to Gipsy Rose Lee

May 31st: David Essex, pictured here with Scots-born actress Katy Murphy, is back on our screens in the popular comedy series *The River*. David plays a handsome lock keeper who gets into lots of scrapes.

It's the same in real life for the docker's son from Canning Town who was actually born David Albert Cook and went on to become a four-dimensional superstar — films, stage, rock and songwriting.

A few years ago while living at Furnace Mill Farm Hall in Four Elms, near Tonbridge, David and his friends were locked in a Westerham restaurant called the *Marquis de Montcalm* after disputing the size of the bill. The police were called and eventually calm was restored.

David Essex has many connections with Kent. He is a great-nephew of Gipsy Rose Lee, the famous Romany fortune-teller who lived at Farnborough for many years. As a young boy he used to spend holidays in the Kent hopfields and remembers sitting around open fires in the evenings with the billy cans boiling and the flames lighting the faces of the gipsies.

In his early adult life he spent years out of work, almost penniless searching for the break into show business that never seemed to come his way. It all changed in 1972 when he was one of two thousands hopefuls who auditioned for parts in the stage production of *Godspell*. He was offered the leading role, playing Jesus. It became the most talked about London show of the era and the *Sunday Times*' Harold Hobson compared Essex's performance with Laurence Olivier.

Since then he has topped all other rivals of his generation with great performances in such shows as *Evita* and *Mutiny* and films like *Stardust* and *That'll be The Day*. Alongside that he has 23 chart-topping hits to his credit.

Kent captain Gerry Chalk (second left) leads his team out to field in one of his last matches as captain of Kent in the summer of 1939. With him are Peter Foster, Brian Valentine, Hopper Levett and Alan Watt.

Boy's arm ripped off by chimp

Controversy continues to follow Zoo owner John Aspinall with the tragic news that a two-year-old boy has had his arm ripped off by a chimpanzee at Port Lympne, near Hythe.

Matthew McDaid was enjoying a family day out when he went to the back of an enclosure, put his arm through the bars and was grabbed by a 28-year-old chimp called Bustah.

Doctors fought in vain to sew the arm back on but have said that brave Matthew will have to wear an artificial limb. Mr Aspinall is shattered by the incident and said he will puts tens of thousands of pounds into a trust fund for the little boy. ***See page 150***

Pilot's skeleton still in his Spitfire

June: A group of French aviation enthusiasts have unearthed the remains of a Spitfire which was shot down near Calais — and, still sitting in the cockpit, the skeleton of Flight Lt Gerry Chalk, former captain of Kent Cricket Club.

Chalk, who led the side brilliantly in 1938 and 1939, was killed on February 17th, 1943. No trace of him or his plane was found and it was assumed he had crashed into the sea. He was officially declared "missing, presumed killed".

A few months ago French civilians located his Spitfire at a village called Louches, near St Omer. An identity disc, service number and clothing enabled the pilot to be positively identified as F.G.H. Chalk of 124 "Baroda" Squadron.

His Spitfire was one of four to be shot down by Focke-Wulf fighters and it is now known the pilot who killed Gerry Chalk was Adolf Glunz, famous for his 71 wartime "kills".

Chalk, who scored a century at Dover in the last match before war was declared in 1939, will be buried with full military honours in a war cemetery at Terlinchtun. Among the mourners will be friends from Kent Cricket Club and his widow Rosemary, who has since remarried and is living in New Zealand.

The owner of an Old People's Home at Margate has been convicted — then cleared on appeal — of ill-treating residents. The trial was the result of a long-running controversy provoked by an ITV documentary *The Granny Business*, which alleged widespread abuse of the elderly in certain homes.

Long hot summer and The Strand is back in business

A long hot summer, which began in May with no rain at all in Tunbridge Wells and an average of more than 10 hours of daily sunshine, was suddenly interrupted in June by a furious hailstorm.

For two hours on June 6th several inches of melting ice covered parts of the Medway Towns. Traffic was halted as drivers dug themselves out and children took the opportunity to hurl hailballs at each other.

It didn't last long. Blue skies and hot sunshine returned and, in July, the temperatures surged into the nineties. It was a long hot summer in other senses. A series of rail strikes made life miserable for Kent's commuters but petered out as the railwaymen slowly drifted back to work.

There was some good news. The Strand at Gillingham, believed to be one of the oldest swimming pools in the country, has reopened following pressure from scores of families.

The Strand opened in 1896 after Thomas Cucknow, a local baker, spent £1,000 to build a pool rather than see local people struggling in the river. In the early part of the century people came from all over the country to spend their holidays in Gillingham and trams brought visitors from the Medway towns.

The pool stayed open through two world wars and when it closed in 1988 the Strand Action Group was formed. 300 regulars linked arms around the "redundant" pool and 10 members leapt into the Medway to persuade the council to think again. Their efforts have been worthwhile.

Frankie Howerd is seen here with the Reverend John Neal recently, when he opened the renovated church hall of St Barnabas at Well Hall on the Progress estate in Eltham. The ever popular comedian lives locally in Arbroath Road. It has been decided that it will be known as Howerd Hall and the Frankie Howerd community centre.

High speed rail link to the tunnel ?

December: For thousands of people across Kent, fury has been replaced by relief. Taken aback by fresh estimates that have tripled the cost of the high-speed rail link from King's Cross to the Channel Tunnel, British Rail have shelved the entire plan for a year.

Nobody doubts that the line will be built but protestors have a breathing space in which to redraw their battle plans. Their determination is immense.

This year saw the biggest protest movement ever known in the county of Kent. Marches, demonstrations and public meetings were held. Members of Parliament were lobbied, petitions drawn up and normally peaceful villages became hotbeds of militant resistance.

It was in January that British Rail drew up plans for four possible routes for the "essential" rail link. By March three

of the variants had been eliminated but the outrage among thousands who claimed their properties were blighted continued unabated. The most vociferous were the residents of South Darenth, Horton Kirby, Istead, Cobham, Bearsted, Hollingbourne and Tutt Hill near Ashford.

Rail chiefs who attended meetings with the "information roadshow" were shouted down. And 10,000 people marched through Maidstone in the biggest demonstration the county town has ever seen.

In September protestors invaded London, massing around Trafalgar Square for an even bigger rally. Families, worried about a railway through their back gardens, demanded compensation and received promises from British Rail that they would put much of the route in tunnels

and recompense all householders who may be blighted.

Then came the news that the costs for the £1.7 billion project had risen by £500 million. The Channel Tunnel Bill bans the use of public money, so who was to pay? That's a problem British Rail will now address next year.   *See page 182*

Photograph above shows two sections of the emphatic NO campaigners, on their protest march through Kent. They include villagers from South Darenth and Horton Kirby, Joydens Wood, Wilmington, Eynsford and Longfield. They claim that British Rail's indecision may result in years of worry — a moral issue which their Members of Parliament must tackle immediately.

All night vigil to save the Rose Theatre

May 15th: Actors, archaeologists and theatre-goers staged an all-night vigil and dawn protest yesterday in a bid to stop the demolition of the remains of the Rose Theatre, Southwark.

The demonstration was led by theatrical dames Peggy Ashcroft and Judi Dench. Singing *We Shall Overcome* they formed part of a human wall designed to prevent developers' lorries entering the site of the only Elizabethan theatre ever uncovered — where Shakespeare himself frequently performed.

Today Nicholas Ridley, the Environment Secretary, announced a one-month breathing space in building works.

October 12th: The remains of Shakespeare's Globe Theatre have been found on Bankside.

10 soldier musicians killed as IRA bomb devastates Marines barracks, Deal

September 22nd: Ten young soldier-musicians were killed today when a pre-timed package of Semtex exploded at the Royal Marines' School of Music, Deal. The IRA has claimed responsibility. It is their worst outrage in the south-east.

The bomb, planted in a plastic bag and placed in the staff rest room, exploded with devastating results. The building collapsed like a pack of cards, trapping the musicians under tons of rubble. Ten young men, all with a bright future as members of the Marines band, were killed immediately. Twenty-two others are in hospital, including one who is seriously injured.

The explosion occurred at breakfast time and the emergency services were quickly on the scene. So was a team from Television South who flew a helicopter over the scene. The Ministry of Defence had set up an air exclusion zone while the rescue operation continued but the cameras still managed to capture the frantic efforts to remove the rubble and get to those trapped underneath.

Help came from a wide area. Infra-red image intensifiers were used to locate bodies or survivors hidden from view and a giant crane from the Channel workings at Dover was used to remove great slabs of concrete.

Condemnations of the mass murder came from Tom King, the Defence Secretary who flew in to Deal and from George Churchill-Coleman, head of the Anti-Terrorist Squad. Sir Martin Garrod, the Royal Marines Commandant, paid tribute to his young musicians. The Prime Minister Mrs Thatcher will visit the scene tomorrow.

In the hours that followed the blast, hundreds of floral tributes piled up at the entrance to the barracks. Most came from the people of Deal who know the young musicians well. Tomorrow the Town Mayor Marion McNicholas will launch an appeal to help those families who have lost a loved one or whose sons have been injured.

Questions are being asked about the level of security at the School of Music. It is believed the perpetrators climbed over a low wall to get into the barracks. Security was largely in the hands of a private company and it would not have been difficult for the IRA to ascertain the daily routine of the guards as they patrolled the area.

The future of the Royal Marines School of Music in Deal has been uncertain for a number of years. David Shaw, MP for Deal and Dover, has spearheaded a lengthy battle to ensure that the Marines stay and the latest statements in Parliament give hope to his cause.

September 28th: An inquest at Dover was told that the ten Marines died of severe or multiple blast injuries. One body was recovered from the roof of an adjoining building and one was killed as he walked into the complex having just arrived at the barracks.

Those who died were as follows: Corporal Trevor Davis, 39, of Trinity Place, Deal, Musician Richard Jones, 27, of Middle Deal Road, Corporal Dean Pavey, 31, of Sandown Road, Deal and Musician Michael Ball, 24, of Turner Street, Ramsgate were found in the rest room where they had been changing into their uniforms.

Corporal Andrew Cleatheroe, 25, of Albert Road, Deal had taken his girlfriend Natalie for a walk and was near the changing room when the explosion occurred.

Corporal David McMillan of Hamilton Road, Deal was in the workshop office. The building partially collapsed and his body wasn't recovered until 10 am.

Also in that building was Musician Mark Petch, 26, of Station Road, Deal, who was born in Ramsgate. His body could not be identified visually.

The body of Musician Richard Fice, 22, who was single and lived at the barracks was found on the roof of the locker room and Clarinettist Timothy Reeves, 24, of Jarvest Place, Kingsdown was found trapped in the entrance doorway.

Musician Robert Simmonds, 34, of Delane Road, Deal died from his injuries in Buckland Hospital.

The Memorial Gardens in honour of the musicians who died was established at Deal soon after the bombing. The Royal Naval School of Music came to Deal in 1930. Evacuated during the war it returned in 1950 and was restyled The Royal Marines School of Music. Its function was to form and train bands for service on ships and for ceremonial occasions, providing military, orchestral and dance bands.

Hundreds of people lined the streets for the funeral procession of the Marines who died at Deal.

Kent's new life-saver takes to the skies

December 21st: Kent has become one of the first counties in England to acquire an Air Ambulance. Thanks to an extraordinary network of supporters who have been raising vital funds for many months, a helicopter carrying a trained paramedic took to the skies today on its first emergency mission.

It is common knowledge that the sooner a patient receives treatment the better are his or her chances of survival. The air ambulance flying in a straight line at an average of 130 mph will be able to reach the scene of an accident in an average of 7.6 minutes.

With Kent's network of motorways and the inevitable queues which form after an accident, it is obvious that many lives are going to be saved. The service, however does not come cheap. Appeals organiser Kate Chivers and her team may need to raise more than £30,000 every month.

The helicopter will operate from Rochester Airport thanks to an arrangement between McAlpine Helicopters and GEC. *See page 179*

Bye-bye Betteshanger. The men were among the proudest miners in the country and now they are redundant. Some will work on salvage and others will go north. Many believe the colliery will be privatised.

A century of mining in Kent comes to a bitter end

August 26th: Betteshanger Colliery, like Tilmanstone and Snowdown, will soon be an industrial tomb. The last shift of miners climbed forlornly from the condemned pit at lunchtime today, knowing the next men down will be salvage teams winding up the remnants of more than 100 years mining in Kent.

Last week about 100 members of the Betteshanger branch of the NUM agreed to accept British Coal's 6 pm deadline for redundancy pay. That means that men with more than 15 years' employment will receive a lump sum of £7,500 in addition to the company's normal payment based on age and experience. Those who do not accept redundancy will be offered jobs in the North East.

Two years of uncertainty have taken their toll on the workforce of Kent's last colliery. After so much bitterness, so much futile negotiation most of them want their redundancy payments and peace.

British Coal blames the closure on the unions. A survival plan was drawn up but "the miners then reneged on undertakings to give full support to management proposals".

'You have a nightmare vision of a Europe teeming with ill-intentioned people scheming to extinguish democracy' — Sir Geoffrey Howe to Margaret Thatcher during his resignation speech.

January 30th: Rioting greeted the rebel England cricketers as they arrived in Johannesburg today. The team, led by Mike Gatting, defied a ban on tours to South Africa.

February 11th: Nelson Mandela has been freed after 27 years in prison. On his release he said: "I greet you all in the name of peace, democracy and freedom for all."

February 14th: Mortage rates have risen to 15.4 per cent.

February 16th: A poll shows that 73 per cent of the voters oppose the Government's proposed poll tax or community charge.

February 21st: Men working at Britain's nuclear plants are being advised not to have children following a link between exposure to radiation and the incidence of leukaemia in children.

February 23rd: Ambulance workers ended their bitter six-month old pay dispute today, during which police and troops manned emergency services.

March 1st: England beat West Indies in a Test Match in the Caribbean today for the first time in 16 years.

March 8th: More than 3,000 Britons have fully developed AIDS, it was revealed today.

March 23rd: The Duchess of York has given birth to a daughter, Eugenie Victoria.

March 31st: A huge rally in Central London by poll tax protesters turned into a full-scale riot with hundreds of arrests. The poll tax or community charge is due to be introduced tomorrow, April Fool's Day.

April 1st: Rioting prisoners in Manchester's Strangeway Prison overpowered the guards and released about 1,000 men. Police may now storm the building.

May 4th: South Africa's President F.W. de Klerk and Nelson Mandela, leader of the ANC, today took part in historic talks about the country's future.

Builders excavating the centre of Canterbury where the Longmarket once stood have exposed more of the Roman city of Durovernum, including the remains of a town house and numerous artefacts. The area is being prepared for a new shopping centre. **See Page 147**

May 8th: Billy Cartman has become the sixth Briton to die building the Channel Tunnel.

May 10th: The Ministry of Agriculture has revealed that a cat, put down a few weeks ago, was suffering from BSE or "mad cow disease".

May 11th: Conservative party candidates took a battering today in local elections in Kent. The introduction of the community tax is partly to blame.

June 3rd: With just 6,200 members the Social Democratic Party has become too small to function effectively, Dr David Owen announced today.

July 8th: West Germany tonight won football's World Cup, beating Argentina 1-0. England lost in the semi-final to the Germans after a penalty shoot-out.

August 2nd: The oil-rich country of Kuwait has been invaded by its neighbours, Iraq. Defences were rolled over by tanks and aircraft which had massed near the border. The President of Iraq plans to annexe Kuwait.

August 3rd: Today was the hottest ever known as temperatures reached 99F in Cheltenham. This beats the previous highest set at Canterbury in August 1911.

August 28th: Ernest Saunders, the former chairman of Guinness, has been jailed for five years along with four former directors. They were at the centre of a massive fraud.

August 30th: Irish hostage Brian Keenan has been freed after 1,597 days of captivity. He says that another hostage, John McCarthy, is alive in Beirut.

September 2nd: A French lorry driver was dragged from his cab near Dover today and assaulted by three men armed with wooden staves. The incident is linked to attacks on British lorry drivers carrying consignments of British lamb imports into France.

October 3rd: 45 years after the end of the Second World War Germany is united again. Its rebirth was celebrated today with a triumphant peal from the Freedom Bell at Schoneberg city hall.

October 23rd: Edward Heath, former Prime Minister and MP for Bexley, returned from Baghdad today with 33 hostages whose release he had secured from Saddam Hussein.

November 22nd: 15,000 British troops have been sent to the Gulf.

November 22nd: Mrs Thatcher failed to win outright in the first ballot for the Tory party leadership and has decided to quit. She will see the Queen tomorrow.

November 27th: John Major is Britain's new Prime Minister. His opponents in the second ballot, Douglas Hurd and Michael Heseltine, withdrew after he won 185 votes from Tory MPs.

GREAT HITS OF 1990
Sacrifice
Nothing Compares 2 U

Six lorries toppled over and several others were blown off course as they attempted to cross the M2 motorway bridge at Rochester during the storm.

Another great storm lashes Kent

January 26th: Experts said it would never happen again in our lifetimes — but it has. A deep, explosive, fast-moving depression hit the Kent coast on Thursday and produced winds in excess of 100 mph. Again thousands of trees were felled and countless country roads were blocked. Homes were blacked out, phone lines severed and there were many amazing escapes.

By the time the gale had subsided there were more people dead in Britain than any other single weather-related event since the floods of 1953. Of the 47 deaths, 36 were a direct result of the storm. That included a woman who died at Hunton when a tree toppled onto her florist's van.

The high number of fatalities was attributed to the fact that the storm struck during the day when there were more people out and about than in the 1987 storm.

In Ashford more than 1,400 buildings owned by the local council were damaged. In Maidstone the nine-storey Coleman House in King Street was evacuated after occupants claimed it was swaying. A large chimney toppled over at the King's Head Hotel, Wye and Kent County Council's nursery at Challock was devastated.

The storm coincided with a national ambulance dispute but striking men refused pay and answered 999 calls during the crisis after a special appeal on Radio Kent. Calls to Kent police and fire service came in at the rate of 100 an hour.

British Telecom workers struggled day and night to repair the 6,500 faults in the Mid Kent and Weald areas alone. Nationally, the storm will cost insurance companies in excess of £2 million.

January 12th: It is believed arsonists were responsible for a blaze which forced passengers to evacuate their burning train at Headcorn on Saturday. The Charing Cross to Dover service was stopped 400 metres short of the station after a passenger in a first class compartment pulled the communication cord.

British Rail employees attempted to fight the blaze after 28 men, women and children had been led to safety. By the time emergency crews from all over Mid Kent had arrived on the scene one carriage had been gutted.

As British Transport investigators sifted through the wreckage it seemed increasingly likely that the fire was started deliberately, possibly by football hooligans.

Manslaughter charge against P&O dismissed

The trial at the Old Bailey, in which P & O European Ferries made legal history by facing charges of manslaughter, has been halted after just five weeks.

Three and a half years after the Zeebrugge disaster, P & O and seven current and former employees, including the *Herald of Free Enterprise* captain, David Lewry, faced a trial that was expected to last most of the year.

In the event the case was dismissed and a prosecution for corporate manslaughter seems unlikely to be attempted again.

March: People from the Kent and Sussex border villages were among the 5,000 marchers protesting about the closure of Rye's Memorial Hospital. The rally was led by Paul and Linda McCartney who live at Peasmarsh. They appealed to the Health Secretary to reverse the decision.

July: Less than one year after the IRA bomb which killed eleven Royal Marines at Deal there has been another atrocity. Five pounds of explosives hidden in his Montego car killed the driver — Ian Gow, MP for Eastbourne, who had outspoken views on Northern Ireland and was a friend of the Prime Minister.

November: The Queen Mother has unveiled a bronze statue of Sir Winston and Lady Churchill at his former home Chartwell which is now owned by the National Trust. The ceremony marked the 50th anniversary of Churchill becoming Prime Minister. The Queen Mother is President of the National Trust and Lord Warden of the Cinque Ports.

Another thrilling bestseller for Ashford's super author, Frederick Forsyth.

Ashford lad with the million seller touch

February 1st: Frederick Forsyth, best-selling author and son of an Ashford furrier, has now launched his eagerly awaited latest novel, *The Negotiator,* which focuses on a plan to psychologically destabilise the US President. Even before it is published it is on course to emulate the extraordinary success of his earlier books.

Forsyth, who was born in Ashford and whose parents still live in Willesborough, has led a life almost comparable to one of his heroes.

At the age of 19 he became the youngest jet pilot in the RAF before leaving to work as a journalist. He joined the Reuters office in Paris and was in the country in the 1960s when several attempts were made on the life of General de Gaulle.

This provided the basis for *The Day of the Jackal,* a novel which took six years to research, checking every minor detail to achieve authenticity. The book brought him about £100,000 in film and hardback rights and later he sold 1.25 million paperback copies — putting him in the same super-author bracket as Harold Robbins and Leon Uris.

Forsyth achieved an equally convincing level of documentary realism in *The Odessa File, Dogs of War* and *The Fourth Protocol.*

Now living in Hertfordshire with his wife and two sons. he still remembers his days in Ashford and particularly the modest second-hand sports car which he drove. Today in his spare time he enjoys game fishing and parachuting.

Remembering that "miracle of deliverance" — the "little ships" gather at Dover. Facing page: A few of The Few.

50 years on — they remember their finest hour

October: This has been a year of wartime memories as the people of Kent look back 50 years to the days of sandbags and shelters, gas masks and ARP wardens and the chilling prospect of a Nazi invasion somewhere between Ramsgate and Dungeness.

By June 1940 the defeat of the RAF seemed certain. The British army had abandoned much of its modern equipment in France. The London Division responsible for the defence of the coast from Sheppey to Rye had no anti-gun tanks, no Bren guns, only eleven 25-pounder field guns, four 18 pounders and eight 4.5 inch howitzers from the Great War. Morale was low, Royal Navy and merchant ships were under constant attack and the greatest threat to the invaders, when they arrived, was likely to come from the new people's army, later known as the Home Guard.

So 50 years on Kent had plenty to remember starting with Anthony Eden's clarion call to men "not presently engaged in military service between the ages of 17 and 65 to come forward".

Home Guard reunions were followed by the 50th anniversary of the evacuation of Dunkirk when a thousand small boats and many larger ones crossed the Channel to rescue the beleaguered troops of the British Expeditionary Force.

In June, 80 of the original "little ships" mustered at Dover and Ramsgate for an anniversary crossing. The "miracle" was not repeated. Facing a stiff north-easterly breeze several boats had to turn back including the steam vessel *African Queen*. The Dunkirk spirit, however, prevailed for most and the flotilla reached Calais with only one minor casualty.

In September came the Battle of Britain reunions with the return to Biggin Hill, Manston, Hawkinge and West Malling of some of our greatest fighter aces — and they were not all British. Americans, Poles, Dutch, Belgians, Czechs, Norwegians, the French and the pilots from the Commonwealth countries shook hands, kissed and hugged their former colleagues as they recalled their one successful common aim — to beat back and then crush the Nazi menace.

Pilots' sadness as RAF plan to leave Biggin Hill

A few of The Few returned to their old fighter station at Biggin Hill in the summer to take part in a TV programme recalling the part they played in the defence of Britain during that long hot summer of 1940.

Among those in the photograph with presenter Danny Baker (kneeling) are Group Captain Des Sheen (second left), a distinguished Australian pilot who destroyed a Heinkel over the North Sea in October 1939 and became one of the first pilots to make "a kill". He arrived at Biggin Hill with 72 Squadron in the summer of 1940 and later commanded RAF Manston.

Squadron Leader Henryk Szczesny (third left), at one time the most decorated flight lieutenant in the RAF, is a Pole who escaped from his country in 1939, fought in France, made his way to England to join the RAF and ended the war in Stalag Luft Three alongside Squadron Leader Ken Campbell (fourth left) who was shot down in the Channel in the summer of 1941 and later helped to plan The Great Escape.

Wing Commander Brian Kingcome (fifth left) briefly commanded 92 Squadron, one of the most renowned in Fighter Command with more than 130 "kills".

On the extreme right is Wing Commander Ian Cosby who served with both 610 and 72 Squadrons at Biggin Hill and is currently leading the fight to save the old station from closure. Unlike his efforts 50 years ago he is fighting a losing battle.

The RAF is due to pull out of Biggin Hill in 1992.

1990

July 16th: *For years Donald Sinden has been an actor closely
linked with the Royal Shakespeare Company. Today, he is
widely known for his versatility in a number of television series,
including* Our Man at St Marks *and* Two's Company.
*Here he is seen with his actor sons Jeremy and Marc for
the first day of filming ITV's* Never The Twain *in which he
plays a very British antique dealer.*
*Away from the cameras antiques play a large part in
Donald Sinden's life. In the mid-50's he bought a dilapidated
cottage for £200 in an isolated part of Romney Marsh near
Tenterden which he and his wife Diana lovingly converted.*
*He laid on water, electricity, telephone and quickly found
himself immersed in the delights of life on the Marsh with
neighbours, who were still living in the cottages where they
were born and had never been to London.*
In his autobiography, Laughter in the Second Act, *Sinden
tells of Old Wilkie who invited Donald and Diana to his
cottage for a drink of his home made cider. "I took a sip
politely", he writes, "but it felt as if I had thrust a red-hot
poker into my mouth: it was too late to stop the process of
swallowing and the 'poker' seared its way down my throat. I
looked at Diana but it was too late for her also. She was
spluttering and tears started from her eyes..."*
*Old Wilkie and his wife had briefly moved out of their village
after they were married but soon came back. " 'That were up
Rolvenden way', he said in a voice as scornful as if he had
been to Alaska. Rolvenden is three miles away."*

Kent wilts in the sunshine

October: For the second successive summer
Kent has been bathed in almost continuous
sunshine, introducing the issue of global
warming to everyday conversation.

The warm weather, in fact, began in
February when dormant plants came into
bloom and the mercury rose to the mid sixties.

The weather continued to grab the headlines.
In March there were only three days of rain
and, by April, Bewl Water — which augments
Medway's flow — was only 70 per cent full.
May was the driest on record and hosepipe
bans were introduced throughout.

July was entirely dominated by a vast area
of descending dry air, an anticyclone, which
set the stage for the sensational day of August
3rd when the British record temperature of
98F, held by Canterbury, was beaten by
Cheltenham with 99F.

In the tinder-dry conditions there were
many blazes including a thatched home in
Lenham and a hop store at Paddock Wood.
A fireman died at Tiffenden and two men
were drowned in a lake at Horton Kirby.

Racing driver's murder linked to underworld

July 5th: The disappearance of millionaire garage owner Nick Whiting and the theft of five high performance cars from his showroom at Wrotham Heath led the police to suspect that Whiting was linked to the London underworld and a possible associate of Brinks Mat robber Kenneth Noye.

That has now been discounted. Yesterday, almost a month after he was reported missing, Whiting's badly decomposed and handcuffed body was found on Rainham Marshes, Essex, by conservationists taking soil samples. He had been badly beaten, stabbed and shot through the head.

Detectives are now working on the theory that Mr Whiting, aged 43 — a legitimate businessman — was driven to the remote spot alive in the boot of a car by at least two men who broke into the All Car Equipe garage at about 6.30 on the evening of June 7th. They also believe the abductors are members of a mercenary hit squad believed to be already responsible for 20 murders.

The former Brands Hatch racing driver who lived in Oldbury Lane, Ightham, with his wife Phillipa and children Mark and Nicola had built up a successful business specialising in high performance vehicles.

All the stolen cars have been recovered. Two were abandoned in St Mary's Platt and the others dumped in different parts of London.

Police say the men who killed Whiting were probably not those who wanted him dead. They were hit men acting on the orders of others. Although the murder remains a mystery new information is trickling in. *See page 164*

Dame Vera Lynn returns to Hellfire Corner and the White Cliffs of Dover to open the secret tunnels beneath Dover castle and 'meet again' with a few of the veterans.

Dame Vera opens secret tunnels

May: As the Forces sweetheart, Dame Vera Lynn worked tirelessly throughout the war to help cheer both servicemen and civilians. This year she has been in great demand again and such songs as *We'll Meet Again* and *The White Cliffs of Dover* are being heard at scores of reunions across the county.

This month Dame Vera opened Kent's latest tourist attraction — the secret tunnels under Dover Castle which served as one of Churchill's bases during the war. From 1940 the tunnels assumed great importance as naval headquarters with liaison officers from the army and airforce. Gun batteries were controlled from the tunnel HQ and the navy employed fluent German speakers who worked next to the cipher room listening to wireless transmissions from Germany.

The caves and tunnels also provided a safe haven for the people of Kent's most bombed town, for Dover was the hottest part of hellfire corner.

Sir Geoffrey and Lady Elspeth Howe with the rector, the Rev Maurice Hewett, after a service at St Botolph's Church, Chevening .

Sir Geoffrey's speech may topple Mrs Thatcher

November 14th: Sir Geoffrey Howe will soon be leaving Chevening, the stately home at Sevenoaks where he and his wife Elspeth have lived since he became Foreign Secretary in 1983.

Howe, who became leader of the House of Commons last year, is no longer a Government minister following a resignation speech of astonishing vehemence against the Prime Minister.

Yesterday in the Commons, Sir Geoffrey accused Mrs Thatcher of having a "nightmare vision" of a Europe "teeming with ill-intentioned people scheming to extinguish democracy".

A cabinet minister since he became Chancellor of the Exchequer in 1979 and frequently tipped as a future Prime Minister himself, Howe resigned from the Goverment two weeks ago because he could no longer agree with policy on Europe.

The man who has served Mrs Thatcher faithfully for 11 years said she had an implacable opposition to the European economic union which undermined all her colleagues' attempts at negotiation. He said: "It's rather like sending your opening batsman to the crease to find...that their bats have been broken before the game by the team captain."

Sir Geoffrey's outburst has opened the door for a leadership challenge which is almost certain to come from Michael Heseltine or Douglas Hurd with John Major as a possible alternative.

The former Chancellor and Foreign Secretary, who is MP for Reigate, is well known in the Sevenoaks area and particularly in the village of Chevening. He worships regularly in St Botolph's Church and is friendly with the rector, the Rev Maurice Hewett.

Sir Geoffrey's criticism of Mrs Thatcher's style of leadership is almost without precedent. He has been likened to a sheep in wolf's clothing. Today she is acting like a wounded animal. *See page 113*

January 10th: White witches are planning to lead a ritual on Romney Marsh in a bid to stop war breaking out in the Gulf. The date for the rite, which will be near a military training ground, is Tuesday January 15th — the deadline given by the United Nations for Iraq to withdraw from Kuwait. About 20 members of Kevin Carlyon's coven of Earth Magic will be directing positive thoughts for peace.

As war in the Gulf becomes inevitable the Rt Rev David Smith, Bishop of Maidstone, has warned Kent clergymen to prepare for calls from servicemen's families.

January 17th: Iraqi diplomats are expelled from London. Operation *Desert Storm* has begun.

January 31st: Israeli cities have been hit by 26 Scud missiles from Baghdad. Western powers fear retaliation from Israel.

February 15th: Opinion polls have shown John Major to be one of the most popular Prime Ministers since the war.

February 16th: A peace offer by Saddam Hussein has been dismissed by President Bush as a "cruel hoax".

Seven thousand gay rights protesters held a rally in Hyde Park after marching on London.

February 20th: Superintendant Dave Hatcher, who appears regularly on the popular BBC programme *Crimewatch UK,* has been appointed superintendent in charge of Ashford.

February 21st: Dame Margot Fonteyn, British ballerina, has died penniless aged 71 in Panama.

February 22nd: Iraqi forces have set Kuwaiti oilfields on fire.

February 26th: Saddam Hussein's elite Republican Guard divisions have been crushed by Allied forces, ending the Gulf War.

February 28th: Kuwait has been liberated from Iraq. 16 Britons and 148 American servicemen died.

Graham Fagg from Folkestone and Phillippe Cozette from Sangatte shake hands beneath the English Channel, or should we say La Manche, at the moment of the historic break-through. **See page 126**

March 6th: Dr George Carey has been enthroned as the new Archbishop of Canterbury.

March 14th: Six Irishman, known as the Birmingham Six, who were jailed for the murder of 21 people in 1975, have been set free following a Court of Appeal decision.

March 16th: England's rugby union team has ended the season unbeaten in the Five Nations championship.

March 21st: Environment Secretary Michael Heseltine today unveiled details of a new property tax to replace the hated poll tax.

March 30th: Seven million people are at risk in a new famine in Sudan. Western relief workers are now pouring into the country.

April 3rd: Graham Greene, author of such books as *Brighton Rock* and *The Third Man*, has died in Switzerland aged 86.

April 19th: It is believed that 500,000 Kurdish refugees are living in appalling conditions on the Turkish border having fled from Iraq.

May 3rd: A 145 mph cyclone which hit Bangladesh has left 125,000 dead and millions homeless.

May 18th: Hundreds of Kentish supporters travelled to Wembley to see Tottenham Hotspur beat Notts Forest to win the FA Cup.

A long stretch of the M20, "the missing link" between Maidstone and Ashford, has been opened to great acclaim.

Mick Jagger of the Rolling Stones, who lived in Dartford and went to the local Grammar School, has married his long-time partner, Jerry Hall. The Texan model is the mother of four of Jagger's children. They first met in 1977.

July 14th: Nigel Mansell today won the British Grand Prix. It is his 17th Grand Prix success — more than any other Englishman.

August 17th: John McCarthy, the longest held British captive in Lebanon, has finally been released.

August 19th: President Gorbachev of the Soviet Union has been toppled in a dawn coup.

August 21st: The Russian coup collapsed today signalling the end of communist rule. Thousands have answered Boris Yeltsin's call to raise barricades against troops and tanks.

August 27th: Eltham-born Bob Hope today unveiled a plaque at the Bob Hope Theatre. He was born in Craigton Road in 1903.

October 17th: Margaret Thatcher's memoirs have been bought for £2.5 million.

November 5th: Robert Maxwell, the British publishing tycoon who disappeared from his yacht, has been found dead.

A multi-million gas-fired power station has been approved by planners for the Isle of Grain.

December 7th: It has been revealed that Robert Maxwell transferred more than £400 million from the Mirror Group pension fund to stave off a debt crisis.

December 25th: Mikhail Gorbachev resigned today as leaders of Soviet Union countries announced their vision of a Commonwealth of Independent States.

GREAT HITS OF 1991

I'm too Sexy
Everything I do

Beleaguered commuters told: 'It's the wrong type of snow'

February 10th: Radio Kent's famous "snow line" — last used in January 1987 - has once again served the county well as bitterly cold air from Russia has sent temperatures plummeting below zero.

Continuous snow showers have forced the KCC Highways Centre in Maidstone to declare an emergency as roads become blocked, making conditions difficult even for gritting lorries and snowploughs.

Kent's railway commuters have suffered badly with many trains cancelled and a few even abandoned. Officials had a ready explanation. "It is the wrong type of snow", they announced. "Its powdery consistency has penetrated electric motors, clogged up the conductor rails and even caused doors to seize bringing trains to a halt."

As daytime temperatures fell to the lowest February reading of the century, 23F (-5C), giant icicles began to appear across the county, growing and growing until they hung like stalactites. Several fell causing injury.

This has been the first snowfall in Kent since the legendary January of 1987. Global warming, of course, has been blamed. For very small children, who have never seen snow or experienced the delights of tobogganing, this has been an exciting month.

Standing passengers 'like ears of wheat'

March 7th: A London orthopaedic specialist told the Cannon Street crash inquiry today that passengers standing in a rush hour train were wafted around the train like ears of wheat blowing in the wind.

Two people died and 542 London-bound commuters were injured when the 7.58 am from Sevenoaks rammed into the buffers at Cannon Street station in January.

The train was so crowded that many of the injured were standing and most of them suffered broken jaws and fractures to their facial bones. Alan Lettin, the consultant surgeon who also gave evidence to the Moorgate inquiry said: "The tops of their bodies went through a large arc while the lower part went through a smaller arc. Many suffered from crash volume and kidney failure caused after circulation was restored to their muscles."

At first it was thought the brakes had failed on the engine which was pulling carriages up to 60 years old but that has now been discounted.

Petts Wood commuter 24-year-old Martin Scrivens was killed in the crash and Pat McKay, a woman passenger, died four days later.

British Rail said this week they have no control over passengers who wish to travel standing in a compartment.

Richard Durtnell and Sons of Brasted — the oldest established firm of builders in the country and possibly Britain's oldest business of any kind — are celebrating their 400th anniversary this year.

It was in 1591 that John Durtnell, the youngest of four brothers, moved to Brasted, near Westerham and applied his skills as a carpenter to making timber-framed Wealden houses.

His first house at Poundsbridge (pictured above) in 1593 was a new rectory for his father, then vicar of Penshurst. By the time he died John was a renowned master carpenter and his workshop at Brasted employed some of the finest craftsmen.

Twelve generations later, in a line directly from father to son, the John Durtnell who is today's chairman of R. Durtnell and Sons carries on the same business on the same site.

Speaker of the House of Commons since 1983, Bernard Weatherill has become a popular figure in the village of Ide Hill, near Sevenoaks, where he lives with his wife, Lynn. Since debates in the House of Commons were first televised last year he is also more familiar to the public than any of his predecessors.

Three new murder inquiries — and no clues yet

December 31st: Three more murders, two of them dramatically connected, have completely baffled Kent police, whose investigations this year have already occupied thousands of hours.

On Easter Monday two men, who had earlier been seen cruising in a large American car through the village of Monkton, knocked on the front door of quantity surveyor Alan Leppard and killed him with a shotgun. He died in the arms of his girlfriend, Brenda Long, who bravely faced the camera a few days later to appeal for help in finding the killers.

Just after Christmas, Brenda's body was found in the bath at her flat in Whitstable and the circumstances were just as mysterious. At first it was assumed she had taken her own life, unable to face Christmas alone. A post mortem, however, revealed the anaesthetic ether in her blood and bruising round her face.

The inquest jury returned a verdict of unlawful killing.

The third murder is that of Rochester girl Glenda Potter whose semi-naked body was found in undergrowth behind the United Reformed Church in Crow Lane, Rochester on May 14th. She had been strangled.

Glenda, who was banned by the courts from seeing her two children and was disowned by her family, was a prostitute who worked in the streets in Medway.

Her boyfriend Alan Shepherd said he had tried to persuade her to join him on a weekend trip to Cornwall. She refused and he left without her. When he returned she was dead.

He said: "She loved her job and used to say to me that she had been put on earth to please men. Whenever she didn't come home I used to ring the police to see if she was in the cells. I'd ring the hospitals. I could have married that girl. Maybe I could have saved her."

Kent hails the heroes of 'Desert Storm'

January 31st: For hundreds of Kent families with relatives in Middle East-based forces it has been an anxious start to the year as they waited for Saddam Hussein to get out of Kuwait. As we now know, compromise deals offered by the UN, France and King Hussein of Jordan all failed, the January 15th deadline passed and the war that everyone tried to avoid is now well under way.

Operation "Desert Storm" began on January 16th when an F-117 Stealth fighter evaded Iraqi radar and destroyed Saddam's telecommunications centre. This week Allied planes have continued bombing Baghdad and Saddam has retaliated by launching Scud missiles on Israeli cities.

Servicemen from Kent are playing a big part in the Gulf War and are among the 700,000-strong Allied force — of which 25,000 come from Britain.

Among them is Adrian Nance, aged 35, of Beadon Road, Bromley, captain of the Type 42 destroyer *HMS Cardiff* which has already been in the thick of action. Last week helicopters from his ship sank a convoy of Iraqi patrol boats which were attempting to land commandos on the coast of Saudi Arabia.

Two Folkestone mothers, whose sons are in the Gulf, have set up a support group for families of other servicemen and women. Christine Close and Sylvia Keeler want parents, wives and sweethearts to meet occasionally and read each other's letters just to find out what is going on.

One who has already written home is Trooper Russell Haffenden of Broadstairs who is serving with the Queen's Royal Irish Hussars. The 21-year-old from St Peter's says that morale is high but it's very cold in the desert. His mum Denise told the *Isle of Thanet Gazette* that she feels dreadful about his mission. "Because there is little work available in Thanet I encouraged him to join the Army," she said.

Airmen and women from RAF Manston are also in the Gulf and this week the station commander Wing Commander Alistair Montgomery thanked the people of Thanet for "their kind offers of assistance during these early days of the Gulf War. It reflects", he said, "the wonderful community spirit which exists here."

He may take up the offers of help for 200 expatriates, who managed to flee from Iraq, have arrived at the Kent International Airport in three flights. Manston says it is prepared to receive other evacuees at a moment's notice.

One evacuee who is now at home with his family in Shipbourne is Eddie May who was held at an Iraqi chemical plant for several months after the invasion of Kuwait as part of Saddam's "human shield". His wife and family, desperate for news, were overjoyed when Eddie, a well-known member of the village cricket club, was set free just before Christmas.

Parents of a young Deal soldier poised to go into battle when the ground troops are deployed say they think about their son every minute. Terry and Sue Austin's son Mark is a gunner serving with the 2nd Field Regiment, Royal Artillery. He is part of a gun crew likely to be in the front line.

Also in the front line are husband and wife Chris and Joy Hopkins from Lydden, near Folkestone. As members of the Royal Air Force Auxiliary and trained medical assistants they were among the first reservists told to report for duty. "It is what we were trained for", said Chris. "We joined knowing this could happen at any time."

One young Gulf soldier wrote to the *Folkestone Herald* informing them he could win a competition among his pals in the Middle East with their help. To win the contest, he said, I have to be the first to get my name in the local paper. A few days ago Gary Stannage of Folkestone collected his prize.

Lieut Claire Smith of Eythorne, who is with the Queen Alexandra's Royal Nursing Service, has written to her concerned but proud parents to tell them about life aboard the hospital vessel *HMS Argus*. "A terrific sense of humour and love of nursing is keeping her cheerful", said her mother. "She was on board on January 15th when the alarm went off and a voice announced that this was not a rehearsal but war."

February 28th: Kuwait tonight is wild with celebrations. After six months and 25 days of brutal occupation the country has been liberated. Today Allied armoured columns rolled into a city shrouded in the smoke of burning oil wells.

The Gulf War is now over. President Bush announced on American television that Kuwait is liberated and Iraq's army defeated. "Exactly 100 hours since ground operations commenced and six weeks since the start of Operation Desert Storm all United States and coalition forces will suspend combat operations."

The victory is not complete despite the fact that Saddam's land forces have been crushed. The Iraqi leader still rules in Baghdad and retains military capabilities.

March 16th: Kent MPs are supporting the ceasefire resolution which Prime Minister John Major will discuss with President Bush this week. The resolution, prepared for the UN Security Council, will leave strict economic sanctions in place enabling the Allies to keep pressure on Saddam Hussein without renewing military action.

Eddie May, Shipbourne cricketer and Saddam's 'human shield', is re-united with his family in time for Christmas.

Waiting for war. Sapper Colin Mottram, 18, of the 21st Engineers Regiment is seen here with some of the huge excavation vehicles which will be used to prepare the ground for the tanks. Colin, of Rainham, sent this picture and others to his girlfriend, Tracey Edwards, with vivid letters describing army life in the desert before the action.

October: *They are known as the tunnel tigers — the British and French workers who are hacking away at the chalk face deep under the English Channel. A few months ago the two countries came face to face for the first time as the last inch (sorry centimetre) was bored through by Graham Fagg from Folkestone and Phillipe Cozette from Sangatte. That was in one of the service tunnels. This month came the historic breakthrough in the train tunnel, completing the undersea link- up and proving that this "once impossible" chunnel can be built. As the tigers continue with the toughest of jobs, the money men in London are getting quite nervous. On the drawing-board the estimated cost was £4.9 billion. Today it's just under £9 billion and a multi-million pound dispute is raging between Eurotunnel and builders TML. More money has to be found and British Rail has been denied permission to build a high-speed rail link from the tunnel to central London.*   ***See page 146***

Pluckley murder: TV documentary casts doubts

June: A recent Granada television documentary, called *In Suspicious Circumstances*, has reconstructed the murder, in October 1980, of Miss Gwendoline Marshall of Pluckley and the imprisonment of Peter Luckhurst who had confessed to the crime.

Following the programme, which threw doubt on the evidence of the Luckhurst case, the Home Office has called for another report. It will hear from villagers how Luckhurst once confessed to vandalism in Pluckley. Despite the fact that most people knew who the culprit was, Luckhurst was taken before a juvenile court and fined. There has been a concerted campaign in the area supporting Luckhurst's innocence in the Marshall case.

A display by fireboats and biplanes accompanied the opening of the Dartford Bridge.

A BRIDGE TOO HIGH

October 30th: Drivers who suffer from vertigo say the new £86 million Dartford Bridge, which was opened by the Queen today, is far too high and they will not have the option of using the tunnel.

The cable-stayed bridge is 62 metres high and, with a span of 2,872 metres, the longest of its kind in Europe. Both the tunnel and the bridge will be oneway, the bridge taking traffic south while the tunnel traffic will run north.

Of the 'Bridge Too High', as it is being dubbed, a police spokesman said: "It could get frightening up there. The biggest problem will arise when cars are stationary in a tailback and drivers feel the structure swaying in the wind."

The bridge was built by Trafalgar House which has created a new administrative company The Dartford River Crossing Ltd. 500 guests saw the Queen declare the bridge open.

• *The first Dartford tunnel was opened in November 1963 for £13 million. A second tunnel commenced in 1972 and opened in 1980 for £45 million. The bridge has cost £85m.*

Terry Waite released

November 19th: After spending nearly five years chained to a wall in Beirut Terry Waite has been released along with the Scottish-born American, Tom Sutherland. Mr Waite was the last remaining British hostage in Lebanon.

The special representative to the Archbishop of Canterbury flew to RAF Lyneham to be welcomed by his family and by both Lord Runcie and the present Archbishop, Dr George Carey.

Mr Waite said he had seen no-one and spoken to no-one but his guards for four years. His clothes had been taken away and he had no window in his cell or pen and paper on which to write. In an emotional account of his imprisonment he said his Christian faith had sustained him.

Prayers were said in Canterbury Cathedral and churches throughout Kent for the safe deliverance of Mr Waite who has plans to write a book.

'An annus horribilis' — Queen Elizabeth, on the 40th year of her reign in November, referring to the domestic problems faced by three of her children and the Windsor Castle fire.

January 15th: The European Commission today recognised the independence of Croatia and Slovenia, signalling the end of Yugoslavia as one nation. The move came a week after Bosnian Serbs created their own republic closely allied to Belgrade.

February 9th: Paddy Ashdown, leader of the Liberal Democrats, has admitted he had an affair with his secretary five years ago. His rating in the polls has risen by 13 per cent.

February 10th: Russia and the newly independent states, now in the grip of a harsh winter, are receiving food and medical aid in an operation similar to the Berlin Air Lift in 1949.

March 25th: The humorous magazine *Punch* is to close after 150 years of publication.

Pakistan today defeated England by 22 runs to win the World Cricket Cup in Melbourne.

March 26th: Mike Tyson, the world's youngest heavyweight boxing champion, has been sentenced to five years imprisonment for rape.

Water restrictions are still in force in much of Kent as water reserves drop to their lowest level ever. It is the same over much of Britain and scientists fear this could be an early sign of global warming.

April 10th: An easy Labour general election victory was predicted but John Major was surprisingly returned to power today with a Tory majority of 21 seats.

April 13th: Neil Kinnock has resigned as Labour's leader.

Princess Anne and Captain Mark Phillips, who have been legally separated for two years, are to start divorce proceedings. Buckingham Palace has confirmed that the Duchess of York is also seeking a divorce.

May 18th: An inquest on the deaths of nine British soldiers has ruled that they were killed by

1992

October 10th: **Archaeologists have discovered, beneath a new road link in Dover, the remains of a large wooden prehistoric boat belonging to the Bronze Age, when metal was first used in Britain.**

Two weeks ago, Keith Parfitt, project field director for the Canterbury Archaeological Trust and Dr Martin Bates of the Institute of Archaeology in London, were working in a deep (six metre) waterlogged hole in Bench Street when they came across an odd-looking piece of wood. Work on a storm water pump was halted and urgent telephone calls made to the Department of Transport. A six-day break in construction gave the team time to excavate what is believed to be the best preserved prehistoric boat ever found in Britain.

About one and a half times as long as a double-decker bus it would have been capable of crossing the channel, carrying a cargo of supplies, livestock and passengers and propelled by at least 18 paddlers.

The discovery throws new light on the possibility of a brisk, prehistoric seafaring trade between Dover and Calais as long ago as 2000 BC.

"friendly" fire and American pilots were responsible.

June 10th: Baroness Thatcher today took her seat in the House of Lords.

June 24th: Hundreds of "Lloyds' names" — businessmen who have invested with Lloyds of London — were told today that the company's losses amount to more than £2 million, the worst in its 300-year-old history.

July 9th: Chris Patten took office as the new (and last) governor of Hong Kong today.

August 9th: Linford Christie (100 metres) and Sally Gunnell (400 metres hurdles) have won gold medals for Britain in the Barcelona Olympic Games.

August 15th: The International Red Cross has denounced the Serbs' policy of "ethnic cleansing". The sight of emaciated prisoners held in Bosnian prison camps has shocked the world.

August 20th: The Daily Mirror today published a photograph of the Duchess of York by a swmming pool in the South of France. She was topless and alongside was John Bryan from Texas sucking her toe!

Herne Bay's impressive £8 million seafront scheme has been completed. There are now gardens for half a mile along a new promenade.

August 27th: A 19-year-old Northern Irishman became the 300th victim today of sectarian violence. It is 23 years since a Catholic was shot dead by the now-disbanded B-Specials.

September 24th: Heritage Secretary David Mellor, known as "Minister for Fun", resigned today following revelations of his affair with actress Antonia de Sancha.

October 21st: A plan to close a further 31 pits across the country and make 300,000 miners redundant has been abandoned in the wake of massive demonstrations and a protest march on London. The Government has said that only 10 pits will now close.

October 26th: Canada has voted against a constitutional proposal to give French-speaking Quebec a special separatist status.

October 28th: With the failure of the £1.5 million computerised system for directing emergency ambulance calls, the London Ambulance Service has reverted to manual control.

November 4th: Governor Bill Clinton of Arkansas today became America's new President. The 46-year-old is the first person born after the Second World War to become President.

November 11th: The Church of England has voted to allow women to be ordained as priests.

November 14th: England today beat South Africa at Twickenham in the first game between the two countries since sporting relations were broken by apartheid in 1964.

The State Apartments and the roof of Windsor Castle have been badly damaged by fire.

GREAT HITS OF 1992

Tears in Heaven
Why?
The Days of Our Life

Steve Backley warms up for Barcelona

January: Steve Backley, the javelin thrower from Park Road, Chislehurst, has recaptured his world record with an astonishing throw of 91.46 metres — proving that he is on course to win a medal at this year's Olympic Games in Barcelona.

Steve has lived in the Bromley area for many years and his supporters have been watching closely his keen rivalry with Jan Zelezny of the Czech Republic, whose record he has taken.

His meteoric rise to fame began in 1986 when he won the javelin event in the Kent Championships and finished second in the English Schools Championships.

Since then he has won gold medals in the Commonwealth Games and European Championships, twice gained the world record and was voted, in 1990, the IAAF Athlete of the Year.

His greatest psychological tactic, which he learned as a teenager and has employed in competition ever since, is to get a good throw in as quickly as possible and put pressure on your opponents.

He gives much credit to his father who helped to create in his mind that burning desire to win. "Champions", he was told, "are born, not in competition, but in the training sessions."

Steve Backley studied Sports Science, including sports psychology at Loughborough.

December: An injury to Steve Backley has put his future as a javelin thrower in great jeopardy. Having won a bronze medal at Barcelona his shoulder has seized up and an operation is necessary. He said this week that it is agony even to throw money into the automatic trough at the Dartford Tunnel. *See page 161*

Steve Backley from Chislehurst — one of Britain's most popular and widely admired athletes — enjoys a promotion for Parcelforce during the Children in Need Appeal.

April 9th: *Money collected from around the world after the tragedy in 1951 when 24 marine cadets were mown down by a double-decker bus in Dock Road, Chatham has been finally freed.*
After a series of setbacks and a campaign lasting more than 40 years the High Court has released the remaining £7,338. The former cadets, now in their 50s, want the money spent on medical bills to treat injuries still giving trouble. Spokesman for the surviving 28 men, who formed the marching column in 1951, is Mr Roy Lyall of Exeter Walk who said there is still a long way to go as the Government could decide to give the money to charity.

Witnesses refuse to identify pub gunman

November: A man who was shot in the leg just before closing time in the Kings Arms pub, Meopham, in August is the brother of a murder victim. Nelson Brown was shot dead two years ago during a feud on a caravan site in Gravesend.

Harry Brown of Culverstone was luckier. He was taken to West Hill Hospital, Dartford, confident that several pub customers had seen the assailant who would soon be brought to justice.

One by one, however, 12 witnesses have refused to identify the gunman and police now believe they have been subject to threats and intimidation. Mr Brown, in fear of his life, has moved to another part of the country.

Grieving father takes his revenge

October: One of the most sensational trials ended at Maidstone Crown Court this month when Stephen Owen from Sittingbourne was acquitted of the attempted murder of Kevin Taylor who was shot at twice by Owen and seriously injured.

Taylor, a one-eyed lorry driver who didn't even have a driving licence, had been responsible for the death of Mr Owen's 12-year-old son Darren. After running over him he then drove off. He was later found guilty of reckless driving and sentenced to 18 months.

Owen, bent on revenge, waited for Taylor to be released. When the two men met in the village of Kemsley, Owen had a shotgun. He fired twice at Taylor who was badly hurt and needed emergency surgery. Owen, who then went on the run, was not found for three days.

At his trial Owen pleaded not guilty. He said that Taylor had shown no remorse over his son's death and his jail sentence was too light. He admitted having a gun and shooting Taylor but did not intend to kill.

The jury found him not guilty of attempted murder. He left the court a free man, waving his hands and claiming "this was justice from God".

Maidstone United — a team picture taken in 1987.

End of an era: Maidstone United is laid to rest

November 11th: Three seasons after savouring the euphoria of election to the Football League Maidstone United has gone into liquidation. Chairman Jim Thompson told his loyal supporters today that all the toils, the endless planning meetings and the impassioned wrangling had come to nothing. Maidstone, as a Barclays League side, was being laid to rest.

"It was all about sacrifices", he said. "We made sacrifices. The council didn't. That's what killed the club."

The decision to put the club in the hands of the receivers brings to an end months of speculation about the future of the 94-year-old football club.

In 1988 the directors, dreaming of promotion to Division Four of the Football League, sold the London Road ground to MFI for £2.8 million. That gave the club capital to relocate and achieve entry to the league the following year. As they negotiated with the council for a new site, Maidstone played all home games on the Dartford ground.

Ambitious plans for a multi-purpose leisure and stadium complex were outlined and possible sites investigated. One, at Hollingbourne, was considered to be so promising that the directors believed they would soon have one of the finest football stadiums in the Fourth Division.

One by one the sites were rejected, the planning officer pointing out that there was nowhere, except perhaps on the moon, where a stadium could be sited without opposition.

In the meantime, before dwindling crowds at Dartford, Maidstone United's precious £2.8 million was being

The Stones and the highlights

1893: A consortium of local businessmen pay £6,500 to turn a hop garden into the Athletic Ground sports stadium.

1907: More than 5,000 see Maidstone United lose 5-2 to Newcastle in a friendly.

1922: Scottish international Jimmy McMullan signs for the club

1923: Maidstone beat Sittingbourne 3-2 in the Kent Senior Cup before before a crowd of 12,000.

1925: England beat Ireland 6-4 in an amateur international on the ground.

1954: Maidstone becomes the first amateur club in the country to install floodlights.

1970: Jim Thompson becomes chairman. The club turns professional and joins the Southern League.

1980: Maidstone draw 0-0 with Gillingham in an FA Cup second round replay in front of 7,465.

1987: Ground badly damaged in October storm. £100,000 of damage. Crowd capacity is reduced.

steadily eroded. The dream eventually died today (November 11th) when the latest plans for a site at Woodcut Farm was thrown out.

One former player devasted by the news is David Sadler who played for Maidstone when his family owned the Two Brewers pub in Yalding. "It was the first football ground I ever saw", he said. "My own Wembley at the age of 10."

Sadler made such an impact in the seasons between 1961 and 63 that he won English amateur caps and had league scouts swarming around the Athletic Ground. Matt Busby and Manchester United won his signature and Sadler reached the heights when he played in the European Cup Final in 1968, which Manchester United won and was selected for England.

December 5th: Charlton Athletic Football Club has returned to The Valley. After seven long years as refugees, five at Selhurst Park — the home of Crystal Palace — and two at West Ham, The Addicks are back at their spiritual home where they have played since the club entered the Football League in 1921. The ground, once little more than a swamp with banked terraces, will eventually include a new west stand with 4,500 seats, a restaurant, hospitality suites and executive boxes. The north and south stands have been refurbished. New seating has become compulsory in the wake of the Hillsborough disaster. In time it will become an all-seater stadium. The capacity is now less than 20,000 and only older supporters can remember the occasions when more than 50,000 regularly crowded into the ground. In 1938,

*75,031 spectators watched the match with Aston Villa. The next aim for club chairman Roger Alwen and managers Alan Curbishley and Steve Gritt is promotion to the senior division. **See page 175***

Jennifer's ear became an election issue

April 10th: A Labour victory in yesterday's general election was widely predicted but, unexpectedly, John Major returns to Downing Street with a majority of 21 seats — in the middle of a recession.

The Bennett family from Faversham found themselves at the centre of the biggest controversy of the election campaign when a Labour broadcast, criticising the long NHS waiting list, picked out the case of Jennifer Bennett.

The little girl was waiting for treatment on her ear but her surgeon said this wasn't because of a shortage of funds — but an administrative blunder. Jennifer's mother, a Conservative supporter, criticised the broadcast. Her father, a Labour supporter, defended it.

The war of Jennifer's ear became the big election issue and many believe it was the turning point of the closest election campaign for years.

Tonight the IRA marked the Tory victory by detonating a van loaded with 100 pounds of Semtex in the City of London. The blast killed three people and injured 91.

1992

Charles and Diana to separate: the fairy tale is over

December 26th: At the time it seemed like a fairy tale. A shy girl, who went to school in Sevenoaks and worked for the town's Voluntary Service Unit, was to marry the Prince of Wales and live in the stately mansion at Chevening. People would take her to their hearts; she would become a much-loved future Queen of England.

Today, it's all over. Earlier this month Buckingham Palace announced that the Prince and Princess of Wales are to separate after 11 years of marriage. The Palace made it clear that their decision had been reached amicably and there are no plans for divorce. Charles and Diana will share the responsibility of bringing up their sons William and Harry.

The separation follows the storm which has been gathering over the royal family since the publication in June of the book *Diana: Her True Story* by Andrew Morton, a royal reporter.

In the book he claims she has made five attempts to commit suicide in desperation over the uncaring attitude of Prince Charles. Morton refuses to confirm rumours that Diana herself collaborated but says the information for the book came from her friends.

The book also outlines her battles with bulimia and claims that the Princess felt trapped in a loveless marriage. Those close to Charles have retaliated by saying that Diana is unstable.

Her friends in Kent believe she has had difficulty in adjusting to the constrained life of a member of the royal family with its rigid protocol. Her inability to put formality before feelings has contributed to her unhappiness. They also say that she resents the influence that her husband's old friend Camilla Parker Bowles exerts on him.

William Deedes, the former Daily Telegraph editor who lives near Ashford, says that Princess Diana's heart has been laid bare for all to see. "True, she came to impart her inner feelings to certain people without even desiring confidentiality, let alone imposing it. Naturally the Press pricked up its ears. And when it came to the sort of scene enacted outside the Taj Mahal in May when Diana sat alone, they picked up their cameras as well."

Andrew Morton's biography has been condemned as an unforgivable intrusion into the affairs of the royal family. The Queen has declined to talk about it publicly but in November, after the Windsor Castle fire, she referred to this year as an "Annus Horribilis", the only good news being the wedding of the Princess Royal to Tim Laurence.

See Page 136

October 21st: *Showing no sign of the strain and bravely hiding her obvious unhappiness behind a constant smile, the Princess of Wales performed one of her less arduous royal duties today by opening the Royal Victoria Place — a giant*

new shopping complex built on three levels off Calverley Road, Tunbridge Wells. Diana was welcomed by the Mayor of Tunbridge Wells and the chairman of the company which developed the shopping mall. A huge crowd lined the streets to greet her and she was presented with a cheque for £2,500 for the Mayor's charity, Headway, of which she is national patron.

Kent traffic policemen couldn't believe their eyes. A three wheel Reliant Robin was in the fast lane of the M20 overtaking much more powerful cars. The policemen gave chase, checked their speedometer and rubbed their eyes again. The Reliant was clocking 108 mph! Driver Clive Richley has admitted speeding. He has also admitted the car's engine wasn't the original and is capable of a much greater speed.

Ramsgate-born Freddie Laker who became a hero with the travelling public for pioneering cheap air travel — particularly with his £59 Skytrain service to the States — has sued the major airlines, including British Airways. His company collapsed in 1982 and Laker claims it was caused by a conspiracy to force him out of business. British Airways and other defendants have now settled out of court, giving him personally in excess of £5 million as well as paying all his creditors. The Thanet entrepeneur is back in business, setting up a new Laker Airways, flying from the Bahamas to various US cities.

Former Sevenoaks pupil marries Princess Anne

December 12th: Good news at last for the royal family. The Princess Royal was married today to Commander Tim Laurence, a former pupil of Sevenoaks School, during a private ceremony in the tiny stone church at Crathie, near Balmoral.

The 37-year-old bridegroom is well-known in Kent. He lived with his parents Barbara and Guy Laurence in the White House, Copthall Road, Ightham, and used to be taken to the local primary school on the back of his mother's bicycle.

Tim entered Sevenoaks School on an entrance scholarship in 1968 and went on to gain 10 'O' and three 'A' levels, mostly in high grades. He won a scholarship to the Royal Naval College, Dartmouth and later read Geography at Durham.

For Princess Anne, who has two children — Peter and Zara — by Captain Mark Phillips, this was a far cry from her first marriage in Westminster Abbey.

'You are presiding over a chaos that is leading the Church of England into terminal decline' — Ann Widdecombe MP for Maidstone in an open letter to Dr Carey, Archbishop of Canterbury.

January 1st: The European Commission's Single Market came into being today. It encompasses 375 million people generating £4.5 trillion. Britain, Denmark, Greece and Ireland are the only countries in which travellers will require passports — "necessary to fight terrorism".

January 5th: *The Braer*, an 89,000-ton tanker, has run aground at Quendale Bay in the Shetland Islands and is spewing its cargo of oil in the sea. Thousands of seabirds and otters are now threatened.

February 11th: The Queen has volunteered to pay income tax and capital gains tax on her private income.

February 19th: Frostbite and weightloss has forced Sir Ranulph Fiennes and Michael Stroud to call off their historic crossing of the Antarctic iceshelf after a 1,345-mile trek that took 95 days.

February 22nd: Two 10-year-old Liverpool boys have been charged with the murder of toddler James Bulger. His battered body was found near a railway embankment.

April 3rd: The world's greatest steeplechase, the Grand National, was declared void today after two false starts. £75 million will have to be refunded.

April 29th: To help pay for the damage to Windsor Castle, Buckingham Palace is to be open to tourists for a fee of £8 a head.

May 1st: Pierre Beregovoy, the former Socialist Prime Minister of France whose party was humiliated in the March general elections, today committed suicide.

May 27th: Prime Minister John Major has dismissed his Chancellor, Norman Lamont and appointed Kenneth Clarke, aged 53.

Restoration work on the 17th century Tyland Barn at Sandling, near Maidstone, was completed in time for the Prince of Wales to perform the official opening. Tyland Barn is the headquarters of the Kent Trust for Nature Conservation.

June 24th: Michael Mates, junior minister for Northern Ireland, has resigned following allegations of links with the fugitive tycoon, Asil Nadir.

July 16th: Stella Rimington, the first woman head of MI5, today revealed to the press details of her organisation's work. She said her aim was to dispel "the fanciful allegations about her once secret service".

July 18th: Ian Botham, one of England's greatest all-rounders, now playing for Durham, has announced his retirement.

August 2nd: The Maastricht treaty was today ratified by the Queen.

Kent's new cricket captain is their outstanding and immensely reliable opening batsman, 34-year-old Mark Benson, who has played in one Test match for England but deserved many more. Averaging over 40 with the bat he has rescued his side time and time again and is a brilliant player in one-day games. In the County championship Mark has consistently made more than 1,000 runs in a season.

August 11th: The number of people waiting for hospital treatment in Britain has risen to more than a million.

Prince Harry visited Buckmore Park, Chatham, to enjoy the karting track. He was presented with a trophy from Formula One racing driver Johnny Herbert.

September 6th: Part of Maidstone East railway station was virtually demolished yesterday after a freight train crashed, dragging five trucks and shedding 900 tons of wire steel. The station will be closed for about two days.

September 13th: Yassir Arafat of the PLO and Yitzhak Rabin, Prime Minister of Israel, today signed an agreement for limited Palestinian autonomy in the Gaza Strip and the West Bank. Peace has broken out in the Middle East.

October 4th: A hardline rebellion against Boris Yeltsin was crushed by the Russian army today. Dozens of people are feared dead inside the besieged White House which was occupied by commandos.

October 15th: This year's Nobel Peace Prize has been awarded jointly to Nelson Mandela and Frederik de Klerk for their work in bringing apartheid to an end in South Africa.

November 17th: Although they beat San Marino by 7-1 England have failed to qualify for the World Cup finals

November 23rd: Graham Taylor, England's football manager, resigned today. A few months ago Graham Gooch resigned as England's cricket captain.

December 15th: John Major and Albert Reynolds, prime ministers of Britain and Ireland, have signed a declaration designed to bring peace to Northern Ireland.

GREAT HITS OF 1993

All That She Wants
That's the Way Love Goes

Maidstone's crusading MP accuses Archbishop

February: Ann Widdecombe, the crusading MP for Maidstone, has already become a national figure for her stance on moral and ethical issues. She opposes women priests, supports nuclear arms and is outspoken on abortion. Her special place in the national consciousness, however, was finally secured this week when television crews and reporters were at Westminster Cathedral to witness her transfer from the Church of England to Rome.

To explain her defection she has written a long open letter to the Archbishop of Canterbury, Dr Carey in which she castigates him for presiding over a chaos that "is leading the Church of England into terminal decline".

She said she left the church in November the minute she heard of the decision to ordain women. She believes the issue of women priests has nothing to do with women's rights. "Theologically", she says, "it is not possible for a women to be a priest."

Born in Bath where her father ran a naval supply depot, Miss Widdecombe's route into politics began with her election to Runnymeade District Council in 1976. Two years later she spoke up for capital punishment at the Tory party conference and co-founded a pro-nuclear movement formed as an antidote to the women of Greenham Common. She was chosen MP for Maidstone in 1987 and became the first woman John Major appointed into a ministerial position.

Her constituents are divided in their opinion of her. Many see her as unsuitable for dealing with purely local affairs and oppose her strong right-wing views. Supporters, however, say she is a driven woman and has campaigned vigorously against such issues as school closures, the high speed rail link and supported hospital funding. They confirm she is a moral crusader with religious zeal, high principles and is on course for a glittering, though controversial, political career. *See page 168*

Globe and Rainbow, Kilndown is a long way from Tipperary!

February: The popular member for Tunbridge Wells, Sir Patrick Mayhew, is another Kent politician with a high profile — not least because he has the most unenviable job in the Cabinet as Secretary of State for Northern Ireland.

Sir Patrick is pictured with schoolchildren in the village of Kilndown, near Goudhurst, where he lives – a community of 400 residents, one shop, a church, village hall and pub, The Globe and Rainbow, where he occasionally downs a Guinness. Compare that to his daily duties in Ulster, his spacious busy office in Stormont and his responsibilities which include security, economic development, agriculture and the setting up of a lasting peace settlement in what is one of the most volatile communities in the world.

Sir Patrick has a second home in the Irish Republic and a great love of the country and of the people who live there — his mother came from a Protestant Irish family from County Cork. His wife, Lady Jean, gave up teaching in London to take on the task as the Province's first lady and now has her own private secretary and busy timetable.

Great-grandson of Lord Goschen, Victorian Chancellor of the Exchequer who left the Liberal Party after Gladstone's conversion to Irish Home Rule, Patrick Mayhew is surrounded by security men whever he goes in the world. He still receives much flak and most of it comes from the Rev Ian Paisley who recently called him "wicked and shameless".

March 25th: *A memorial stone erected by the Metropolitan Police in memory of Detective Constable John Fordham, who was stabbed to death by Kenneth Noye in January 1985, has been vandalised. Police this week found bullet marks on the stone in West Kingsdown not far from the spot where Dc Fordham fell. It is now almost 10 years since the Brinks Mat gold bullion robbery and eight years since Noye was acquitted of killing the 45-year-old surveillance officer in the grounds of Hollywood Cottage, West Kingsdown.*

Damning diaries of Alan Clark

May: It is not only the country's leading politicians who have been savaged. Scores of well-intentioned villagers, who live in the vicinity of Saltwood Castle, have become major casualties of Alan Clark's honest, engaging and intentionally indiscreet *Diaries* which were published this week to great acclaim.

Clark, the former junior minister in employment and trade, tells of the fat wife of a parish councillor whom he caught "stealing" firewood from the castle grounds, the "incredibly tiresome" woman behind him at a Christmas service and her "buffer of a husband who blundered in occasional nicotine tones".

Clark, infamous for his "bongo bongo" land statement, his treatment

of his younger and long-suffering wife Jane is outspoken in his opinions of former colleagues and their place in numerous political dramas.

Michael Heseltine is described as "wild-eyed" and a "zombie". Norman Lamont is "untrustworthy. I can see you weren't at Eton" and Kenneth Clarke is a "pudgy puffball" and "not surprisingly a life insurance nightmare". Sir Alistair Morton, chairman of Eurotunnel, is "aggressive, nasty and stupid".

On the other hand the Lady (Margaret Thatcher) has "captured his heart", the "unclassy" John Major has a "lovely grin" and John Wells, former MP for Maidstone, is a "very splendid

fellow".

Clark, who is the son of *Civilisation's* Kenneth Clark, is well-known in Saltwood where he swims in the moat surrounding his beautiful castle, whizzes around the village in vintage cars and frequently shouts at poorly performing postmen and tradesmen.

A multi-millionaire, who admits living on the interest of his interest, he no longer has a seat in the House of Commons but makes no secret of his desire to return. His *Diaries*, published by Weidenfeld and Nicholson, have entered the national bestsellers list.

See page 154

A memorial for The Few

July 9th: An idea by Wing Commander Geoffrey Page for a permanent national Battle of Britain memorial high above the White Cliffs of Dover has finally come to fruition. As the Queen Mother formally opened the memorial today invited guests recalled those dramatic summer months in 1940 when 507 RAF aircrew were lost and many more civilian and service personnel killed.

Several pilots were shot down in the Channel and Flying Officer Page was among them. In August 1940 he baled out of his Hurricane, badly burned and was rescued by the Margate lifeboat. He underwent plastic surgery in the Queen Victoria Hospital, East Grinstead and was a founder member of the Guinea Pig Club.

Geoffrey Page campaigned vigorously for the memorial on behalf of the Battle of Britain Memorial Trust.

Black youth murdered by 'gang of five'

April 29th: The murder last week of Stephen Lawrence, a black 18-year-old A-level student, outside a bus stop in Well Hall Road, Eltham, is believed to be both unprovoked and racially-motivated. The assailants are a gang of five white youths who surrounded Stephen, called him a "nigger" and stabbed him to death.

With him was a friend, Duwayne Brooks. The boys had been friends since primary school and were going home to Woolwich after an evening together. They were neither causing nor looking for trouble.

After the killing a murder squad from the Metropolitan Police's south-east London area was assembled in Eltham station. A spokesman said they immediately identified five youths as prime suspects, three of whom were named by a police informant on April 23rd.

Stephen Lawrence's parents, who demand justice immediately, are deeply traumatised by the circumstances of their son's murder. So is Duwayne Brooks, who will be asked to name the suspects at an identity parade. ***See page 163***

Stephen Lawrence's parents tell television reporters of their grief and their hopes that justice will quickly prevail.

Rebecca, first woman on top of the world

May 19th: Rebecca Stevens from Kemsing near Sevenoaks has become the first woman to reach the 29,002-foot summit of the world's highest mountain.

The 31-year-old journalist, who gave up her job with the *Financial Times* to attempt an assault on Everest, reached the summit ahead of Sherpa guides at 7.41am UK time on Saturday April 17th. In a radio message Rebecca said: "I am at the top of the world."

She was taking part in the expedition sponsored by DHL which is climbing the mountain to mark the 40th anniversary of Sir Edmund Hillary's conquest on the eve of the coronation in 1953.

Rebecca, the youngest of three sisters, grew up in Kemsing and was a pupil at St John's School, Sevenoaks, before moving to Tonbridge Grammar School and then university. A career in journalism followed.

Four years ago she covered a story of an Everest expedition and that's where her interest in climbing started. She has now conquered Mount McKinley in Alaska, Mont Blanc, Mount Kenya and Mount Kilamanjaro.

She said the hardest thing about Everest was forcing herself to make a second assault on the peak despite appalling weather forcasts. In her first attempt she had been forced back by bad weather and the need to care for a team-mate who was exhausted after reaching the summit without oxygen.

The final climb to the summit took six hours. Rebecca then began her slow, careful descent to the base camp at 17,000 feet. ***See page 145***

Riot police on horseback prepare for action on the Clan Field, Welling.

Welling protest march becomes a riot

October 16th: Race hatred erupted in the streets of Welling today when more than 20,000 demonstrators clashed with police barring their way to the British National Party's "headquarters" in Upper Wickham Lane.

Violence erupted into a pitched battle as police in riot gear and on horseback attempted to divert a march organised by the Anti-Nazi League, Youth Against Racism in Europe and the Indian Workers' Association.

The marchers carried a banner which read: "Unity demonstration. No more racist murders. Close down the BNP." As the throng attempted to push their way forward officers mounted baton charges into the crowd, who retaliated by throwing bricks and smoke bombs. The whole sorry affair ended with 19 police and 48 demonstrators being taken to hospital.

Most of the marchers moved on to a rally in Clan Field recreation ground and scuffles continued there until well into the evening. When the riot eventually broke up it looked as if a tornado had passed through.

October 20th: With Anti-Nazi League supporters chanting outside, Bexley Borough Council town planners spent two hours last night discussing how they could remove the controversial British National Party bookshop from Upper Wickham Lane but eventually decided to accept the status quo and carefully monitor the premises.

'Hangs one that gathers Samphire ...'

Samphire Hoe — the new and exciting part of Kent — made from the spoil excavated to create the Channel Tunnel is attracting hundreds of visitors to see the wild flowers and birds.

It was created when Eurotunnel dumped nearly two and a half million cubic metres of the Chalk Marl at the foot of the Shakespeare Cliff while the rest, another 2½ million, went to France.

The result was a new area of land consisting of 75 acres, made up of material equivalent in weight of 51,580 London double-decker buses. The Chalk Marl was then landscaped and sown with wildflowers and grasses.

The vegetation is already attracting plants from the surrounding countryside, including orchids, and wildlife is abundant. Butterflies, dragonflies, grasshoppers and birds are just some of the species enjoying the new land.

The area got its name last year following a competition organised by Eurotunnel and the *Dover Express*. Hundreds of entries were received from which the judges chose Samphire Hoe.

Rock samphire grows on the Hoe and for many years it was an important plant, collected by locals, cooked and eaten in the same way as asparagus. Today, of course, it is a protected plant.

Samphire is mentioned in Shakespeare's play, *King Lear.*

"...The crows and choughs that wing the midway air
Show scarce so gross as beetles, half way down
Hangs one that gathers samphire, dreadful trade."

Samphire Hoe, the new area of Kent below the massive Shakespeare Cliff.

1993

July: *The Open returned to the sand dunes at Sandwich Bay this month when the Royal St George's provided the venue for the world's major golf championship. The winner was the Australian Greg Norman, seen here with Bernhard Langer, who became only the second player after Bill Rogers in 1981 to complete the 72 holes under par — which proves what a severe test these famous links provide for the greatest golfers.*

Primary Club members are saddened by Johnners' death

January 5th, 1994: Radio and television personality, Brian Johnston, best known in recent years for his brilliant input to the BBC's Test Match Special team and his passion for cakes, has died at his home in London aged 82.

One of the many tributes to "Johnners" as he was known comes from the Primary Club, a charity which raises money for blind cricketers and particularly those who are pupils at Dorton House School for the Blind at Seal near Sevenoaks.

Hundreds of cricketers all over the world belong to the Primary Club. They qualify by their inability to survive the first ball — a personal disappointment but one which immediately entitles them to buy a club tie.

The Primary Club was the brainchild of Beckenham Cricket Club in 1955. At first only club members were allowed to join but as soon as recruitment was thrown open to the world, membership grew rapidly. Today cricketers from most counties, including almost every member of the Kent 1st X1, belong and many thousands of pounds are raised each year.

Brian Johnston was the Primary Club's senior honorary publicity officer, regularly urging his listeners to be proud of a first-ball dismissal and encouraging them to buy and wear the Primary Club tie.

'If the music school ever closed it will tear the heart out of Deal' — Mrs Thatcher commenting on the Royal Marines School of Music which the Government plans to close.

January 1st: Rebecca Stevens of Kemsing, the first woman to climb Mount Everest, has been awarded the MBE.

January 4th: Torrential rain, following one of the wettest Decembers ever known, has caused havoc in many parts of Kent.

February 5th: A single mortar bomb killed 68 people and wounded 200 in Sarajevo today. Bosnia has blamed Serbian guerillas for the attack. They now command the hills above the city.

The Queen visited Shorncliffe Barracks, Folkestone — the home of the Argyll and Sutherland Highlanders Regiment.

February 23rd: Seven bishops and more than 700 clergy have said they will become Roman Catholics following the decision by the Church of England to ordain women priests.

April 18th: The West Indies batsman Brian Lara today took his Test score against England to 375 passing, on the way, Sir Garfield Sobers' record score of 365.

April 22nd: The Red Cross estimate that more than 100,000 people have been killed in two weeks of tribal slaughter in Kigali, the capital of Rwanda.

May 1st: Ayrton Senna, Brazilian Formula One driver and winner of 41 Grand Prix, was killed today when he crashed into a concrete wall during the San Marino Grand Prix.

May 12th: John Smith, leader of the Labour Party, died today of a heart attack. He was 56.

June 6th: Thousands of veterans from Kent travelled to Normandy to celebrate the 50th anniversary of *Operation Overlord.*

June 15th: Railway signalmen, striking over pay and productivity, have brought chaos to the railways.

June 17th: American movie star

January 14th: The Duchess of Kent (seen here in Rochester in 1986 posing for a young photographer) is the first member of the royal family to become a Roman Catholic in modern times. In a private ceremony conducted by Cardinal Hume, Archbishop of Westminster, she was received into the church of Rome. Her husband, the Duke of Kent and their three children, who remain Anglicans, watched the service as the duchess solemnly declared her belief in the Catholic doctrine and was anointed with blessed oil. The Duchess is seen here with the Lord Lieutenant of Kent, Robin Leigh-Pemberton.

and former football hero, O.J. Simpson has been charged with the murder of his former wife, Nicole and her friend Ronnie Goldman.

June 30th: The Prince of Wales, in an ITV documentary, said yesterday that he has no plans to divorce but insists he would not regard divorce as an impediment to becoming King.

July 1st: AIDS cases worldwide has risen to four million according the World Health Organisation.

Yassir Arafat's 27 years of exile from Palestine ended today when he crossed the Egyptian border into the Gaza Strip.

August 31st: The IRA today announced a complete cessation of military operations leaving

the way open for a political settlement.

September 28th: It is feared that 912 people may have died when the roll-on roll-off ferry *Estonia* sank in heavy seas.

October 9th: A campaign is under way to keep the Royal Marines School open in Deal following a Government announcement that it will be sold for development. Mrs Thatcher, when she was Prime Minister, said that if the music school ever closed it would tear the heart out of Deal.

October 14th: Ffyona Campbell today completed her 19,586 mile walk round the world. It has taken her 11 years.

November 19th: Gambling fever today seized the nation with the draw for Britain's first National Lottery. Seven punters will share the prize of £15.8 million.

There were angry scenes at Sheerness Docks today when nine lorries containing 3,000 live sheep and calves arrived for the start of Ferrylink's new export service to Vlissengen.

November 26th: Plans for a £250 million redevelopment scheme has been approved for Port Ramsgate. Proposals include a new marine terminal, hotels, offices and leisure facilities.

December 9th: A plaque in memory of the former world motor cycle champion Bill Ivy was unveiled today in the Chequers Centre, Maidstone. Bill was a former pupil at Oldborough Manor School in Loose Road. He was killed when he crashed during practice for the German Grand Prix in 1961.

December 31st: The company which sailed super ferries from Sheerness to Holland has closed down. Olau Line once employed nearly 700 people.

GREAT HITS OF 1994

Love is All Around
Crazy For You

The huge new terminal at Cheriton near Folkestone

Channel Tunnel: 200 years from concept to reality

May 6th: They said it would never happen. But a 200-year-old dream became a reality at last today when Queen Elizabeth and President Mitterand cut red, white and blue ribbons to open the Channel Tunnel.

It took seven years to build and, in that time, the estimated cost rose from £4.9 billion to more than £9 billion.

The Queen took a train to the terminal at Folkestone and then travelled through the tunnel to Coquelles where President Mitterand was waiting. Having performed the historic ceremony they returned in a royal Rolls-Royce as it was brought to Folkestone on Le Shuttle.

Earlier in the day the Queen had opened the Eurostar terminal at Waterloo. The regular passenger service is due to begin in November when the first Eurostar leaves on its maiden three-hour journey to Paris.

Although ferry companies are saying that many Continental-bound passengers will still prefer the traditional method of travel they are nonetheless concerned about the likely impact on their business and feel that freight companies in particularly will desert the sea route. Airlines also believe their passengers may show a preference for the train, certainly until the novelty wears off — if it ever does. ***See page 164***

The Queen and President Mitterand in Coquelles prepare to cut the ribbon.

Canterbury's Roman city is revealed

Roman Canterbury is alive and well — and attracting massive interest among all those who have been watching builders prepare the footings for the city's new Longmarket shopping centre.

There, under the builders' feet, is part of the Roman town built soon after the invasion in 55 BC. For 400 years the legions marched through the city which was beautifully placed at the junction of the roads which led from London to the great ports of Rutupiae (Richborough), Dubris (Dover) and Lemanis (Lympne) and so to the heart of their Empire.

As the builders work, the hypocaust and tesselated pavement of the Roman town can be seen, attracting archaeologists from all over the country.

The artefacts found on the site with other important Roman finds are now on display in the Roman museum. Exhibits include a collection of silver spoons and two swords.

March: An uncertain future faces Gillingham — Kent's only professional football club. As debts continue to grow, chairman Tony Smith has said he can no longer put money into the ailing club. Gillingham and its famous ground at Priestfield has now been put up for sale with an asking price of around £250,000.

October 14th: Round-the-world walker Ffyona Campbell today reached John O'Groats after a trek that took her across four Continents and into the history books. She began the last stage at Folkestone in September, stopped for the night at Wye and then moved on to Biddenden and Sevenoaks before heading north.

Children examine the Roman artefacts.

Six killed as walkway at Port Ramsgate collapses

September 15th: It should have been a routine sailing to Ostend for the 29,000-ton *Prins Filip*, berthed at Port Ramsgate last night. But as the last batch of foot passengers were crossing the walkway towards the waiting ferry, the lights went out, the middle section gave way and scores of people slid 40 feet onto the concrete below.

Frefighters and paramedics were on the scene within minutes but they were too late. Five people had been killed and a sixth died on his way to hospital.

As the walkway collapsed all the passengers in front were thrown onto a floating pontoon on the quayside.

They were then hit by more people falling on top of them and trapped by the structure. Two Belgians and one Englishman were among the dead. The bodies of two men and a woman are still unidentified.

Eight casualties were taken to hospital in Canterbury suffering from multiple injuires.

The *Prins Filip* was eventually able to sail out of Ramsgate 12 hours later but the inevitable questions were being asked. Why should a purpose-built walkway — built only eight months ago — suddenly collapse?

There will be an inquiry.

An ambitious proposal by the Rank Leisure Group to turn 400 acres of the beautiful Lyminge Forest into a Centre Parcs style development has so incensed local people that a massive protest is gathering momentum. The Save Lyminge Forest Action Group has already collected thousands of signatures on a petition to be delivered to Downing Street. Shepway Council and the KCC approves of the holiday village plan which will create 1,000 new jobs for Shepway and bring a much-needed financial boost to the local economy. Supporters of the scheme also plan to lobby the Government; they fear Rank may prefer its second option which is a site near Boulogne.
The villagers (pictured above) are in a defiant mood.

The courage of Chloe Teacher

Five years ago a horrific riding accident left Chloe Teacher in a deep coma with terrible head injuries. Miraculously she survived the accident, climbed back in the saddle and this summer took over as the new High Sheriff of Kent.

Chloe, 49, lives at Hadlow Place, a 4,000-acre estate near Tonbridge, with husband James — a member of the whisky family — and their four children.

The accident occurred in the summer of 1988 while Chloe was hunting with the Quorn. She was taken to hospital in a deep coma and a neurosurgeon told her husband that her chances of survival were low.

Chloe was unconscious for almost a month but is now gradually making a full recovery.

After 14 centuries of male domination, a girl has been voted captain of Britain's oldest school. Miriam Lwanga, aged 17, a Ugandan, took up her appointment at The King's School, Canterbury, by saying: "It is both terrifying and exciting as a prospect."

A former Chatham dockyard worker, who blamed his work on nuclear submarines for causing his cancer, has been awarded compensation of more than £160,000 against the Government. Other dockyard cancer victims have been told that the MOD cannot accept liability.

A village community was in shock after a man was killed with a shotgun in his local pub, The Blue Anchor at Yalding. Police are still searching the countryside for the weapon that was used to kill 38-year-old Stanley Nicholls.

Darling Buds and those Doodlebugs

November: An unpublished manuscript, written by H.E. Bates — one of Kent's best-loved novelists — has been discovered in the Public Record Office. It is described as one of the most exciting literary discoveries of the decade.

The book, *Flying Bombs Over England* and now in the shops, tells the story of Germany's "secret weapons", the V1 and V2, which were designed to turn the tide of war. It was written by Bates shortly after the vengeance campaign ended but then considered too sensitive, embargoed for 30 years and locked away in the British Public Records Office at Kew.

Bates, best known for his story of the Larkins family in *The Darling Buds of May,* died in 1975 and the manuscript was forgotten.

It lay undiscovered until Kent author Bob Ogley stumbled across it and gained permission from the Crown to have it published.

Madge Bates, the author's widow, donated her royalties to the RAF Benevolent Fund and in three months has seen the fund benefit by more than £10,000.

Rod Hull and his wife with the key to Restoration House, Rochester.

Rod Hull and Emu leave their home: Miss Havisham remains

July: One of Rochester's best-known personalities, the comedian Rod Hull, has been declared bankrupt and forced to leave the home he loves so much.

Hull, aged 58, sprang to fame on the arm of his demented puppet Emu, who became a national institution. The bird "born" in Australia had an unpredictable temper. He once ate the Queen Mother's bouquet and famously wrestled chat show host Michael Parkinson to the ground.

Rod Hull, a brilliant ventriloquist, presented several of his own shows on BBC television. At the height of his celebrity, Emu was receiving more than 200 fan letters a week.

The comedian, who was born on the Isle of Sheppey and went to the County Technical College in Sheerness, made a fortune out of his irascible bird. He bought Restoration House, Rochester, the model for Miss Havisham's Satis House in *Great Expectations* and spent more than £500,000 restoring it. He even preserved the "Havisham Room" created there as the set for David Lean's film in 1946.

Sadly, this expensive exercise has come at a time when his financial affairs have been badly mismanaged. It means bankruptcy for Rod Hull and a smaller home for him and his second wife Cheryl Hilton in Winchelsea, Sussex.

Why Faversham brews the "best ale in the world"

Shepherd Neame's new Spitfire premium bitter has won the gold medal for the world's best strong ale. Employees of the Faversham Brewery also learned this week that the company's Grants Morella cherry brandy is the best liquor in the world.

And to crown a fine year The Chequers, Doddington, owned by Shepherd Neame, has been chosen by CAMRA as the south-east pub of the year.

The Faversham Brewery is almost certainly the oldest in England, founded in the last quarter of the 17th century by Richard Marsh. Ownership in turn passed to the Shepherds and then to the Neames who have continued to manage the family business through five generations.

The awards, given respectively by the brewing industry and the international wine and spirit convention, is confirmation of Faversham's outstanding tradition of quality.

■ A former Kent army captain who bigamously married his second wife in Croatia to save her from a Bosnian war lord, has been given an absolute discharge by Medway magistrates.

Brian Blandford met Jasyenka Perisin soon after flying to Bosnia with the United Nations. She had been raped and left pregnant.

Dodging an attempt on their lives and hiding in a safe house in the mountains the soldier from Chatham and Jasyenka took the baby back to Croatia. He then decided to marry her to give Jasyenka a new identity.

The news reached England and Blandford was reported to the police by the woman he had been married to for 25 years. He is now back in Croatia.

Big cats on the prowl in east Kent

September: Following a number of sightings an animal welfare worker from Studdal, near Deal, believes there are at least three big cats roaming in the wild in east Kent.

Dave Riches who runs a wildlife centre is more and more convinced of their existence and says they may have been living in the area for several generations. In June he saw a big cat in the Ashley area of Dover, gave chase but lost the animal.

Mr Riches is not alone in his sightings of puma or panther-like creatures in the area. According to the book *Kent Unexplained* sightings of mysterious big cats prowling woods, gardens and streets have escalated enormously in the county over the past six years.

In July 1991 staff at a home for the elderly in Southfleet reported several sightings of a black panther in their garden. In the same year another big cat was seen in a garden at Allington and in May 1992 Maureen Tulloch saw a puma in the woods near her home in Paddock Wood.

Further sightings came in January 1993 in Wigmore and, earlier this year, in Snodland and East Malling.

For the third time in 14 years a zookeeper has been killed by a tiger at Howletts. Trevor Smith, aged 21, was seen entering the enclosure and stroking Balkash, a two-year-old Siberian tiger. The tiger rose on his hind legs and put his front paws on the keeper's shoulders pushing him to the ground. He then picked up Mr Smith by his neck and carried him in its mouth to a shed in the compound. Another keeper managed to shut the tigers away but Mr Smith was dead. The latest tragedy has renewed the debate over where the line should be drawn between the need to protect the keepers and the desire to provide captive animals with as comfortable environment as possible. John Aspinall, the owner of Howletts, said his philosophy rests on the belief that zoo animals should be treated as 'honoured guests'.

See page 158

Carriages were balanced precariously above a 300-foot embankment.

Trains collide in the fog on a single line: five die

October 15th: A signalman stood helplessly at his controls today as two trains collided in thick fog at Cowden, near Edenbridge, killing five people and injuring 11.

The signalman knew that the two trains were on a single line but he didn't know the numbers on the drivers' onward mobile 'phones and even if he had, they were switched off to save battery power.

Rescuers, who were quickly on the scene, found part of the wreckage precariously balanced on top of a 300-foot embankment. They risked their own lives in attempting to reach trapped passengers but eventually had to wait for the carriages to be stabilised. Only then were the emergency services able to reach the passengers and retrieve the bodies.

British Rail said that the thick fog had made it difficult for the drivers to see trackside signals and the northbound train had gone through a red light. A union official said an advanced warning system should have triggered alarms in the cabs but there was no automatic system in place. There will be an inquiry.

More lorry refugees are smuggled into Kent

December 17th: Hundreds of lorry refugees seeking political asylum in Britain have been illegally smuggled into Kent causing logistical problems for police, social services and immigration officials.

In March, seven children were among a group of 31 suspected illegal immigrants found huddled in a container lorry at Dover. It was the largest group of illegal immigrants found at any British port.

This week immigration offices at Dover, acting on a tip-off, dismantled a van load of beer and found far more than Christmas cheer. Sticking out from a hollow in the load were four sets of feet belonging to Turkish immigrants.

Police are now double-checking all vans bringing beer from the continent.

The total of illegals found in the last three months has risen to 223. Many have been discovered in the backs of lorries some miles from the ports.

Most, if not all, are expected to claim political asylum in Britain which means their cases for settlement must be heard, a procedure that could take years. ***See page 184.***

Bootleg liquor trade is out of control

December 31st: It's not only the flood of illegal immigrants that are worrying customs officers and police. Since the European barriers came down thousands of pounds worth of duty-free bootleg liquor is coming into the county almost every day.

Customs officials have chalked up some successes. Two weeks before Christmas an undercover operation discovered that a group based in Dover had smuggled so much alcohol into Kent that it cost the Government more than £2 million in lost tax.

Almost 100 officers spent 10 months watching the gang, waiting for the right moment to pounce. The bootleggers rented properties in East Kent and travelled to Calais daily in hired vans. There they bought large quantities of beer and wine at a cash and carry company, returned to Dover and took a van to Deal. From here the alcohol was taken by lorry to warehouses in North London.

Most of them have now been arrested and are awaiting trial.

Shepherd Neame of Faversham, which is among the brewers campaigning for a halt to the bootlegging trade, welcomed the news of the seizure, but said there would almost certainly be another gang to take its place.

Meanwhile customs officials are smarting over the news that 4,000 customs jobs are to be axed. They say the Government must either apply the law of the land to stop the trade or accept that it can longer do so.

See page 174

The girl who shoots for gold

When Dionne Rogers was 14 she accompanied her father to a shooting competition at the Kent County Showground in Detling, entered the Lady's Clay Class for fun and came home with the trophy.

This year 24-year-old Dionne, who lives near Ticehurst on the Kent and Sussex border, has two more trophies in her cabinet — the Ladies World Championship Cup which she won last year in Madrid and the 1994 European gold medal.

In the intervening ten years this remarkable girl, who shoots clays with 12-bore in several disciplines, has made sporting history by winning gold medals in most European cities, including 16 national titles in three years and the overall British championship in 1988 — and the first woman ever to beat the men!

Under the watchful eye of Patrick Lynch, the national coach, she practices at Old Hay shooting school, Paddock Wood, and is sponsored by a management company from Tunbridge Wells.

■ In a remarkable pioneering operation that lasted more than seven hours, surgeons in America have removed a life-threatening tumour from the head of a four-year-old Northfleet boy.

Doctors in Britain said they could do no more for Ashley Fowle but if his family could raise the money there was a hospital in America which might help.

Ashley's mother appealed to viewers on Meridian TV and within three days had collected £70,000, enough to give the boy a chance of life.

■ **April 1st:** In 1969 Robin Knox-Johnston from Downe, near Bromley, became the first man to sail solo round the world in his famous Bermudan ketch.

Today the master marina arrived home to another tumultous welcome after his British and New Zealand crew had smashed the round-the-world record aboard their catamaran ENZA New Zealand.

January 1st: Frederick West was found hanging today in his cell at Winson Green prison. He was awaiting trial, accused of the murder of 12 young women.

January 9th: Comedian Peter Cook, famous for his partnership with Dudley Moore in *Beyond The Fringe,* died today aged 57.

Martin Caldwell, a convicted rapist with a 20-year record of sex attacks who was released early from jail, was found guilty today of trying to kill a woman he kidnapped in Dover.

January 27th: Eric Cantona of Manchester United was fined £20,000 today for attacking a fan who insulted him.

January 28th: A bridal shop in Faversham closed down suddenly today leaving at least 20 would-be brides with little hope of getting the wedding dress they had paid for.

Six minibuses and four double-deckers have been destroyed in a fire at the Maidstone and District bus depot in Chatham.

February 1st: Kent County Council today cut its education budget back by £11 million. That has meant redundancy notices for 170 teachers and 50 administration staff.

February 8th: David Watkins of Leeds, near Maidstone, has been found guilty of running Britain's biggest-ever drugs factory. Primrose Cottage near Wrotham had been raided by the regional crime squad after a 10-month surveillance operation.

February 22nd: John Major and John Bruton, Prime Ministers of Britain and Ireland, today released a document for the future of Northern Ireland.

Following nine years of indecision and delay MPs with constituencies along the proposed Channel Tunnel railway link promised they would fight to win compensation for the people whose lives have been blighted.

Former Tonbridge schoolgirl Kelly Holmes returned to her home in Sevenoaks with two medals from the World Athletic championships. In the 1,500 metres in Gothenburg, the army recruiting sergeant won a silver. In the final of the 800 metres she came away with a bronze.

March 1st: The governor of Swaleside Prison on the Isle of Sheppey has been forced to scrap his plans for a £40,000 six-hole golf course in the grounds of the jail. The prison service said the project was totally unacceptable.

March 18th: England today beat Scotland 24-12 to win the Five Nations rugby championship.

Personalities from the world of sport and showbusiness announced today they are forming a corsortium in a bid to rescue the ailing Gillingham football club whose debts amount to £1million.

April 1st: Two toddlers, Emily Birkett from Gillingham and Ryan McCook from Rainham, have died from an unidentified strain of meningitis.

April 16th: There was more trouble for Eurostar today when a train with 250 passengers got tangled up in overhead power lines. The passengers had to endure a four-hour wait in the tunnel before continuing their journey.

April 29th: Clause Four of the Labour Party's constitution which commits the party to state ownership has been scrapped by Tony Blair after a long battle.

May 11th: Lord Nolan, who lives at Brasted near Sevenoaks, today presented his report on the standards of public life aimed at cleaning up "sleaze" at Westminster.

May 24th: Harold Wilson, 79, the Labour Party's four-times general election winner, died today.

An entrance fee of £2 is being charged for Canterbury Cathedral in an attempt to raise the £7,000 per day needed to run the building.

May 31st: Bosnian Serbs today seized more than 350 UN peacekeepers and military observers as the crisis in the Balkans escalated. President Clinton has offered Nato the "temporary use" of ground troops.

July 15th: Despite a sparkling and defiant innings of 96 by overseas player Aravinda de Silva Kent were beaten by Lancashire in the final of the Benson and Hedges Cup at Lords.

Public support for Howletts Zoo is gaining momentum following Canterbury City Council's decision to ban keepers from tiger enclosures. 52,000 have signed a petition and 12,000 have written letters calling for the ban to be lifted.

September 17th: Kent cricketers today went on a jubilant lap of honour at the St Lawrence Ground, Canterbury, in celebration of the Sunday League title and the £35,000 prize. The previous day they were confirmed as bottom club of the County Championship, a position they last held 100 years ago.

September 20th: 245 passengers were trapped on board Stena Sealink's channel ferry *Challenger* today after she ran aground on the beach near Calais.

GREAT HITS OF 1995
Unchained Melody
Wonderwall
Some Might Say

Thanet MP campaigns against "bent and twisted journalism"

April 25th: Jonathan Aitken, MP for South Thanet, is to take legal advice following "damaging" newspaper and television claims concerning dubious links with the Saudi royal family.

Just hours before a *World in Action* special Mr Aitken called a press conference at Tory headquarters and said he was launching a crusade against certain sections of the media.

He said: "If it falls to me to start a fight to cut out the cancer of bent and twisted journalism in our country with the simple sword of truth and the trusty shield of British fair play, so be it."

Mr Aitken is a former journalist himself and grandson of Baron Beaverbrook, founder of the *Daily Express*. He has the full support of Prime Minister John Major.

He said at the conference: "The time is rapidly approaching when good, honest and talented men and women will begin to wonder whether they should dedicate their lives to public service."

See page 170

Live animals for export: the anger grows

'Get back behind the barrier sir. I don't care if you are Alan Clark, the former Government minister!'

April: More than 200 animal rights protestors have been making a determined, almost fanatical attempt to stop lorries from entering Dover Harbour with live animals for slaughter.

For a long time it looked as if the trade in the export of live animals would be abolished in the face of so much opposition but this week the High Court ruled that Dover Harbour Board is not legally permitted to deny the trucks access to the port.

For the seasoned campaigners this has been almost too much to bear and they plan to continue to lobby, petition and campaign despite what they call "intimidation" from the police escorts and some drivers.

Several weeks ago a lorry carrying more than 400 sheep overturned on the London-bound carriageway of the A2. 184 sheep were crushed or suffocated and the RSPCA had to destroy many others. A mini saloon was crushed between the lorry and the crash barrier and four people were hurt.

Protestors said the carnage would not have happened if the animals has been carried as carcasses rather than live.

Traffic lights melted in the inferno heat

January 21st: Maidstone has suffered more than its fair share of big fires over the years — but the blaze which lit up the town centre two nights ago was arguably the greatest ever known.

In fact the heat was so intense that traffic lights and phone boxes melted, telephone cables were destroyed and scores of people had to be evacuated.

The fire began in a second floor workshop at the back of Clark's furniture store in King Street and spread so rapidly there was a danger of the whole town going up. At its height 200 firefighters attempted to bring the blaze under control.

Arson is not suspected but Bill Dinley of Kent Fire Brigade said they were going to demolish the building, make it safe and carry out a thorough search.

Troubled Tories are wiped off the map

May 5th: Kent has been a Tory stronghold for most of the century. But yesterday, in the local council elections, Labour and the Liberal Democrats rampaged through the Conservative heartland to create sensational front page news in almost every region. In fact not a single chink of blue survives; the Tories have been wiped off the local government map.

Before the elections they comfortably controlled nine of the local councils. Yesterday, they lost the lot.

It was the Labour Party who boasted the largest number of gains inducing one successful candiate after another to declare "the tide is turning. The party will form a national government within two years".

Alongside substantial Labour gains the Liberal Democrats took control of six. There were also plenty of hung councils in areas unused to anything but a Tory landslide. In the "true blue" town of affluent Sevenoaks, for example, the Conservatives lost 14 seats while the Lib-Dems took nine and Labour an amazing ten.

Amid the celebrations there was bitter disappointment. Many defeated councillors felt the elections had been hijacked by the growing dissatisfaction with the government and no consideration had been given to purely local issues and to the many years of dedicated service that some members had given.

The final figures tell the full unbelievable story. Across the entire region the Conservatives lost a total of 259 seats and failed to gain one. Labour won 209 and didn't lose one. The Liberal Democrats gained 73.

The swing to Labour has been decisive and the attention now is firmly fixed on the general election due in the next two years.

Seacats or dogs — they are both very welcome

March 31st: The port of Folkestone, struggling in competition with the Channel Tunnel and ambitious Dover, today welcomed the relaunch, by Hoverspeed, of the Seacat service.

The catamaran, vital to the economy of both Folkestone and Boulogne, was withdrawn from service last year despite having transported a million passengers and 40,000 cars across the Channel in 12 months.

The crossing time is just 55 minutes.

April 1st: Kent police today appealed to the public for new recruits. They must be good-natured, intelligent and have four strong legs. German Shepherds, they said, are particularly welcome. They would enjoy a career in the force.

Meet the Sparrow twins from Goudhurst who have equalled the world record for the lightest babies ever born. They arrived prematurely on February 8th, 1994 and weighed in at just over a pound, measuring eight inches each. Here are Sarah Louise and Anne Marie on their first birthday — an occasion which marked a triumph for medical science.

April 6th: Five years ago Paul and Linda McCartney led a protest to save the cottage hospital near their home at Rye. The hospital closed but the McCartneys and their team refused to give in and raised the £5.3 million required to build another one. Here they are at today's topping-out ceremony. In the background is the memorial to the spirit and determination of the people of Rye.

Big Brother has great success in Gravesend

May: What have the towns of Sandwich, Dartford, Tonbridge, West Malling, Ashford, Dover, Deal, Folkestone, Maidstone and Rochester got in common?

Answer: they are all recipients of a government grant totalling £1 million enabling them to establish closed-circuit television cameras in their town centres.

District and borough councillors have high hopes that the unsleeping eye of Big Brother will cut down the growing number of public order offences, including street robbery, vehicle crime, drug dealing and vandalism.

Gravesend was the first town in southern England to try CCTV. The fall in crime figures was so dramatic that they immediately tripled the number of cameras and recommended that others follow their example.

But not everyone welcomes the innovation. Worried members of the public say the cameras are an intrusion on personal liberty and should be avoided at all costs.

The police don't agree. They say a strict code will operate on who would see the screens. A spokesman said: "By making town centres safer we are convinced people would gain more freedom than they would lose."

Police step up hunt for dangerous bomber

May: People living in the Canterbury area have been warned to beware of a dangerous bomber, who seems to have an aversion to telephone boxes.

Following a third attack at Adisham station this month police have stepped up their hunt for the villain. They are linking it to an explosion at the station in February and to a blast beside the A2 at Nackington in November.

In each case the devices were triggered by command lines.

The first two explosions destroyed telephone boxes. The third was designed to explode beneath a car parked on the approach to the station. The device was placed under the petrol tank and a detonation command line ran 80 yards to a point where it was triggered by the bomber.

In the event only the detonator fired but it was enough to alert the family who lived in the converted railway building.

Kent relives the day it savoured freedom

May 8th: The people of Kent are recovering from a day-long bout of unashamed nostalgia. Yesterday, in honour of the 50th anniversary of VE Day, there were street parties, thanksgiving services, parades and fetes in almost every town, village and hamlet.

Community spirit came alive in the former "front line county" as thousands remembered the Allied victory over Hitler's armies.

For those who had lost loved ones or served in the forces or just survived six years of hardship it was an emotional trip down memory lane. For others it was a good excuse for a party.

Nowhere were the celebrations greater than in Dover, the most-bombed town in England and one that was nearer to the enemy than to its own county town.

The commemorations also brought together many people who hadn't met since the war. Among them was the class of 1940 from a boarding school who were evacuated to Devon at the start of the war. The former pupils met again, journeyed to Devon and relived their memories of the evacuation.

Norman Wisdom throws himself wholeheartedly into the spirit of VE Day — plus 50 years.

Lisa Leeson, wife of disgraced Baring's trader Nick Leeson, has appealed for her husband to be allowed to return to England for trial.

The 28-year-old financial dealer bankrupted his bank by gambling in millions of pounds on the high return high-risk derivatives market in Singapore.

He and his wife, who works at the Elizabeth Tea Rooms in Maidstone and lives in West Kingsdown, had flown to Frankfurt where he was arrested. He was apparently making his way to London, preferring to face a British court rather than stand trial in Singapore.

The results of his gambling have been disastrous for Barings which is one of Britain's oldest and most respected investment houses. It appears likely that it will be taken over — along with debts of £650 million — by the Dutch ING group for just £1.

Many believe that the Barings directors should share the blame for allowing a young man, who lives in a council house, to gamble on such a massive scale.

John Aspinall at play with the animals he loves.

Council bans keepers from tiger enclosures

June 15th: John Aspinall, the former casino owner and now proprietor of Howletts and Port Lympne, has said he will close both zoos unless Canterbury City Council's safety officials withdraw an order banning keepers from tiger enclosures.

The order had been imposed following the death of Trevor Smith last year and a list of previous incidents involving keepers.

Mr Aspinall said that banning animal contact robbed the zoo of its identity. "Part of the ethos of the place", he said, "is to go in and bridge the man-made divide between ourselves and the higher mammals."

The keepers themselves are also backing their boss. "We do this because we want to", said one. "If we were concerned about being injured we'd be sitting in an office."

Mr Smith died of head injuries when a young male Siberian tiger picked him up by his neck. In 1980, keepers Brian Stocks and Bob Wilson were both mauled to death by a tigress named Zeya in separate incidents at Howletts. Later Zeya was shot.

Last year Mrs Louise Aspinall, Mr Aspinall's daughter-in-law, needed 15 stitches after being bitten by a tiger cub. Five years ago, Matthew McDaid, aged two, had his arm ripped off by a chimpanzee at Port Lympne wildlife park. In April the same animal bit off the finger and thumb of Ms Angelique Todd, 25, a student working at the park.

In 1984, Mr Mark Aitken, a 22-year-old keeper was killed when an Indian elephant crushed him against railings.

A telephone poll among Meridian television viewers sympathises with Mr Aspinall. Out of 6,000 people who responded, 90 per cent said they thought keepers should be allowed to go in with the tigers.

This is the moment that Gillingham Football Club went one up against Premier Division Club Chelsea to the delight of more than 10,000 ecstatic fans who thought they would never see another football match at Priestfield Stadium. Threatened with bankruptcy , relegation from the Football League and almost certain disbandment, Kent's only professional football club was saved by businessman Paul Scally. With a few shrewd managerial moves, support from some of the biggest names in the game, a little luck and a fighting fund that caught the imagination of the football world, the Gills survived to play a pre-match friendly against Chelsea who had just signed European Footballer of the Year, Ruud Gullit. The Dutchman certainly brought the fans through the turnstiles and, after Chelsea went behind, displayed some of his magic. Final score: Gillingham 1 Chelsea 3. The future: Rosy.

Flat Oak Tribe versus Thanet Way

August: Most people, especially drivers, believe the Thanet Way bypass is a desperate necessity. Many believe otherwise. They say it is environmentally wrong to carve another four-lane highway through the beautiful Kent countryside and have held protest meetings, lobbied councillors and organised petitions to prove their point.

It's all in vain. Work has already started but a handful of protestors still hope to draw people's attention to the "unnecessary" road building in England and perhaps persuade the Government to abandon the project.

Fifty members of the Flat Oak Tribe — named after the ancient oak tree on the edge of Convict Wood which is the focal point for demontrations — are camped nearby. One member, Vicky Fawcett from Whitstable, chained herself to a drainpipe attached to the roof of a house which was being demolished. She has now been removed — still attached to the drainpipe.

Campaigners remember victims of Hiroshima

August 14th: In a symbolic tribute to bomb victims all over the world, anti-nuclear protestors gathered at Sun Pier, Chatham and threw flowers into the water. They were marking the 50th anniversary of the Hiroshima atom bomb and remembering the thousands of people who lost their lives in the disaster.

The event was organised by the Medway branch of the CND, aimed to raise awareness of the global threat posed by nuclear weapons.

1995

Hosepipe bans and road rage! What a summer

September: Once again Kent is paying the price for the weather. With August already confirmed as the hottest month on record and the summer as a whole expected to be the driest, hosepipes bans are in effect across the county. Lifeboat crews and firefighters have recorded their busiest season ever — and a new phenomena has hit the headlines — road rage.

According to the media this epidemic has swept through the county. It's principally caused by a mixture of ultra-hot weather and political and economic frustration.

So concerned is one minister that he has devised a set of guidelines for the heated motorist. "Don't use horns or headlights unless absolutely necessary", says the Rev Howard Daubney of Rochester. "Refrain from braking in front of cars which are following too closely. If you are singled out by a road rage road hog, remain in the car and lock your doors and windows."

Meanwhile hosepipe bans are causing more consternation. Public anger has been fuelled by the fact that Southern Water is losing almost 20 million gallons every day through leaking pipework. "Engineers are working around the clock to repair leaks", said a spokesman. "Underground, it's like looking for a needle in a haystack."

All water companies in the region have restrictions and they are asking people to grass on their neighbours if they are breaking the ban rather than take the law into their own hands.

One Kent gardener who was spotted using a hosepipe later found it cut into inch-long pieces!

September: A killer whale twice stranded on mudflats near Sandwich has had to be destroyed despite courageous and desperate attempts to save her by a team from the British Divers Marine Life Rescue based at Gillingham.

Queen of the Channel — 27 times

September 4th: **A 31-year-old foreign exchange dealer who works in the City, today swam the Channel in 10 hours 58 minutes to earn a place in the record books for the greatest number of Channel swims by a woman. It was her 27th!**

Alison Streeter, who lives near Lingfield with her family, has a flat in Dover for the swimming season. She already has many records — the first person to swim around the Isle of Wight, the first person to swim from Scotland to Ireland and the only person ever to swim the Channel seven times in one season.

She started swimming when she was young because she had asthma. She said: "The more swimming I did the further I could go and the further I swam the slower all the others got."

Alison now hopes to break the all-time record of 31 Channel swims held by Michael Read.

January 19th: Ian and Kevin Maxwell, sons of the late Robert Maxwell, have been cleared of fraud charges at the Old Bailey.

February 10th: Princess Diana agreed today to Prince Charles's request for a divorce. They had been strongly urged to divorce by the Queen.

The IRA ceasefire which had lasted for 17 months came to an end today when a bomb exploded near South Quays railway station on the Isle of Dogs. Two have died.

February 16th: Medway Police are among the first in the country to be issued with CS spray cannisters for use against violent people and those who resist arrest. All of the 187 patrol officers will start carrying the hairspray-size cans in two weeks as part of a national trial.

March 13th: Former scout leader Thomas Hamilton today shot dead 16 children and a teacher in the worst mass murder in British history. The incident brought horror and grief to the Scottish town of Dunblane. Hamilton eventually turned the gun on himself.

March 17th: Sri Lanka beat Australia by seven wickets today to win cricket's World Cup.

March 22nd: Twelve European countries have banned British beef as unsafe for human consumption because of a possible link between BSE in cattle and a new strain of CJD in humans.

April 11th: Princess Alexandra's daughter Marina has separated from her husband, photographer Paul Mowatt after six years of marriage. The couple have two children.

April 19th: Dover today welcomed the first ship to its £9 million cruise line terminal at the Western Docks. The *Black Prince* of Fred Olsen lines docked with 400 passengers.

A series of bunkers across Kent,

August 8th: There was a hero's welcome for Sevenoaks yachtsman Ian Walker today as he returned home to Kent displaying the Olympic silver medal he won in the men's 470 class in Savannah. Walker, 26 and John Merricks of Hamble clinched silver by just one point in the 11th and final race of the gruelling series which took place in nightmare conditions. The former Sevenoaks School pupil, whose sailing career began at Chipstead Sailing Club, said he was not sure about Sydney 2000. "We finished second in the world championships and now second in the Olympics so we have some unfinished business to do!"

which would have been used if the Cold War had escalated into full-blown nuclear conflict, were linked to a heavily reinforced Command Post at Hawkenbury, near the Government's Land Registry Office. The ending of the Cold War has signalled the demise of the virginia creeper covered building. Few knew of its existence.

April 22nd: Eurotunnel announced a loss of £925 million for its first year of operation.

May 2nd: Chelsea manager Glenn Hoddle has taken over from Terry Venables as manager of England's national soccer team.

June: In the final of the European Football Championship played this month, Germany beat the Czech Republic in extra time.

July 19th: The Centennial Olympic Games opened in Atlanta, Georgia today when Mohammed Ali, suffering from

the ravages of Parkinson's Disease, lit the Olympic flame.

Kent's Steve Backley came second in the javelin event with a throw of 87.44 metres. The gold medal was won by Jan Zelezny.

September 13th: Police officially named the chief suspect in the M25 road rage killing of Stephen Cameron on May 19th. He is currently a fugitive in Spain.

October 3rd: Two ship companies, P and O and Stena have merged their cross-Channel operations to compete with the Shuttle train link through the Channel Tunnel.

October 13th: Six weeks ago Damon Hill was told this was to be his last season with Williams Renault Formula One team. Today he came sixth in the Japan Grand Prix to win the Formula One world championship and emulate his late father.

November 11th: Murderer Mark Aryan has been sentenced to four life sentences for cutting the throats of his ex-wife and three of their children. A jury at Maidstone heard how Aryan flew into a rage when his divorce came through and in the space of a few minutes murdered Gillian and their eight-year-old daughter Shameem and inflicted terrible injuries on their two sons aged two and five at their home in Montgomery Road, High Brooms.

December 4th: Eurotunnel today resumed its passenger service two weeks after the Channel Tunnel fire.

December 5th: Toni Paynter, 18, a young mother, was shot dead in front of her children in the Brook multi-storey car park next to Chatham's Pentagon Centre today. The man, Barry Robinson, 21, then turned the gun on himself.

GREAT HITS OF 1996

Spaceman

Wannabe

1996

Down by the seaside. Water rose to eight feet in parts of Black Bull Road, Folkestone.

Folkestone flooded after 'biblical' storm

August 13th: The people of Folkestone know all about floods. On several occasions during the century the harmless little brook known as The Pent has burst its ancient confines and transformed itself into a wild, destructive, fast-flowing river.

The floods that hit the town yesterday were every bit as dramatic — "more of biblical proportions", said one observer. They followed one of the heaviest rainstorms ever known.

In two hours, four inches (100mm) of rain fell — more than double the usual amount for the whole of August — and caused a deluge that was too much for the drains to handle. Water built up to a pressure that damaged many buildings and left others on the point of collapse.

In central Folkestone levels reached eight feet completely covering front doors. Scores of people moved upstairs where they were rescued by dinghies at first-floor level.

Emergency calls came into fire brigade headquarters every 25 seconds and firemen took amphibious vehicles with them on rescue missions.

In the harbour, quick-thinking fishermen smashed down a wall in order to direct rising flood water into the sea. It helped but still The Pent continued to rise.

As Lord Warden of the Cinque Ports the Queen Mother has sent a message of sympathy to the families whose homes have been damaged and Michael Howard, MP for Shepway, has set an appeal fund rolling with an undisclosed donation.

The mopping up will continue this morning and it will take many weeks. Some irate residents have accused Shepway council and Southern Water of incompetence, blaming beach nourishment work at Sandgate for blocking storm drain outfalls.

A spokesperson said: "Drains burst because of the extreme intensity of the water and the Pent stream broke its banks. Rain and foul water sewers could not cope."

Lawrence family in quest for justice

April: The case against the white youths accused of killing a black teenager outside a bus stop in Well Hall Road, Eltham has collapsed. Neil Acock, Luke Knight and Gary Dobson have been found not guilty by an Old Bailey jury after identification evidence was ruled invalid by the judge. Two other youths, Jamie Acourt and David Norris, had already been cleared by magistrates.

The parents of Stephen Lawrence, whose son was the victim of a racially-motivated killing, were seeking justice in a private murder prosecution following a decision by the Crown Prosecution service to discontinue an earlier case because of insufficient evidence.

The Lawrences have thousands of supporters who believe investigating officers from the Metropolitan Police Force dragged their feet because Stephen was black. They refuse to accept an inquiry report by Kent police officers, on behalf of the Police Complaints Authority, that "the Met officers' behaviour was insensitive but showed no sign of racism".

Arrangements can now go ahead for Stephen's inquest early next year. His parents, however, refuse to lie down. They say the Metropolitan officers obtained no forensic evidence to convict the suspects, they delayed arrests and there were signs of corruption and collusion. Their campaign will continue. ***See page 184***

No more racist killings. Another demonstration by banner carrying Lawrence supporters.

Prolific Lord Ted's 21 million words

April 2nd: With his most recent play *Intent to Kill* set to open in Bromley today, Lord Ted Willis of Chislehurst has earned himself an entry in the Guinness Book of Records as the "most prolific scriptwriter".

Son of a bus driver, Ted Willis was born in London and his first play *Buster* was presented in the capital in 1944 starring Alfie Bass. Since then he has 33 stage plays, 31 feature films, 32 TV series, 13 novels and 21 TV dramas to his credit totalling a mind-boggling 21 million words.

One of the principal founders of the Writer's Guild of Great Britain Lord Willis has earned many accolades including a British Film Academy Award. He lives in Chislehurst with his wife Audrey.

1996

Lorry drivers thought they were going to die

Stephen and his fiancee Danielle, 17. They were engaged at Christmas.

Police seek 'road rage' killer

May 21st: A 21-year-old motorist was left dying by the M25 and M20 interchange near Swanley on Sunday after being stabbed by a "road rage" driver.

At a press conference today the devastated family of Stephen Cameron made an emotional plea for help. They said he had been waiting for the traffic lights to change and somehow became embroiled in a stand-up row with the driver of a Land Rover Discovery. Next to Stephen in the car was his fiancee, Danielle Cable.

The two men fought by the roadside before Stephen was knifed twice in the chest. His killer drove off towards the Dartford Tunnel.

Det Supt John Grace said just before the incident the Land Rover overtook three cars and pulled in front of Stephen before the traffic lights. "As far as we know all Stephen did was to shake his head and say 'that's not very clever'. We are looking for a man in his late 30s to early 50s who was wearing jeans and, possibly, a black bomber jacket."

See page 180

Garage boss riddle a contract killing?

November: According to the Sunday Times Scotland Yard has established a new undercover nationwide police unit which will investigate a mercenary hit squad believed to be responsible for about 20 murders.

Among them is the gangland-style killing of millionaire garage owner Nick Whiting who disappeared in June 1990 on the same night that five high performance cars were stolen from the garage at Wrotham Heath.

His handcuffed body was found dumped on marshes almost a month later. The case was never solved.

All kinds of theories for his disappearance were suggested but Scotland Yard, according to the Sunday Times, now know his was a contract killing by a squad believed to be responsible for many others.

Kent police say there is no evidence to link Nick Whiting with the London underground world.

November 19th: The Channel Tunnel, designed to be safer than any other crossing, yesterday suffered the one disaster that everyone hoped would never happen — a fire.

No lives were lost but it was a very serious event which will prevent any trains using the tunnel for up to two days and will close one of the main tunnels for several weeks.

The fire began near the back of the 700m-long 8.45 train on a freight shuttle from Calais to Folkestone. It is believed that a lorry carrying polystyrene caught fire. Altogether 15 lorries were destroyed.

Safety procedures worked well. All 34 passengers and crew were evacuated within 70 minutes but they suffered from the effects of smoke inhalation. In fact several drivers described how they choked in the smoke and thought they were going to die.

The tunnel is badly damaged. The fire brought down lumps of concrete from the ceiling, destroyed a portion of the line buckling the rails and ruined trackside equipment and wagons.

The financial damage is more serious. Eurotunnel president Patrick Ponsolle said insurers will pay for most of the physical damage but the loss in public confidence could take longer to restore.

It will undermine the current negotiations by Eurotunnel to reschedule the project's debt of £8.7m. The stock market reacted predictably marking down Eurotunnel while P&O shares have prospered.

The Channel Tunnel transports some 1,500 lorries a day with 28 wagons to each freight shuttle. The drivers travel, not with their lorries, but in a separate amenity carriage.

French take over our historic rail network

August 23rd: One hundred years ago the London, Chatham and Dover and the South Eastern Company were locked in bitter rivalry as they competed furiously to attract passengers to the key railway routes in Kent.

What would the Victorian directors of those go-ahead, truly English companies think of the situation on our railways today? A French firm has won the franchise to operate trains in the South East!

The news that Connex Ltd would be taking over has been warmly welcomed by Kent's MPs.

"It's extremely good news", said Sir John Stanley, MP for Tonbridge and Malling. "The group has pledged to replace the entire south-eastern slam-door fleet with new trains, coupled with the best deal on fares that we have ever achieved."

Connex must cap all fares in line with inflation for the first three years of the 15-year agreement. Air conditioned rolling stock will be introduced within three years as part of a 25 million investment programme which also includes improvements to stations, passenger security, new ticketing systems and car parking facilities.

Chairman Colin Webster said: "We believe we can turn this undertaking into a model franchise for Britain."

Steam returns to the Eridge railway line

December: The Tunbridge Wells to Eridge railway line, which closed in 1985 despite furious opposition from a well-organised action group, will soon be open again. After years of dedicated work that action group — now a preservation society — has acquired the line and steam-hauled locos will be running as far as Groombridge.

The Tunbridge Wells to Eridge railway was once part of an extensive network of lines in Kent and East Sussex.

Tunbridge Wells originally had two stations. The first, at Mount Pleasant, was built by the SER in 1846. It serves trains to London and Hastings.

Tunbridge Wells West was built by a rival company, the London, Brighton and South Coast in 1866. Later it was expanded to include a stretch from Eridge to Eastbourne — known as the Cuckoo line.

Rail travellers wishing to use the Channel Tunnel have two choices. They can go to the Eurostar Terminal at Waterloo, alongside Britain's largest domestic station or they can use the International Station at Ashford — the new gateway to Europe.

The station (see above) has been built on the site of the existing Ashford station by extending two central platforms to serve Eurostar trains. Here, full passport control and border entry facilities have been introduced.

This massive project was completed by the Laing Civil Engineering team in August well ahead of schedule. Here "Le Shuttle" — the high speed passenger trains — are provided solely by Eurostar.

Each train is a quarter of a mile long and carries up to 794 passengers. That's the same as two fully loaded Boeing 747 jumbo jets. Power cars at each end are electrically driven and provide up to 16500hp to propel the 18 passenger coaches. The Ashford to Paris run takes two hours and Brussels is 15 minutes longer.

Major surgery for women after missed smear tests

Pathologists at the Kent and Canterbury Hospital have admitted that 91,000 cervical screening tests will have to be re-read because of faulty diagnosis.

The screening errors came to light because three women developed cancer after abnormalities were missed in a routine NHS screening. The hospital discovered deficiencies in the cytology department. The misreporting of the tests, which were carried out between 1990 and 1995, means that early and complete protection from cancer for a number of other women has also been lost.

The discovery of the country's worst screening scandal means that the three women will have to undergo major surgery. They have already suffered from a loss of fertility and "a small but nevertheless statistical reduction in their expectation of life".

As a result of this negligence scores of other women are seeking compensation for post traumatic stress and an independent review has been called for by the Government.

Businesswoman of the year — that's Nicola

Nicola Foulston, the young girl who took over the running of Brands Hatch when she was just 20, has achieved what many said was the impossible. In seven years she has turned the loss-making venture into one with a multi-million pound turnover.

Last year Nicola sold the circuit to a consortium of venture capitalists, APAX Partners and to her great surprise they kept her on as chief executive. In October this year Brands Hatch, now owner of all its freeholds, was successfuly floated and quickly emerged as one of the strongest companies for its size in the leisure sector.

This week came more good news. Nicola has been named as the *Times/Veuve Clicquot* Businesswoman of the Year.

Nicola was 20 when her father was tragically killed testing one of his cars at Silverstone. She begged her mother to be allowed to run Brands Hatch, having left London University without a degree.

There were many low points during the first few years but gradually Nicola turned the company around. She said: "I have never forgotten Margaret Thatcher saying that running the country was no different in essence from running a household. It was all about balancing the books."

She more than balanced the books. This year's turnover is expected to be in excess of £12 million.

See page 184

Nicola with former Formula One world champion, Nigel Mansell.

January 3rd: Snow at last in Kent. After nine snowless Januaries, during which snow lovers had begun to despair, ten centimetres of the fluffy white stuff fell in towns and villages to the east of Maidstone today.

January 9th: British yachtsman Tony Bullimore was rescued from the freezing waters of the Southern Ocean by an Australian frigate today, five days after his boat capsized. The Queen has commended his extraordinary feat of survival.

January 31st: The 50th anniversary of the memorable winter of 1947 has been marked with the driest January since 1976. Kent is once again obsessed with "lack of water" stories and even John Gummer, Environment Secretary, has said the Garden of England will be fit for growing only maize and sunflowers in the next 50 years.

February: Cable Television is coming to most parts of Kent. Among the latest towns to receive the fibre optic network is Folkestone town centre where workmen laying the cable plan to proceed to Hythe then New Romney. Cable TV will give viewers up to 50 extra channels.

February 21st: Three men, who were jailed 18 years ago for the murder of newspaper boy Carl Bridgewater near Stourbridge, have been freed by the Court of Appeal.

February 24th: A research team at the Roslin Institute, Edinburgh has produced the first clone of an adult animal — a sheep named Dolly.

March: Frank Muir has published his autobiography in which he recalls a happy 1920s childhood in Ramsgate. The book is called *A Kentish Lad*.

A giant new £700 million shopping centre near Greenhithe will cause immense damage to nearby towns, it has been claimed. Bluewater is due for completion in two years time.

Kent has invited wicket-keeper Steve Marsh to take the helm and help revive the county's fortunes. The new captain, who takes over from Mark Benson, made his debut in 1982 and won a regular place soon after the retirement of Alan Knott. It was an onerous task because his great rival for the gloves, Stuart Waterman, was a better batsman. Under the watchful eye of Bob Woolmer at Cape Town Marsh improved and was soon scoring important runs. He missed much of the 1987 season through injury but returned to score two centuries in 1988 and play a regular role in Kent's resurgence.

March 20th: Furious protesters have lost their High Court appeal against the decision to build the Oasis holiday village in Lyminge Forest. They accused Shepway Council of using underhand tactics.

April: A new unitary council for the Medway Towns comes into effect this month. This means that, without the Medway members, Kent County Council reverts to Conservative control.

April 6th: The Grand National was abandoned today after an IRA bomb scare.

May 2nd: Labour will have its first government since 1939. At 43, Tony Blair is the youngest Prime Minister in 185 years.

June 19th: William Hague, 36, has defeated Ken Clarke by 92 votes to 70 to become the new leader of the Conservative Party.

June 20th: The builders, managers and designers who are creating the millennium dome in Greenwich have been given several demands by Prime Minister Tony Blair. One of them concerns the exhibition centre which must be a permanent structure.

June has been one of the wettest of the century with average rainfall in Kent measuring 133.7 millimetres. Last June 30 mm fell.

Sir Colin Cowdrey, the former Kent and England cricketer, has received a life peerage in the Queen's Birthday Honours.

October: At the age of 84 the Daily Telegraph columnist Bill Deedes who lives near Ashford has written his memoirs of 66 years in journalism.

The Kent Archeological Rescue Unit has discovered an unknown Roman town on farmland about two miles south of Ashford. The unit has removed about 3,000 objects, mostly pottery, from the settlement which covers at least 25 acres.

November 17th: Six British tourists were among 58 killed today in a terrorist attack at Luxor's Temple in the Valley of the Kings, one of Egypt's most popular tourist sites.

November 20th: The Queen today celebrated her gold wedding with a "people's banquet" hosted by Tony Blair.

December 11th: The Royal Yacht *Britannia* was decommissioned today after 44 years' service to its country.

December 19th: William Hague, the Tory leader, today married Ffion Llwellyn Jenkins in the Crypt Chapel of the Palace of Westminster.

December 31st: 1997 was the hottest year on record according to the World Meteorological Organisation. They have put the blame on El Nino rather than global warming.

GREAT HITS OF 1997

Never Ever

Perfect Day

1997

May 9th: With the last of the general election votes now in, Kent's traditional Tory heartland has been dramatically transformed. Seven of the county's 17 Conservative MPs have lost their seats. A swathe of red now covers eight constituencies.

Casualties include former Government ministers James Couchman, Jonathan Aitken and Bob Dunn. Also gone are Roger Moate, Kent's longest-serving MP, David Shaw and Dame Peggy Fenner.

Anne Widdecombe (Maidstone), Andrew Rowe (Faversham and Mid Kent), Sir John Stanley (Tonbridge

Labour rips through Tory heartland

and Malling), Roger Gale (Thanet North), Julian Brazier (Canterbury) and Michael Howard (Shepway), the former Home Secretary, have survived with reduced majorities.

Three new Tories who defied the great swing to the left are Archie Norman of Tunbridge Wells who stood down as chief executive of Asda to enter politics, Damien Green of Ashford, a former BBC and ITN journalist and Michael Fallon of Sevenoaks, a former education minister and Government whip.

The new Labour members are Paul Clark (Gillingham), Bob Marshall Andrews (Medway) who turned a Tory majority of 8,700 into a Labour one of more than 5,000, Jonathan Shaw (Chatham and Aylesford), Derek Wyatt (Sittingbourne and Sheppey), Chris Pond (Gravesham) who achieved a massive 10 per cent swing, Gwyn Prosser (Dover), Howard Stoate (Dartford) and Steve Ladyman (Thanet South) who easily beat the former Treasury minister Jonathan Aitken.

Michael Howard dangerous, says Miss Widdecombe

The Theatre Royal, Chatham (pictured here in its halycon days) was designed for the famous Barnard theatrical family and opened in 1899 as Kent's showpiece theatre. It once attracted audiences in excess of 3,000 people. Then, in 1955, the theatre went dark, into decay and for 45 years lived with the constant threat of demolition. The Theatre Royal has now been purchased by a charitable trust with the aim of restoring it to its former glory as Kent's largest Victorian theatre. The cost is £8 million but Michael Holden, who headed the team to restore the Globe in Southwark, is ready to create a theatre to continue the traditions of Charlie Chaplin, Max Miller and George Formby who appeared so regularly.

May 16th: Michael Howard's bid to become leader of the Conservative Party has taken a great knock following an astonishing attack from his Tory colleague Ann Widdecombe, MP for Maidstone and the former prisons minister.

According to the *Sunday Times* Miss Widdecombe has damned Mr Howard as "dangerous stuff" and has said "there is something of the night" in his personality.

The member for Shepway is ignoring the remarks. He said: "My campaign for the leadership is going well and I am confident of my chances. I will remain a conscientious MP for Shepway. This is my home."

Miss Widdecombe, who claims she has been the victim of a smear campaign, wants to make a personal statement in the House of Commons but this has been denied. Her future prospects within the Conservative Party are in doubt but she vows nothing will deflect her from her denunciation of Mr Howard whom she says is disturbing and unpleasant.

The political row centres on Mr Howard's sacking of the prisons chief Derek Lewis, whom Miss Widdecombe has always supported.

Avon lady killed neighbour in struggle

February 6th: David Stutchberry, a cleaner at the Eurotunnel terminal at Folkestone, was killed yesterday in a struggle with 36-year-old Wendy Hertz at her home in Densole. He was believed to be carrying a knife when he knocked at the door. There was a fight in the hallway and he died from a single stab wound. Mrs Hertz — the village Avon lady and wife of a bank manager — is being treated in hospital for knife injuries.

It is clear that Stutchberry, aged 49, normally a mild mannered man and known in his community as a model husband and father, had launched a savage sex attack on his victim and she courageously fought him off.

He had failed to turn up at his early morning Tuesday shift where he drove road sweepers and emptied dustbins. He was seen hanging around the village before he knocked at the door of another woman's house. Refused admission he then called at the home of Mrs Hertz.

Police say there was no relationship between her and Stutchberry and she merely knew him as the husband of Linda Stutchberry, headmistress at Temple Ewell Primary School, Dover and father of a 14-year-old daughter.

Detectives are still waiting to talk to Mrs Hertz about the attack but they are assuming it was self-defence. Technically, however, she could be charged with manslaughter and a report may be submitted to the Crown Prosecution Service. Forensic scientists have visited the home which is still under police guard.

Shocked families in Densole have been helping to piece together the events that preceded the fatal struggle. *See page 176*

May 16th: Jon Lindbergh, whose famous father Charles was the first aviator to fly solo across the Atlantic, visited Kent today to see the house where his mother and father settled during the traumatic years which followed the historic flight.

When Jon's eldest brother was kidnapped, held to ransom, then murdered in 1932, his grieving parents flew to England and rented, from Harold and Vita Nicolson, their rambling home at Long Barn, Sevenoaks Weald. Jon, who made many friends in the village and loved the surrounding countryside returned with his wife, Karen, for the first time in almost 60 years. He even travelled to Sissinghurst where he met Nigel Nicolson to explain why his father supported appeasement 59 years ago.

Eco-warriors dig in at Lyminge

April 17th: Eco-warriors — veterans of the Newbury bypass and M11 protests — are digging in at the site in Lyminge Forest which is earmarked for Rank's 400-acre Oasis holiday village.

Elaborate tree houses are being constructed high above the forest floor, tunnelling is underway and pits are being dug so the protestors can "lock on" when the time comes for police to try and drag them away.

The campaigners say their aim is to prevent environmental damage to a beautiful woodland area. They claim to have supporters in nearby villages who have pledged food and drink.

Despite a ferocious campaign by those villagers opposed to Rank's plans, the scheme was approved by Shepway District Council and work is imminent. "Building at West Wood", say the hardliners, "will act as a catalyst and change the nature of the whole area." The Forestry Commission is seeking an eviction order to remove the illegal occupants.

When Reggie wed Roberta

July 15th: The illuminated message of romance shone brightly in Maidstone on Sunday evening "Married in the morning", it read, "Reggie and Roberta."

And true to the laser lightshow promise gangland killer Reggie Kray married 38-year-old Roberta Jones in a quiet ceremony in the prison chapel.

Kray, who is in the 29th year of a 30-year sentence for the murder of Jack "The Hat" McVitie, met Miss Jones, an English literature graduate a year ago when she visited the prison.

The couple fell in love, got engaged and Roberta moved into a flat in the Boxley Road to be nearer to her fiancee.

The bride was certainly impressed by the illuminated show which showed wedding bells projected onto the prison wall in a rainbow arc of light.

Kray is expected to move to an open prison in Norfolk soon. A friend said: "Roberta does not condone what Reggie did in the past but he has served his time and now wants to be with the woman he loves."

Cheerful Charlie may 'stand easy'

June 26th: Cheerful Charlie Chester, the veteran entertainer who has lived with his wife Joan at Chestfield near Whitstable for more than 20 years, has died in a nursing home aged 83.

Charlie, pictured after receiving the MBE, has been associated with BBC radio since 1937 when he made his first broadcast. He became a star of his own programme, Stand Easy, *on the old Home Service and went on to present* Housewives' Choice *and latterly* Sunday Soapbox *on Radio 2 which began in 1969.*

Controller of Radio 2 James Muir said today: "The world of entertainment has lost one of its more enduring and popular stars. After 60 years in the front line of broadcasting, cheerful Charlie may now stand easy."

Charlie, a former King Rat, was a familiar figure in Whitstable where he was known as a generous man who did a lot for charity.

Aitken's libel defeat will cost £2million

June 21st: Following new evidence by the defence counsel, Jonathan Aitken, the former Cabinet minister, has abandoned his libel action against the *Guardian* newspaper and Granada Television. He faces legal costs of £2 million.

Documents show that the former Tory MP for Thanet South had lied on oath over the details of a weekend spent at the Ritz Hotel in Paris.

Aitken had sued the newspaper following its claims that he was financially dependent on the Saudi Arabian royal family, had procured prostitutes for Arab businessmen and was involved in illegal arms deals.

The former MP, who lost his seat last month, said that a *World In Action* documentary also "butchered his personal, political and professional reputation".

Aitken and his wife of 18 years, Lolicia, have now separated. "Recent events have shattered me and broken our family", she said.

The libel action was adjourned on Thursday shortly before Mrs Aitken and her twin daughters were due to give evidence. ***See page 190***

Tony Blair will return Bernie's £1m gift

November: Bernie Ecclestone is well known at Brands Hatch, Silverstone and other international racing circuits throughout the world. He is also well-known at Biggin Hill following his purchase of a significant part of the former RAF fighter station.

Otherwise, few people know of the 67-year-old businessman who has always kept an ultra-low profile.

All that has been completely shattered by the news that the boss of Formula One donated £1 million to the Labour Party shortly before the June election. And that most generous gift was surprisingly followed by a decision to exempt F1 from a ban on tobacco advertising in sport.

Ecclestone and his Croatian wife Slavica have been persistently pursued by the media who claim that Labour are as bad as the Conservatives when it comes to accepting gifts for favours. But such has been the furore that Tony Blair has said he'll return the cash.

Bernie Ecclestone will refuse to take it back. He says no favours were involved; it was a gift for a party on course to form a Government.

Perhaps he doesn't really need the money. Since 1989 Ecclestone has taken £142m in salaries and dividends from his various companies. He also intends to float F1 which will produce an estimated £750m in cash for trusts controlled by members of his family.

Visit the Roman house

May 12th: The Roman Painted House, discovered in 1970 during a massive programme of excavation across ancient Dover by the Kent Archaeological Rescue Unit, is now open to the public. Described as "Britain's Pompeii" the house formed part of a great mansion or hotel for travellers built about AD200. It stood outside the naval fort of the Classis Britannica.

Tom Baker — lots of literary festivals

Tom Baker and the girls with double-barrel names

October 7th: *Who on earth is Tom Baker?* That may be the title of his new book but most people in England and certainly all those who live in the village of Lenham know this charismatic three-times married actor who is best known as the ultimate *Dr Who.*

Tom, who has lived in the Wealden village for several years and is a great devotee of the local pub, is still reeling from the shock news that Harper Collins liked his manuscript, printed 80,000 copies and booked him on a 50-city publicity tour.

Delighted that he's going to be a "famous author", he told *The Independent* this week: "I'm getting letters from girls with double-barrelled names — which has always been good for my libido — asking me to come and talk at literary festivals. I went through a phase where I could only shag girls with double-barrelled names — twice the pleasure I thought."

Tom Baker has been married to his third wife Sue Jerrard for almost 10 years. In the church near to his home in Lenham is a gravestone, "engraved", he says, "for the moment of my great escape."

See page 180

Diana in Kent

May 1983: Canterbury (where she opened flats for the elderly and lifts for the disabled).

December 1985: Ashford (the William Harvey Hospital as patron of the National Rubella Council).

September 1989: Deal (to open a new charity shop at the Deal Centre for the Retired).

March 1990: Tunbridge Wells (visit to Barnados Ravensdale Day Care Centre).

October 1990: Chartham (visit to St Augustine's Psychiatric Hospital as patron of the charity Turning Point).

October 1990: Tenterden (to open the town's new leisure centre. On that day Diana also visited the perfume manufacturer Quest International at Ashford).

April 1992: Sevenoaks (the marriage guidance charity, West Kent Relate).

October 1992: Tunbridge Wells (to open The Royal Victoria Place shopping centre).

October 1992: Ashford (to open the Paula Carr Diabetes Centre).

October 1992: Aylesford (the official opening of the Heart of Kent Hospice at Preston Hall).

June 1993: Canterbury (Howe Barracks to inspect the Princess of Wales Royal Regiment).

May 1995: Canterbury (to present new colours to her Regiment).

August 1993: Buckmore Park, Chatham (where Prince Harry met Johnny Herbert).

The tragic death of

September 5th: Kent, like the rest of the nation and most of the world, is a county in mourning this week following the tragic death of Diana, Princess of Wales in a car accident in Paris. Her boyfriend, Dodi Fayed, who lives in Oxted, also died at the crash scene in a tunnel near the River Seine.

The Princess's strong links with the county go back to the days when she was a schoolgirl at West Heath, Sevenoaks in the late 1970s. Former headmistress Ruth Rudge described her as a "lovely, lovely girl and very helpful". Her piano teacher said she was "quite naughty with a lovely sense of humour and a quick wit".

Throughout Kent flags are flying at half-mast and books of condolences are filling up as people prepare for Saturday's funeral at Westminster Abbey. Hundreds of thousands of mourners have crammed into London-bound trains clutching a wreath of flowers to place around the gates of Diana's home at Kensington Palace. There, a forest of tributes spreads ever outwards. All week the Palace has been the focus of a torrent of emotion.

In almost every community throughout Kent people have their own special memories of Princess Diana and the charm and radiance which she brought to every visit.

Prominent though are the memories of those teachers and former schoolfriends at West Heath who recall her love of sport and dancing and her work with the town's Voluntary Service Unit. When her engagement to Prince Charles was announced in February 1981 the school was thrust firmly into the limelight.

Princess Diana made several visits to West Heath — official and unofficial. One was to open the new sports hall and another was as a surprise guest when headmistress Ruth Rudge retired in 1987. Today, West Heath school itself is closed, a controversial decision, made only a few months ago.

The Princess was also closely connected with Canterbury — as Colonel-in-Chief of the Princess of Wales Royal Regiment, formed in 1992 by the amalgamation of the Queen's and the Royal Hampshire Regiments. On several occasions she inspected the troops at Howe Barracks and showed deep affection for the regiment by always asking with disarming informality: 'How are my boys?'

About 350 men, women and children of the Princess of Wales Regiment held a memorial service this week conducted by the padre the Rev Jonathan Ball who said: "In her death we have lost not only a Colonel-in-Chief but a listener, a mother, an encourager, an ally and a supporter."

The people of Cranbrook remember how Diana turned up at Dunstan's Church in April 1989 where her cousin Edward Berry was marrying Joanna Leschalles, youngest daughter of the former High Sheriff Kent, Anthony Leschalles.

Hundreds of people thronged Cranbrook's streets as the Princess appeared in an eye-catching red and white sailor suit and three cornered hat. Her sons William and Harry were page boys.

Many businesses across Kent will close on Saturday as the nation pauses as a mark of respect to the Princess they loved so much. Sports and leisure centres will close early, sports fixtures will be postponed and flower shows cancelled. English Heritage properties in the county will shut all day and churches will hold special services.

Among them will be Canterbury Cathedral and Rochester Cathedral. In a tribute the Archbishop of Canterbury, Dr George Carey, has said: "Diana was a vibrant and beautiful woman but also a very vulnerable human being. Out of that vulnerability came lots of strength, her passion and her commitment to people." There will be a special service at St Mary's Kippington, Sevenoaks — the church where Diana was confirmed.

Many are also remembering Dodi Fayed who lived near his father's mansion in Oxted. His half-sister Jasmine has been a pupil at Sevenoaks School since 1992 and just completed her GCSEs. Headmaster Tommy Cookson has sent a message of condolence. *See page 180*

Diana — Princess of Wales

Diana inspects the Princess of Wales Regiment at Canterbury. At the parade ground the band played: Hey, Look Me Over.

Booze-cruise smugglers have closed 50 Kent pubs

December: For some years now Faversham's long-established brewing company, Shepherd Neame, has been campigning vigorously against "booze-cruise" imports from Calais supermarkets which are flooding the county. With the duty rate 1/7th of the UK supermarket price for the same product they argue that the competition is unfair — particularly with legitimate UK businesses that have paid UK duty.

Chancellor Gordon Brown's penny-a-pint tax rise was almost the last straw. Shepherd Neame — forced to close 50 Kent pubs because of the continuous hammering from the "Calais-runners" — challenged the Government's increase in the High Court claiming that the excise duty was a breach of European law and a "threat to British beer".

This week came the news that Shepherd Neame has lost its legal battle — but not its will to fight. As an appeal is prepared, Customs and Excise said they had lost a massive £120m in revenue to the smuggling industry.

October 24th: Michael Stone, an unemployed man of Skinner Street, Gillingham, has been charged with the murders of Lin Russell and her daughter Megan who were bludgeoned to death as they walked along a quiet bridleway at Chillenden, near Canterbury on July 6th last year.

He is also charged with the attempted murder of Lin's older daughter 10-year-old Josie Rusell who lay clinging to life for more than eight hours until she was found by a passer-by.

The horrific murder and the bravery of Josie has been a dominant feature of the Kent news for more than a year.

Mrs Russell, 45, had picked up her daughters from Goodnestone primary school and they were on their way back to their cottage at Nonington when they were attacked.

Doctors at a London hospital told Dr Shaun Russell, a university lecturer, to fear the worst — if Josie did survive she was likely to have lasting brain damage. But Josie made an astonishing recovery. Within a month she appeared in public at Howlett's Zoo, Canterbury. She went back to school last October and in December she received a Children of Courage Award.

Sixteen months on she is still unable to speak but her infectious smile has won the hearts of millions of people who have closely followed her courageous battle.

Much of Josie's recovery is due to the patience of her teacher, Lynda Roberts from Goodnestone, who has been named this year's Teacher of The Year.

The courage of Josie, the girl who was left for dead

Dr Shaun Russell and Josie after the funeral of Lin and Megan Russell.

'The countryside is being eroded by urban people. Like the Government they show a lack of respect' — retired hop grower during the great countryside protest.

January 2nd: Frank Muir, one of the best-loved figures in broadcasting, died today aged 77. Muir, from Ramsgate, wrote many comedy series for TV and radio often in partnership with Denis Norden.

January 21st: An investigation has been launched into whether Bill Clinton had an affair with a White House internee and then asked her to lie about it under oath.

February 6th: A judge has halted the trial of two people accused of causing the death of an 11-year-old girl. Michelle Shields suffocated when the car she was in was crushed by a lorry at the Dartford crossing toll booths in 1996.

March 5th: Thirty National Front and anti-fascist protesters were arrested today after a series of scuffles with police at Marine Parade, Dover. They were protesting at the influx of Czech and Slovakian asylum seekers.

March 11th: Roger Tompkins, chief of an engineering company from Tonbridge, told the BSE inquiry today how his "stunning" 24-year-old daughter Clare was dying from the human form of mad cow disease. The inquiry is investigating the origins of BSE and its connections with a new variant of CJD which has killed 23 people.

March 21st: Dover, Folkestone and Ramsgate are among the top entry routes in the country for "class A" drug traffickers. There has been a marked decrease though in seizures of LSD, ecstasy tablets, cannabis 'skunk' and amphetamines.

March 23rd: Controversial reggae star Judge Dread collapsed and died on stage at the Penny Theatre, Canterbury yesterday. Dread, real name Alex Hughes, lived in Snodland and hit the headlines in the 1970s with a series of raunchy reggae tracks.

March 24th: *Titanic,* the most expensive movie ever made, dominated today's Oscar ceremony taking 11 Academy awards.

September 5th: When radio and TV personality Gloria Hunniford was looking for a home near London, she settled on a leafy road in Sevenoaks so she could be near her son Michael at Sevenoaks School. Gloria, then divorced from her husband, soon became involved in local affairs and was always a familiar figure in the town. Today Gloria, 58, was married to Stephen Way, well-known celebrity hair stylist at St Peter and St Paul Church, Hever. Among the many guests were Terry Wogan, Sir Cliff Richard and Anthea Turner.

April 4th: Health chiefs confirmed this week that there are three suspected cases of Creutzfeld-Jacob Disease (CJD) in south-east Kent. These latest cases follow the death of a 29-year-old woman in the Kent and Canterbury Hospital in February.

April 10th: Political parties have finally agreed to a peace settlement for Northern Ireland. Unionist and Nationalist parties have come together for the first time after 30 years of bloodshed.

May 15th: With success in the play-off matches, Charlton Athletic has won promotion to the Football League Premiership.

May 28th: As Emperor Akihito began his state visit to England today, former prisoners of war staged a protest against the failure of the Japanese Government to apologise for its behaviour towards British PoWs during the war.

June 9th: The Rolling Stones have cancelled four British concerts in

order to become tax exiles and avoid facing a £12 million tax bill for the proceeds of their recent world tour. Mick Jagger and Keith Richards were once at school in Dartford.

August 6th: Bill Clinton's presidency entered its most perilous stage today when Monica Lewinsky testified before a Grand Jury about her alleged relationship with the President.

August 11th: A car bomb in Omagh today killed 28 people.

August 15th: Forty environmental protestors are occupying 12 acres of Crystal Palace Park to object to Bromley Borough Council's proposed development of a £58 million leisure complex.

August 18th: Beowulf, the Anglo-Saxon dragon slayer, performed his most heroic deeds in the muddy wetlands off the north Kent coast, according to a new archaeological study. It is believed that the charred remains of a 60 foot longboat discovered at Faversham may have been the funeral pyre for the nobleman.

September 21st: The House of Representatives today voted to broadcast Bill Clinton's video-taped grand jury testimony about his affair with Monica Lewinsky.

December 12th: More than 100 Romanians, including children and babies, were intercepted at Dartford today after arriving there fromn Zeebrugge. It is the biggest single arrival of illegal immigrants smuggled into Britain.

December 15th: Zandra Rhodes, the fashion designer who lives at Kemsing, near Sevenoaks, has made a fairy to adorn the Queen's Christmas Tree at Buckingham Palace. Like its creator, the fairy has pink hair.

GREAT HITS OF 1998

Stop

Angels

Densole's Avon lady will not be charged

January: Wendy Hertz, the Avon Lady who stabbed to death a man who sexually assaulted her, will not be charged with manslaughter, the Crown Prosecution Service has decided.

David Stutchberry, a 49-year-old road sweeper who lived 200 yards from the Hertz home in the village of Densole had a history of psychiatric problems and had been convicted 29 years earlier of attacking a woman in South London. She had been battered about the head but survived.

Stutchberry's wife Linda, a primary school headmistress, knew nothing of his violent background

Police are now looking at the possible link between the attack on Mrs Hertz and the murder of two women in Bedgebury Forest in 1979 and 1982.

Family lifts the veil over famous ashes

April 14th: Cricket's hotly contested prize for The Ashes has a history which goes back to 1883 when the England captain, the Hon Ivo Bligh, returned from Australia with an urn, supposedly containing the ashes of a burned bail from the deciding Test.

Bligh, later Lord Darnley, placed the urn on his mantlepiece at Cobham House where it remained until his death in 1927. It was then bequeathed to the MCC and kept at Lords.

This week Rosemary, Dowager Countess of Darnley said the ashes are not those of a bail but a veil — and it was all the result of a simple mishearing.

She said her mother-in-law, as a young lady, was called Florence Murphy. She and her friends burned the veil, put the contents in the little urn and presented it to Ivo Bligh whom she later married.

David Frith, author of *England versus Australia* says the story makes a lot of sense. "A veil would be much easier to burn than a cricket bail. Until Lords open the urn we shall never know."

Peter Sissons, whose brush with death was 30 years ago.

Forsyth, Sissons and an ambush in Biafra

December 11th: Frederick Forsyth, the thriller writer who was brought up in Ashford, described this week how he saved the life of the BBC's long-serving Nine O'Clock News presenter, Peter Sissons.

Thirty years ago they were reporting the Biafran War, Sissons as an ITN reporter and Forsyth as a freelance journalist.

The two men walked into an ambush and Sissons, badly wounded, was just about to be finished off when Forsyth managed to nudge the gunman's rifle skywards.

Peter Sissons, astonished by Forsyth's recollections, still believes he owes his life to ITN's cameraman Cyril Paige who took off his shirt and made a tourniquet while bullets were still flying. He then lifted Sissons onto a plank of wood and bribed a Nigerian to take him to hospital 60 miles away.

Today, Sissons, 56, and Paige, 77, both live in Sevenoaks and meet most weeks in the town's market. They rarely discuss the episode in Biafra in October 1968.

Boom town Ashford — Kent's link with Europe

The boom town of the future that everyone predicted for Ashford seems to be coming true. The international railway station and its links with Europe, the creation of the 80-acre Eureka Science Park beside the motorway, the £6 million southern orbital road, has now been accompanied by an enormous influx of companies to the area. The petitions, the protests and the anger of the 80s seem to have been forgotten.

(Above) Donald Downs, countryman par excellence, practises his fly fishing skills in the Serpentine on the day the country came to town. (Right) Part of the Weald contingent gather at Staplehurst station on their way to the march.

Kent countryfolk march on London

March 1st: Three special trains, each pulling 18 coaches and crammed with country people from almost every village and hamlet in Kent, pulled into the London commuter stations today at the start of a countryside protest that was quite bewildering.

Farmers from Buckland, Burmarsh and Brook, smallholders from Sturry, Snodland and Staplehurst, kennel owners from Whitfield, Woodchurch and Wouldham joined conservationists, huntsmen and gamekeepers and all those supporting field sports. They travelled also by car, bike, horse and cart — and hundreds walked.

From the Embankment this column of protesters marched to Trafalgar Square where speaker after speaker made clear their feelings about the threat to their sport and, more important, their way of living. All the speakers emphasised that if things don't change they will be back — in even biggers numbers.

For many the protest began on Thursday evening with a chain of bonfire beacons across the county which could be seen for miles.

Farmer Tim Phillips of Guston said: "The march was an amazing sight. There were thousands and thousands of people from every corner of the country. On my farm we can't produce enough to make a living so I have do so something else for six months of the year."

One of the biggest contigents came from the Weald. Kitted out on wax jackets, flat caps and walking boots they took their concerns about country life to the city. Rupert Hodges, a retired hop grower from Goudhurst, said: "The countryside is being eroded by urban people. Like the Government they are showing a lack of respect and understanding of the countryside."

Staplehurst farmer Roger Munn, chairman of the local branch of the NFU said: "We want the Government to listen to what we say and not make policies without fully understanding the issues."

Sandy Bruce-Lockhart, leader of Kent County Council and a fruit farmer at Headcorn for 30 years, said farming is under threat from Government and European policy — all our farmers want is a level playing field on which to compete. "Government funding", he said, "favours urban areas."

1998

Mother's body found under garden patio

January: When a pretty young mother mysteriously vanished after taking her two children to school in Sevenoaks in January 1995 there were various theories about what may have happened.

Her car was found abandoned in Lakeside Shopping Centre. But had she run away, committed suicide or been kidnapped? Investigating detectives spent hundreds of hours and interviewed scores of people in attempting to unravel the mystery.

They now know the answer. Diana Goldsmith, the estranged wife of a successful Westerham businessman, Derek Goldsmith, had been murdered. Police, responding to a strong tip-off, found her body under the patio of a house in Bromley.

Detectives, thwarted by cover-ups, mysterious deaths and unbelievable bad luck have already charged a man with conspiracy to murder Mrs Goldsmith but another man, Ian Colligan, who they arrested and charged with being involved in the kidnap plot, has committed suicide in prison, a key witness has been killed and Mrs Goldsmith's boyfriend — Sevenoaks councillor Charlie Hatt — has died of cancer a few days after giving evidence to a special court set up by his hospital bed.

It appears that Diana Goldsmith was kidnapped after taking her children to school. She was bundled into the back of her own car and killed sometime afterwards. Her body, bound with plastic ties and rope, was found earlier this year and she was still wearing the clothes in which she had last been seen. A post mortem has been unable to determine the cause of death.

See page 186

April 9th: Foreign Secretary Robin Cook, who completed an acrimonious divorce from his wife of 28 years last month, was due to marry Gaynor Regan at Chevening House — his official home near Sevenoaks - next week.
Fearing a media circus because of the publicity surrounding his "affair" with Miss Regan, Mr Cook brought his wedding forward by 10 days and staged it today at the register office in Tunbridge Wells. The traditional civil marriage ceremony was conducted by the superintendent registrar Wendy Young and the witnesses included Jim Devine, Mr Cook's constituency agent. When they emerged from the ceremony the couple were delighted to find no waiting cameras. Mr Cook was seen to punch the air and exclaim: "YES!"

Sergeant's sadness

February 10th: Sergeant Trevor Walker of Gillingham, who lost a leg while on United Nations peace-keeping duties in Bosnia, has lost his claim for compensation against the Ministry of Defence.

Mr Justice Lathan ruled that, although the Serbian tank attack which caused Sgt Walker's injuries was a crime of violence, it also amounted to "military activity" and fell within the exception of the compensation policy.

Air Ambulance crashes on the hillside

July 26th: A pilot and two paramedics were killed last night when the popular and busy Kent Air Ambulance helicopter hit 11,000-volt overhead power cables and crashed into woodland near Bluebell Hill.

The three men had responded to an emergency call following a road accident. They were returning to base after being told they were not needed when the tragedy happened.

The French-made twin engine Aerospace Squirrel came down half a mile from the M2 outside the village of Burham, near Rochester — about a mile from its base at Rochester Airport.

The men who died were pilot Graham Budden, 40, paramedic Mark Darby, 37, and paramedic Tony Richardson, 47, who was only on that shift because he had swapped with a friend.

Their deaths and the loss of the helicopter has left a question mark over the future of the air ambulance service which relies on the public to fund its running costs of almost £500,000.

In the nine years since the helicopter first took to the skies it has flown on thousands of life-saving missions. The service, however, does not come cheap. Chief Executive Kate Chivers and her team need to raise £37,000 every month and have struggled for years against seemingly impossible odds to raise the money.

In a joint statement the Kent Air Ambulance Trust and the Kent Ambulance NHS Trust said: "This has come as a great shock to us all. We have lost three exceptional men in tragic circumstances. At this time our thoughts are very much with their families."

Investigators sift through the wreckage at Burham.

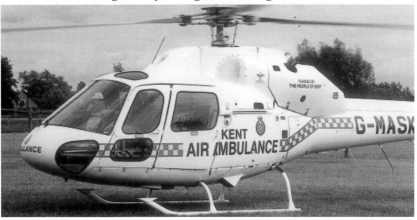

Kent's first air ambulance — funded by the people of Kent.

A new helicopter — the service goes on

September: In tribute to the three men who died in July's tragedy, the Kent Air Ambulance Service has had another helicopter delivered with the letters KGMT painted on the front — K for Kent, G for Graham (Budden), M for Mark (Darby) and T for Tony (Richardson).

The charity's Chief Executive Kate Chivers said the aim now is a 365-day service.

Technicians at the Medical Aviation Services based in Gloucestershire pulled out all the stops to get the replacement chopper delivered in time.

Al Fayed generosity saves Diana's old school

The name of the mystery benefactor who has put in a multi-million bid to turn Princess Diana's old school, West Heath, Sevenoaks, into a centre for traumatised children, has been revealed — Harrods boss, Mohamed Al Fayed, the father of Diana's boyfriend Dodi who also died in the Paris car crash.

Mr Al Fayed hopes to save the school from the grasp of property developers and set up a millennium gift for children in crisis run by Valerie May, head of the Beth Marie Centre in Sevenoaks.

The school closed some months ago and Mr Al Fayed, who lives a few miles away at Oxted, has offered to buy it, totally refurbish it and guarantee its financial future — as a living memorial to Diana and Dodi.

The BBC newsreader Peter Sissons who lives in Sevenoaks said: "It is an act of profound generosity and catches exactly the mood of what a memorial to Diana should be all about. There is no reason why everything should not fall into place."

Lord Weatherill, ex-speaker of the House of Commons will be a patron of the school with the Princess' former head Ruth Rudge and author Susie Orbach who counselled Diana.

Farmer Brown — an 'honorary Geordie' from Tunbridge Wells

December 5th: Most people were under the impression that the new agriculture minister Nick Brown was an anti-fox hunting Geordie who was more at home pulling pints than milking a cow.

In fact he comes from Tunbridge Wells and his grandfather had a farm on the Kent Sussex border. He broke away from the rural idyll to become a student at Manchester and then a researcher in Newcastle before winning the city seat. Today he is an "honorary Geordie".

This week he has been in the news for two reasons. First he beat the *News of the World* by admitting he was gay and secondly he managed to persuade Chancellor Gordon Brown to give British farmers an extra £120 million.

His next mission is to get the beef ban lifted.

July 26th: Louis Bleriot, grandson of the first man to fly across the Channel, crashed into a lake near Calais today moments after beginning an attempt to repeat the feat for an anniversary tribute. M Bleriot, 54, was in a replica aircraft made of wood and canvas which took off from Bleriot-Plage. The pilot was unhurt.

Flowers mark the spot where Stephen died. Left to right Martin Cook and his girlfriend, Ellie Cameron (Stephen's sister), Ken Toni and Maressa Cameron, aged seven.

Rage suspect fights extradition

September 1st: A well known criminal — now Britain's most wanted man — is fighting extradition from Spain following the news that he is wanted for questioning over the road rage murder of Stephen Cameron.

Yesterday he told a judge in Puerto de Santa Maria that police had no evidence linking him with the murder of Stephen on the M25 slip road at Swanley in May 1996.

The suspect, who lives near Sevenoaks, disappeared after the murder and was eventually traced to Spain.

Stephen's father who lives in Swanley appealed on TV for him to come forward. He said the murder of his son had ripped his family's lives apart and left Stephen's fiancee Danielle Cable utterly heartbroken.

Love drug pioneered at Sandwich

September 16th: Viagra, the impotence drug which has received its long-awaited licence, was pioneered by British scientists based at the Pfizer headquarters in Sandwich.

Yesterday the European Commission gave it a marketing licence for a prescription medicine and made the drug "adult only" for men over 18.

Pfizer scientists are delighted to receive the licence but disappointed by the Department of Health decision which bans Viagra on the NHS. Until further notice it will be available only on private prescriptions.

Dr Gill Samuels, one of the scientists who has worked on the Viagra project from its inception in 1985, says the NHS spends up to £12 million a year on erectile disfunction and it is difficult to understand the Government's refusal to issue it on the NHS.

Pfizer has already received thousands of letters from satisfied customers. One read: "This medication has had a substantial positive effect on my life and marriage. It may be difficult for someone who has not suffered impotence to comprehend the effect on one's life. The word 'devastating' comes close."

The Sandwich Viagra team which has worked on the project for 17 years consists of 1,500 people. Each tablet costs £4.84. It is being hailed as a great British achievement.

See page 183

Stamps commemorate the closing of the North Foreland — the last manned lighthouse in Britain. The old telescope and barometer will be sold to a museum.

Light goes out on maritime history

November 26th: The five dedicated keepers of the North Foreland lighthouse at Broadstairs have been replaced by a computer — so ending more than 2,000 years of maritime history.

Today the flag on the last manned lighthouse in the British Isles was lowered by Dermot Cronin, the principal keeper. Once again technology has made an enormous impact on working lives.

Trinity House said this week that automation has brought savings of £5 million a year. New equipment will be installed and monitored from a base station at Harwich. The only visitors now will be emergency engineers.

It was in 1634 that Sir John Meldrum was given permission to light bonfires to warn sailors of the hazardous Goodwin Sands. A lighthouse followed and it has been in operation ever since.

This way for the Continent. John Prescott, Secretary of State for the Environment, prepares for the rail link.

Work starts at last on the Channel Tunnel rail link

November: The long saga over the route of the Channel Tunnel rail link has finally reached a conclusion. Today, deputy Prime Minister John Prestcott performed the official sod-turning ceremony and work began on the £4.3 million line.

The first section will run from the Channel Tunnel to Fawkham junction, a distance of 43 miles. It is due to be completed in 2003 when Railtrack will acquire the line after receiving overwhelming backing from its shareholders.

Railtrack has an option also to buy the second section between Southfleet and St Pancras including Ebbsfleet station, due for completion in 2007.

It is the first major new railway in Britain this century and it will attract something like 54,000 new jobs.

Drug-crazed burglar who fantasised about torture

October 24th: Michael Stone, aged 38, of Gillingham — jailed for life for the murder of Lin and Megan Russell — was a known thief, burglar, knife attacker and armed robber who fantasised about torturing and killing innocent people.

At his trial in Maidstone which ended this week the jury heard references to his heroin addiction but had no way of knowing that Stone was a violently disturbed man with a long medical history.

Stone was born at Pembury and spent most of his early life moving around Kent. His schooling was chaotic, there was much truancy and he ended up in several care homes. Eventually he became locked in a cycle of drugs, petty crime and violence that was to shape his adult life.

It was a convicted killer Mark Jennings who heard Stone confess in Christmas 1996 that he had "hurt someone bad". He told the jury that Stone was capable of murdering women and children.

Mr Justice Kennedy warned the jury that The Sun's money may have loosened Jennings' tongue but "it is up to you to decide".

Rothermere — last great Press baron

Viscount Rothermere, owner of the Daily Mail and Northcliffe Newspapers, who has died aged 71, was known as the last great Press baron and one of the richest people in England.

It was his great uncle, Alfred Harmsworth (later Lord Northcliffe of Broadstairs), who began a newspaper dynasty when he founded the Daily Mail in 1896.

The village of Benenden was later home to the Harmsworth family in what is now Benenden School.

They established a series of foundations in the 1920s in memory of two Harmsworth sons killed in the 1914-18 war.

Viscount Rothermere's son Jonathan succeeds to the title.

Kent couple's Gambian dream

When Michael and Annie Strand of Nonington, near Dover, took a 10-day holiday in Gambia they were given such a vivid glimpse of the realities of the Third World that they decided to help.

The result is a fully-equipped elementary school at Sukuta Sanchaba near Banjul.

With the help of individual sponsors the Strands have funded the complete project and today are paying for the upkeep and running of the school which houses 180 pupils.

Each month from Nonington they write cheques to pay the staff and twice a year they visit the school which bears their name.

'It means I will trust Edward to make decisions that are good for the family' — Sophie Rhys-Jones on her decision to keep the word 'obey' in her wedding vows.

The Sandwich-based company, Pfizer, which makes the drug Viagra, is to challenge the Government ban on prescribing the drug on the NHS. A High Court hearing is due to begin in the summer of 1999.

January 16th: Jerry Hall, who alleges that Mick Jagger has ruined their marriage by committing adultery with an "unknown woman", has filed for divorce. The former Dartford schoolboy is worth an estimated £145 million.

January 31st: The 12-strong choir at the Church of All Saints, Woodchurch, has been sacked because of its preference for traditional hymns.

February 18th: The Dartford River Crossing should be free of toll charges by the year 2002. The Government announced this week that construction costs for both tunnel and the QE2 bridge will be paid for by then.

Margaret Cook, the former wife of the Foreign Secretary, has triggered a political storm by writing a book about Robin Cook's "serial infidelity and heavy drinking". The couple lived at Chevening before their separation.

March 18th: Larry O'Connell, the boxing judge from Hartley, who deemed the world title clash between Lennox Lewis and Evander Holyfield a draw, has been at the centre of an enormous controvers*y. The Sun* dedicated two pages to Mr O'Connell's role in "boxing's night of farce".

March 24th: Nato today launched air strikes against Yugoslavia as Serb forces continued to drive Albanian refugees out of Kosovo. It is Nato's first major campaign in its 50-year history.

Three black rhinoceros calves have been born in captivity at Port Lympne Wild Animal Park in five months, raising hopes for the survival of the species.

April 8th: Traffic on the M25

Kelly Brook, 19, from Rochester — a former Medway Carnival Princess — has been chosen to replace Denise Van Outen on Channel Four's Big Breakfast. She joins another Medway girl on the show, fashion correspondent Ashley Rossiter.

came to a halt today when a suspicious package was found at the Dartford crossing toll booth. As bomb disposal experts prepared to carry out a controlled explosion, traffic built up for several miles in Essex and Kent. It was eventually discovered that the "package" was a cool box containing ham sandwiches!

April 9th: Russian President Boris Yeltsin today warned Nato of a "world war" if they attempted to seize Yugoslavia.

Matthew Fleming, a former captain in the Guards, is the new captain of Kent Cricket Club. Andrew Symonds is the overseas signing and Trevor Ward the beneficiary for 1999.

April 20th: Combat 18, a far-right racist group, is believed to have planted the nail bomb which injured 40 people at Brixton. A 999 call claiming reponsibility was made to police from a telephone box in Well Hall Road, Eltham where Stephen Lawrence was stabbed to death.

April 26th: Television personality and presenter of *Crimewatch UK*, Jill Dando, was shot dead today on the doorstep of her home in Fulham. Detectives are considering a number of potential motives for the murder.

Kent Cricket Club has decided on the nickname Spitfires for the new National one-day league competition. It derives, of course,

from the famous fighter aircraft that played such a vital role during the war in the skies above Kent.

May 4th: The Bank Holiday weekend was the third hottest on record. Temperatures at coastal resorts in Kent exceeded 72F.

With the death of Godfrey Evans, aged 78, one of Kent's mighty oaks has been felled. The great wicket keeper played 91 Tests for England and was a member of England's strongest postwar team.

May 13th: More than 800,000 Kosovars have now fled to an uncertain future in refugee camps after experiencing the horrors of ethnic cleansing.

May 12th: Following a successful amendment by Lord Weatherill 92 hereditary peers will win a temporary reprieve from Labour's plans to remove all 750 of them from the House of Lords.

Bob Geldof of Davington Priory, Faversham, is launching a new travel internet company called Deckchair.com. His last business venture, Planet 24, was the company that launched the *Big Breakfast*. It was sold to Carlton for an estimated £18 million.

June 6th: As details of a peace deal between Nato and Yugoslavia is thrashed out it is reported that the rebuilding of Kosovo is likely to cost £2.5 billion.

June 12th: British paratroopers massed on the Macedonian border today ready to move into Kosovo.

June 20th: Bob Woolmer, South Africa's Tonbridge-born cricket coach, says the defeat by Australia in the most dramatic circumstances after the match was tied will haunt him for the rest of his life. Australia went on to win the World Cup by eight wickets.

GREAT HITS OF 1999

No Regrets

Baby One More Time

Grand Prix returns to Brands Hatch and Bernie is delighted

May 15th: The British Grand Prix is returning to Brands Hatch after 13 years. Alongside the official announcement today came details of a proposed expansion and development of the track where Nigel Mansell won the last Formula One European Grand Prix in 1986.

The news has stunned the British Racing Drivers' Club who felt that Silverstone would continue to host one of Britain's biggest sporting events. But, under the guidance of Nicola Foulston, the Brands Hatch Leisure Group has been built into a formidable company and has £30 million in backing to support funding from Sevenoaks District Council.

The ruling body, the Formula One Administration, has approved the new circuit designs and awarded a contract for six years.

Bernie Ecclestone said this week that he looks forward to making the 2001 Grand Prix the most successful ever. "It is a circuit with a lot of history and people in the business like it."

Dartford scouts die in avalanche

January 15th: Thanksgiving services have been held this week for four young scouts who died under an avalanche on Ben Nevis.

Among them were sweethearts Emma Ray, aged 29 and Paul Hopkins, 28, from Meadow Walk and Warren Road, Wilmington. They were buried together following a joint service at St Michael's Church.

The other victims were Matthew Lewis, 30, of Sutton-at-Hone and Ian Edwards, 28, of Dartford. Tributes have been pouring in for the scouts who were victims of a tragic accident.

Sarah Finch from Longfield and her boyfriend Steven Newton from Dartford survived the avalanche.

March 11th: More than 50 battle-hardened eco-warriors have now left Crystal Palace Park — their makeshift home for more than a year. They have been living in almost mediaeval squalor in a defiant effort to save the park from being turned into a £55 million leisure complex. Of the 50 activists who began the protest, three are still squatting in the underground tunnels. Bromley Borough Council, which owns the site, removed four tons of waste before eviction. One eco-warrior said it was quite ironic that Bromley should complain about rubbish. "By chopping down trees", he said, "they have ruined the natural habitat."

Lawrence inquiry: a damning indictment

July 22nd: Ben Bullock, the only officer to face serious disciplinary charges after the failed Lawrence murder investigation, was punished with a caution today for two breaches of police regulations. He now retires from the Metropolitan Police after 30 years.

Earlier in the year the Lawrence inquiry, led by former High Court judge Sir William Macpherson, produced a damning indictment of "the bungled police inquiry, the poor leadership of senior officers and a force infected by institutionalised racism."

The inquiry lasted for 69 days, received 100,000 pages of evidence and heard 88 witnesses including the five men suspected of killing Stephen at a bus stop in Eltham in April 1993.

The legacy of the tragedy was the biggest shake-up of race relations legislation for decades. Home Secretary Jack Straw said the inquiry's 70 recommendations would serve as a watershed in attitudes to racism.

Stephen's father said: "These recommendations have to be implemented so we can see that racists who go out and kill people don't get away with it. If we lose this opportunity it will be like my son has died in vain."

Crisis for Kent as more and more refugees seek asylum

February 10th: **With the arrival of 160 illegal Romanian refugees who were recently intercepted in Dartford, Kent County Council is now supporting some 1,200 asylum seekers — and the figure is growing dramatically each week.**

Social services chiefs say the KCC has been forced to spend £3.8 million of public money on dealing with the continuing influx.

As an accommodation crisis grows the county is urging neighbouring authorities to share responsibility for the refugees. Many hostels in the county are full. Premises at Ashford and Dartford are already being used to house recent arrivals while a further hostel at Maidstone is on standby.

In addition, some London boroughs are continuing to place their refugees in Kent despite appeals for them not to do so. More than 500 children already need school places and Kent police are hoping for extra cash to help pay for their role in the asylum seekers' crisis.

March 16th: A disused quarry (right) almost hidden by towering 50-metre high chalk hills in north-west Kent (right) has been transformed into Europe's largest and perhaps most innovative retail and leisure complex.

Bluewater opened today. Inside this retail cathedral are three malls, more than 320 stores and a greater shop frontage than London's Oxford Street. The site is surrounded by a landscape of lakes, parkland and trees. Bluewater employs 6,700 people recruited through a vast advertising and roadshow programme and presents a competitive challenge to traders in surrounding towns and especially to the giant Lakeside complex on the other side of the River Thames.

This remarkable shopping complex is owned by the Australian Developers Land Lease Corporation which has spent £30 million improving surrounding roads leading to the site.

'London Manston' says farewell to the RAF

April 1st: The RAF today flew out of Manston Airport leaving behind evocative memories of the days when Britain's finest pilots flew from this famous old forward fighter station.

The Wiggins Group, which already owns the civilian airport within the site and the Manston Business Park, now takes control of the whole airbase.

The new airport is to be renamed London Manston. The owners plan to build a new £10 million terminal able to handle up to 1.5 million passengers a year with business people flying direct from Kent to Europe and North America on scheduled services.

The Wiggins takeover has upset many aviation enthusiasts and local people who recall the days when the airfield was heavily bombed but recovered to play a major role in the Battle of Britain and beyond.

At a public meeting earlier this year more than 1,000 people turned up to complain about likely noise and pollution and plans to create a huge commercial development on the 600-acre site.

Millionaire is not guilty of wife's murder

May 13th: Who killed Diana Goldsmith? One of Kent's most absorbing murder inquiries remains unsolved following the collapse, this week, of the case against her 62-year-old former common-law husband, Derek Goldsmith.

The millionaire inventor who lives at Crockham Hill was found not guilty at Maidstone Crown Court of murder and not guilty of conspiracy to murder. He left the court a free man with costs estimated to be in the region of £750,000.

Diana Goldsmith, 44, was abducted from her Sevenoaks home on January 25th, 1995 and was not seen again until her body was discovered buried in a Bromley garden in March 1997.

The trial jury was told that her husband was behind a "calculated and wicked" conspiracy to kidnap and murder her in order to regain custody of his children. He was accused of enlisting the help of his former son-in-law and two other men in the plot to rid himself of Diana in return for £20,000 "up front".

One of those men, Ian Colligan, committed suicide. The second, Michael Fitzpatrick, formerly of Westerham, has pleaded guilty to conspiracy to murder and is awaiting sentence. **See page 193**

When 21-year-old Stephen Cameron was the victim of a frenzied knife attack on the Swanley intersection of the M25 motorway, police believed he was a road-rage victim and soon identified a prime suspect, then living in Spain. Extradition orders took time but were eventually secured and the man, a Kent resident, appeared before magistrates at Sevenoaks. Police took no chances and marksmen were employed to keep an eye on this well-known former criminal. His trial is due in the autumn of this year..

Girl from Brenchley becomes a Princess

June 19th: Sophie Rhys-Jones, the girl from Brenchley who once worked part-time in the village pub, was married to Prince Edward at St George's Chapel, Windsor Castle today. Scores of friends from the village were among those invited to this glittering occasion.

As a little girl Sophie, now 34, lived with her parents and brother David at Church House, Brenchley and is remembered as a "lovely little girl and real chatterbox". After completing eight O-levels at Kent College in nearby Pembury, Sophie attended West Kent College for Further Education to do a secretarial course.

During this time she worked part time at The Halfway House and, according to customers, "pulled a generous pint and was always chatting to the locals".

Sophie's parents, Christopher and Mary who now live in Homestead Farmhouse, Brenchley, were astonished when they first heard about their daughter's relationship with Prince Edward. "It was the first time in my life", said Mr Rhys-Jones, "that I needed a gin and tonic before 10 o'clock." Since then Edward has visited Sophie at Brenchley regularly but the couple avoided detection by travelling to the farmhouse separately. However, villagers said they had seen Edward at the local golf club and occasionally roaring past the post office in his Range Rover.

Early speculation that the wedding would take place in the 800-year-old village church was soon dismissed and the new Duke and Duchess of Wessex chose Windsor. Favouring tradition at the core of the marriage proceedings, Miss Rhys-Jones promised to "obey" Edward as the Bishop of Norwich, the Rt Rev Peter Nott, read the vows.

Paul Scally, Gillingham's chairman, at Wembley before the match. Can the Gills pull it off? Scally thinks so. So does manager Tony Pulis.

Gillingham's Wembley nightmare

May 31st: Gillingham Football Club's first-ever appearance at Wembley ended in heartbreak for the team and 35,000 supporters yesterday when they lost to Manchester City after one of the most dramatic turnarounds in soccer history.

With just a few minutes of stoppage time remaining in the play-off final for a place in Division One of the Football League, Gillingham were leading by 2-0. Somehow City scored twice, forced the game into extra time and then won in a penalty shoot-out.

The nation watched on television as the agony replaced ecstasy. Many City fans had already left and were trudging dejectedly down Wembley Way when their club scored the dramatic late goals. Division One glory had been cruelly snatched from Gillingham's grasp.

Although Gillingham lost in the final they have enjoyed another brilliant season. No-one in the Medway Towns has forgotten that the club was facing bankruptcy and disbandment just four years ago. They were rescued by businessman Paul Scally who helped manager Tony Pulis assemble a team that gained promotion from Division Three and then came within minutes of a place in Division One, alongside the likes of Blackburn and Notts Forest.

See page 193

Manchester City and Gillingham were in deadlock until the 81st minute. These were the dramatic moments that followed:

4.36: Carl Asaba scores and jumps over the advertising boards in delight. Gillingham one-up.

4.45: Gills fans ecstatic as Bob Taylor nets a second. Nearly all over.

4.48: Terry Horlock scores for City. Just 5 mins of stoppage time remain.

4.52: Paul Dickov equalises for City. Someone up there loves Manchester.

5.30: Deadlock again after extra time. Down to a penalty shoot-out.

5.45: City win 3-1 after the penalties. Gillingham's chairman, manager, player and 35,000 fans are hearttbroken. A dream is over.

The fans at Wembley. The proudest moment in Gillingham's topsy-turvy history.

Jonathan Aitken on his way to The Old Bailey.

Former Thanet MP "wove a web of deceit" says judge

June 8th: Jonathan Aitken, former MP for Thanet South, was jailed for 18 months today for perjury and perverting the course of justice. For the 56-year-old former Chief Secretary to the Treasury it completes his "self-inspired professional, political and personal ruin."

Aitken's 18-year-old twin daughters Victoria and Alexandra burst into tears as he was sentenced. They had arrived at the Old Bailey with Petrina Khashoggi, their father's illegitimate daughter by Soraya Khashoggi, and his mother Lady Aitken.

The former Tory MP, once so popular and well-respected among his constituents, admitted that he had lied when he told a High Court case in 1995 that his wife Lolicia had paid the bill for a weekend stay at the Ritz Hotel in Paris. In fact, Said Ayas, an adviser to Prince Mohammed of Saudi Arabia, had paid the £1,000 bill.

Mr Justice Scott Taylor told Aitken: "For nearly four years you wove a web of deceit in which you entangled yourself and in which there was no way out unless you were prepared to tell the truth."

The court heard of Aitken's deep sense of remorse, especially over his action in persuading his daughter Victoria to sign a statement in an attempt to salvage his libel action against the Guardian newspaper and Granada Television, who made a *World in Action* documentary about his affairs.

In a statement admitting to his lies Jonathan Aitken said that for the rest of his life he would bear the burden of having misled and manipulated some of those close to him to lie on his behalf.

Widdecombe gets the post she coveted

June 16th: Maidstone's robust, barnstorming MP, Ann Widdecombe has been invited by Conservative leader William Hague to join his shadow cabinet as shadow home secretary.

It is the portfolio she has coveted since the Tories' election defeat in 1997 cost her a ministerial job in the Home Office.

Then she was working as a middle-ranking minister alongside Michael Howard. His decision to stand for the Tory leadership allowed her to deliver the devastating verdict that he had "something of the night" about his character".

The Shepway MP, like most of his former cabinet colleagues, does not have a place in Hague's top team.

Another Oscar nomination for the working-class girl from Ramsgate

March 22nd: It's a long way from Ramsgate to Hollywood but Brenda Blethyn has made the journey following her nomination for an Academy Award as Best Supporting Actress in the film *Little Voice*.

Brenda, 52, was raised in Thanet by working-class parents who taught her "not to whinge but get on with the job". She did. After the breakdown of her marriage to a graphic designer whom she met when working for British Rail, she enrolled at Guildford drama college and, in time, has become one of Britain's finest character actors. She is a firm favourite with the two Alans, Bennett and Ayckbourne and director Mike Leigh adores her.

After 20 years on the stage Leigh galvanised Blethyn's special talent in his film *Secrets and Lies* for which she received a Oscar nomination.

And with that rare ability to make the lives of ordinary working women seem compelling she has pulled it off again in *Little Voice*.

Asda chief Archie Norman

Back the pound: a mission for Archie Norman

June 16th: Archie Norman, MP for Tunbridge Wells, former Conservative Party chairman and chief executive of Asda, the giant super market chain was appointed shadow minister for Europe in William Hague's summer reshuffle of his shadow cabinet. His chief mission is to persuade business to back the policy of keeping the pound.

Last year Mr Norman was positioned 41st in a national newspaper league table of the country's most influential people.

Designed to measure "how successful you are in getting people to do what you want" he was placed above both the Pope and Richard Branson.

Mr Norman told the *Courier* newspaper: "It was ludicrous. I was put higher than Chris Evans but he's a great deal more powerful than I am. I don't have much power in my own household let alone the country."

Brenda Blethyn arrives in Los Angeles wearing a sleeveless blue sequinned dress by Escada.

The Millennium Dome on Greenwich Peninsula — due to be opened by The Queen on December 31st.

Polluted site is now "the greatest show on earth"

September 22nd: The Millennium Dome, costing £758m, built on land once known as Busker's Cove and later the site of the biggest, ugliest gas works in England is designed to draw millions of people to the Greenwich Peninsula and what is described as "the greatest show on earth".

The lottery-funded dome, as big as a dozen Albert Halls in an area that could contain Trafalgar Square and 117 tennis courts, is divided into 14 zones.

The most controversial zone is The Body, which features two massive reclining figures. A moving staircase will give visitors a voyage of discovery through the human machine while multi-media techniques describe development in medicine, lifestyle, health and beauty.

The 300-acre Greenwich Peninsula was once London's largest derelict and polluted riverside site. The location of the Dome on the northern tip has triggered the development of the whole area, including the 1,400-home Millennium Village and Skyscape, a major performance venue,

displaying the largest cinema screen in Britain.

Construction began on June 23, 1997 when the first of 8,000 concrete piles were driven into the ground. By October the cable netting, which provides the support for the Dome's canopy, began to take shape. Specially recruited abseilers spent three months on the site putting the cables into place.

The Jubilee Line's new North Greenwich Transport Interchange, the largest underground station in Europe, is alongside the Dome. For those who prefer a river journey, boats will run frequently from central London direct to the Experience Pier.

The British Tourist Authority estimates that the Millennium Experience could generate up to £500m through additional overseas visitors. As a tourist attraction it will be a rival to the Eiffel Tower; in fact the Eiffel Tower could lie on its side within the Dome!

Maidstone-based Gurkhas gave lives for others

June 22nd: Two Gurkhas, based at the Invicta Barracks, Maidstone, were killed today when unexploded Nato cluster bombs blew up as the soldiers were preparing to destroy them 20 miles to the west of Pristina, capital of Kosovo.

The tragedy occurred some days after the Serb forces had left and Nato forces were clearing the area, prior to the rebuilding of the province.

The soldiers were Lt Gareth Evans from Bristol who was serving with the 69th Gurkha Field Regiment, part of the 36th Engineers Regiment and Sgt Bala Ram Rai of the Queen's Gurkha Engineers.

The cluster bombs had been dropped during the Nato air campaign against Serbian troops and police units in the disputed region.

A spokesman for the British Forces in Kosovo said that Lt Evans and Sgt Rai were "two brave men who were well aware of the dangers of dealing with explosives but were prepared to risk their lives to make life safer for others."

Gurkha Major Damar Ghale of the Queen's Gurkha Regiment said he knew Sgt Rai well. "He was a fine soldier, a high flier and will be sadly missed." Major Andy Edington of the 36th Engineers said that Lt Evans, one of the few British officers serving with the Gurkhas, was "an excellent officer and a super bloke who loved working with the Gurkhas. Everybody is terribly shocked and saddened by the news."

It was Lt Evans who made the decision to demolish the cluster bombs after removing them from near a primary school in a village called Orlate but somehow the devices exploded prematurely.

Run faster Donald, run faster — shouted Bob in his nightmare

June 21st: The South African cricket coach Bob Woolmer is no stranger to success. As a key member of the Kent squad in the 1970s and 80s he knew what it was like to contest a one-day final and twice helped his team win the county championship pennant. He also played 19 games for England and scored two centuries in the great Ashes series of 1977.

All the medals, all the success will now pale into insignificance alongside his memories of the 1999 World Cup campaign when he guided South Africa brilliantly towards the final at Lords and then saw his greatest dreams snatched away in a moment of madness.

With the South African and Australian scores level and the last ball about to be bowled Allan Donald was dramatically run out. The glory of winning cricket's greatest prize was snatched away from Woolmer in what has been described as "the greatest one-day match ever played."

Bob Woolmer, 51, was inconsolable. This was his last match as South Africa's coach; five years of dedication and hard work were shattered.

"For several nights afterwards", he said, "I kept waking up telling Donald to run faster. It was a moment that will haunt me for the rest of my life."

Woolmer began his cricketing education at Yardley Court and Skinners' School and won a place in the Kent side after several successful seasons with Tunbridge Wells in the Kent League. On retirement he ran a sports shop in Tonbridge but also accepted a coaching position with Warwickshire and turned them into one of the most combative county squads ever known — and the first to win three trophies in one year.

The five-year South African job followed and he was favourite for the job as England's coach in succession to David Lloyd. But Woolmer, in need of a holiday, turned that down.

Blair promises: hunting will be banned

June: Rural and pro-hunting groups throughout Kent have condemned Tony Blair's decision to ban hunting "before the next Parliament" and said it amounted to a "declaration of war on the countryside".

June: Cross-channel passengers said farewell to duty-free perks which officially ended at midnight on Wednesday June 30th. Before the deadline thousands of bargain hunters packed ferries and hovercrafts to stock up on cheap drink and cigarettes.

July: Tony Pulis, manager of Gillingham Football Club and the man who guided the Gills to Wembley, has been dismissed by chairman Paul Scally in July for "alleged gross misconduct". Peter Taylor, the former England Under 21 manager, has been appointed in his place.

July: In a High Court hearing Jerry Hall accepted a £10 million financial settlement from Mick Jagger.

July: Linda Currie, sister of Diana Goldsmith, says she is disgusted by the five-year jail sentence imposed on Michael Fitzpatrick for his part in Diana's abduction. She said: "The truth of my sister's murder will come out one day."

August: The worldwide ban on exports of British beef has ended — almost three and a half years after it was imposed by the EU at the height of the BSE crisis.

August 11th: Parties were held all over the county today as thousands watched the final solar eclipse of the Millennium. In Kent the eclipse was not total but in most places heavy clouds stayed away enabling dedicated watchers to see the moon play hide and seek with the sun and an eerie band of darkness fall across the county.

Kent — the pollution and the progress

My exhausting but exciting and, I hope, worthwhile millennium project for the county of Kent is over.

The highlights of the century from the scorn that greeted those early motoring pioneers to the controversy that preceded the opening of the great dome at Greenwich is committed to four volumes, totalling 800 pages and illustrated by more than 600 photographs.

During the last four or five years I have visited almost every town and village in my quest to capture the changing social and cultural life of a county — by reportage rather than analysis. It has been great fun.

A few years before the 20th century began geologists said that coal existed in Kent and the race was on to look for more. At the same time politicians were arguing that a tunnel under the Channel was, and always would be, a threat to the nation's defences.

By 1905 Ashford's great railway works were supporting a community of nearly 3,000 — all involved in the construction of Britain's finest locos. That year the world's biggest battleship, *HMS Africa,* slipped gracefully down the slipway at Chatham Dockyard accompanied by a military band and the rendition of *Rule Britannia.*

Automobiles were then a novelty and "only for the rich or very sporty". Moving pictures were a faraway pipedream and who really believed in the concept of flying machines?

Now, at the end of the century, Kent's rich coalfields have gone, Ashford's loco works have closed and Chatham Dockyard is a museum. Many families think nothing of flying abroad for their holidays; they frequently own two cars and a pattern of motorways takes traffic through our county to the Channel Tunnel terminal at Folkestone.

For most of this helter-skelter century the pace of change was dictated by politicians. For the final 25 years scientists were in control and science continues to transform the experience of everyday living.

When I was a boy I used to climb the North Downs, or the Greensand Ridge, and sit on top of the world between skies of blue and fields of gold, surrounded by wild flowers and songbirds. Below was God's great canvas — the county of Kent.

Today, a great stretch of the North Downs and the Greensand Ridge sits on the edge of surburbia. A six-lane motorway takes traffic on its orbital route round London and on to the Channel Ports. Millions of new houses have meant more roads, more cars, more waste and more pollution of light, sound and air. Many of our lovely cherry orchards and hopfields have disappeared.

The siege continues. Advertising signs litter the county and motorists drive at breakneck speeds on minor roads.

No longer is it possible to cycle safely down village lanes. Giant jets pollute the air. Country people with country lifestyles are becoming rare. In places the green fields are a sickly yellow. Worse, much worse, the Green Belt is in danger of being broken up to accommodate four and a half million new homes.

Today, because of the noise and fumes and physical danger, the clamour is for bypasses. Lamberhurst, Riverhead, Hadlow, Bethersden, High Halden, Newenden, Rolvenden, Sturry, Tenterden, Northfleet, Borough Green, Meopham, Staplehurst, Linton, Goudhurst, Hawkhurst, and Headcorn — to name a few — are looking for Whitehall funding in order to get through traffic out of their village, but again the precious countryside will be eaten up.

More homes, more roads and a high-speed rail link, funded by private sector loans, means more stolen land and ultimately more noise, more waste, more pollution etc. Where will it all lead? Only time can tell.

But, there is much that is positive.

Conservation groups of all kinds — particularly the high profile Kent Trust for Nature Conservation — are strongly supported and every year more nature reserves are created to protect habitats for our threatened wildlife. The Council for the Protection of Rural England (CPRE) is encouraging people to work together to protect the countryside from the effects of heavy lorries, to help save local shops under threat, to safeguard the distinction between town and country and to recognise the importance of a balanced agricultural system.

Southern Water has spent £1 billion to bring waste water treatment up to European standards and that has involved the building of new pumping stations at Folkestone and Dover to provide cleaner bathing waters and flood protection.

On the page opposite we have shown that the dawn of the new millennium will break close to the Langdon Cliffs at Dover. Here, on a clear day, you can see France 21 miles away and the new cruise ships which call regularly. The docks either side of Dover's harbour form the busiest roll-on/roll-off port in the world and there are plans to extend the harbour wall to meet a rise in traffic of as much as 100 per cent.

Such ambitions stretch across the county. Nicola Foulston will realise a dream to bring the British Grand Prix back to its spiritual home at Brands Hatch in 2001; Gillingham chairman Paul Scally plans a £60 million multi-purpose complex at Priestfield fit for premiership soccer and the massive Ebbsfleet International and Domestic passenger station near Northfleet will serve the new rail link across Kent creating 26,000 new jobs and 3,000 new homes — all in the name of progress.

Bob Ogley

MILLENNIUM DAWN

THE first people in England to see the dawn of the new millennium will be those standing near the South Foreland lighthouse a mile or two from the Langdon Cliffs at Dover. Thousands of sightseers will gather on this famous landscape to welcome the first chink of light — and maybe even the sun — at 07.58 hours on January 1st, 2000. For years astronomers claimed that Lowestoft, on the most eastern part of Britain, would have the honour but, due to a slight tilt of the earth at that time, the White Cliffs will be the actual location. The Royal Greenwich Observatory revised its official estimate. The South Foreland lighthouse was decommissioned some 10 years ago but is now maintained in full working order by the National Trust. A lighthouse has existed on the site since 1635 but the present white tower is 150 years old.

Charles Rolls completes the first return flight across the English Channel.

White Cliffs — a beacon of resistance and hope

THE White Cliffs have acquired symbolic status as the last and first glimpse of England; a beacon of resistance and hope. They have evoked mystification, wonder, delight and gratitude. They represent the front door of Britain.

Julius Caesar headed for the White Cliffs in his reconnaissance raid of 55 BC and William, Duke of Normandy made it his target after defeating the English at Hastings in 1066. A century later Henry II came here to supervise the building of the great castle — ordered by William I after the conquest — in Kentish ragstone and aslar dressing from Normandy.

Below and beyond the cliffs are the memorials to the pioneers — Captain Matthew Webb who was the first to swim the Straits of Dover in 1875, Louis Bleriot who made the first flight in 1909 and the Hon Charles Rolls (of Rolls-Royce) who completed the first return flight in 1910.

The White Cliffs of Dover have a powerful association with two world wars; they represent the most dramatic years in England's history.

These include the gallant men of the Dover Patrol who kept open the vital cross-Channel link with the British forces fighting on the Western Front in the Great War and those who later masterminded and carried out the miracle of Dunkirk — the evacuation of the British Expeditionary Force.

It was above these cliffs that the Battle of Britain pilots harried and finally drove the Luftwaffe back to France and it was here the clifftop gunners carried on the fight until freedom was secured — a triumph so evocatively predicted in Vera Lynn's memorable song *The White Cliffs of Dover.*

How suitable that this famous Kentish landscape will be the first place in Britain to greet the dawn of the new millennium — at 07.58 hours on January 1st, 2000.

SUBSCRIBERS

The following kindly gave their support to this book

Pauline Abraham
Doreen Allibone
Charmian Amos
Iain H Anderson
Sally G Anning
Jim Armstrong
E R Arnold
Roy Arnold
Graham Ashby
Vic Ashlee
Yvonne Atkinson
Mrs F E Austen
Jonathan Balcon
Mrs S Balderstone
Charles F Baldwin
Kathleen & Tony Ball
R A Barham
E Barnett
Denise Barr
S R & S M Beck
Robert Beck
Heather Bell
Francis Bellingham
H Belsey
D E Bengeyfield
Dick & Pamela Bennett
Eric Bennett
W Beresford
A F Betts
Madeline Beverton
Mrs B Birtwistle
Melville Edwin Bishop
Karl Bloomfield
Mr R Bolton
Miss M V Borner
Paul M Boulton
B Bowman
G R Boxall
K Brackley
Violet Brand
Julian Branson
David Brattle
Wendy Brazier
Ruby & Mary Breeds
W J Brenton
Miss M A Brett
Mr & Mrs M A Brett
Mr & Mrs R Brickell
Violet Brook

R J Brooks
Mrs Dinah Brown
Peter T Brown
Mrs Rosemary Brown
B J Buchanan
Ann Buckett
Jean Bunnett
Sidney W Burvill
Carol Ann Bush
David Bushell
A K Butcher
Alan Butcher
Colin Butcher
Mrs M C Button
John Byrne
Ron & Joyce Cambridge
Robin Carden
Joan Carlier
Joan & Ian Carver
John Castle
Mrs Causton
Nicholas P L Chalk
Mrs Janet Chambers
Mr & Mrs C A Chapman
Anne Charlier
Christopher Chase
Marjorie & Rex Cheesman
Mrs R Child-Osborne
Mr E A Childs
John & Brenda Childs
Betty J Church
Mr & Mrs T Churcher
Mr M A Churches
Dennis Clare
Margaret & Sydney Cliffe
Arthur Clipstone
Marjorie Cocker
Mr N R H Cole
Dennis Collins
Dr J W Comper
J M Cook
Mrs H Coomber
Mr G A P & Mrs P Coombs
Mrs Evelyn Copland
E Craker
Cyril & Iris Crane
Mr & Mrs Cresswell
Mrs Jean Crisfield
L J & P A Cropper

Richard P Cross
E M Crosse
Ivan Curtis
Jean Cust
Simon Daniel
John Darby
Stan Darnell
A Davidson
Glenys Davis
Mr R S Dawe
John Dawson
Alan Deares
V Dennett
John E Denton
M J K Dodsworth
John F Dorling
Clive Douglas
N O Durdant-Hollamby
A J Dutton
Mark Dutton
Mr C Dyer
Mr D Dykes
Stan & Barbara Edgell
Eric Edghill
Bernard M Edwards
Mrs Janet Edwards
Douglas Elks
Pamela Ellis
Rachel & George Elvery
P Entecott
Mrs Evelyn Evans
Barry Everett
Richard Ewing
Jennifer & David Eyre
Mr & Mrs M Feltham
Mrs Melanie Felton
Denis Fentiman
Harry Fenton
The Finney Family
Edgar Fitzgerald
Mike Flight
Mr N Folkard
Bill Foster
Mr Rae Fowler
Mr C H Fox
Emerald Frampton
Valerie Fry
Mr Bernard Fuller
Marion Furner
Doug Furrents
Mrs Leila Gardner
Edwin & Gloria Garrett
J Garrett
David A Giles

Michael Ginn
R Goddard
Mr M Godfrey
M H Gosby
Mrs Iris Gosling
Peter & Eileen Gray
R B Griggs
Eileen Gunnell
Yvonne & Terry Hagreen
Marion Hall
P J Hamill
Kenneth William Hammerton
Neville Hammond
Helen Hankey
Alan Hankinson
Angela & Barrie Harber
Muriel Emma Harker
A V Harlow
Dave Harris
Derek Harris
R C Harris
Sheila Harris
J C Hart
Ken Hayes
Alan & Marian Healey
Marjorie Hewes
M G Hewett
J Hickling
E Hickmott
Joyce Hickmott
George R Higgs
Neil Hilkene
Herne Bay Historical Records Society
Guy Hitchings
David Thomas Hobbs
Jenny & Norman Hocknell
Vic Holdaway
Angela M Holness
Bob Holness
B A Holyland
Jim Homewood
Roy & Audrey Hooker
Bryan Hopkins
Doreen Hopkins
Mrs Edith Hopkins
John Hori
Molly Horn
William Horne
Miss A E Horner

M Hover
Mr L Howard
John Howcroft
D Hudson
Mr Peter Hughes
Sue & Chris Huke
Alan Humphrey
Maureen Humphrey
Joyce Jackson
Elizabeth Jaecker
Mr H W M James
Kenneth James
Maria Jarvis
Gary & Bobbie Jarvis
A R Jeffrey
Mr A Jeffreys
Mr & Mrs F W Jenns
Jean & Tony Johns
Mrs J Johnson
Mary L Johnson
Andrew G Jones
Ray & Brenda Jones
Mr T I Jones
Mrs C L Jones
Barbara Jones-Thomas
Lynn Jung
Alan M Kay
Peter & Patricia Kearin
Margaret Keatley
Derek Kemp
Eric Keys
Peter J Kiff
Sue Kirkham
A J Ladd
The Langridge Family
Mr David Lewis
Freda Lewis
S J Lewis
Mrs Iris Lilly
C Lindsay
Mrs Linton
Gordon Linton-Smith
Dorothy Loft
John London
Gary Long
Brigid Longley
Martyn Longstaff
Jeanne Loveland
Gordon Luck
Lyminge Historical Society
Ron Machen
Colin Mackinlay

SUBSCRIBERS

J Macro
Leslie Male
John Marsh
Pat Marshall
Valerie & Simon Marston
Peter Martin
Ian Martin
Josephine Martin
David J Mason
Miss E Mason
B L & J F Matthews
C N Matthews
C P Matthews
C S Matthews
M S Matthews
N J Matthews
Philip Maytum
James J McGrane
Timothy F P McGrane
Diane Melaugh
Mrs P Meridew
Beryl Miles
Chris Miles
C K A Miller
Pat & Lal Mineham
John Miskin
Caroline Mitchell
Clive Mitchell
J Mitchell
Elaine Moody
Peter Morgan
M Morris
Queenie Mortimer
W Morton
Mr & Mrs A R Mount
Tony & Maralyn Mulcuck
P E Murphy
Anne Nash
Brian & Muriel Neal
Frederick G Neville
Mr R A Newport
Brian Nobbs
Mrs Adrianne Norris
Mrs Majorie Norris
D C Nowers
Mrs Nunn
Pam Nye
June O'Connor
Peter O'Sullivan
George & Sheila Obermuller
Len Olive
Pam Osborn

Mrs P Owler
Alison Painter
Mrs E Palmer
Stephen Palmer
Elaine Parker
H & R Parkes
Mrs Lilian M Parrish
G Parsons
Ian D Patterson
Mr & Mrs B B Payne
Reg & Gwen Pearce
Margaret Pearce
Mollie & Tony Pearce
Allan Pearce
L Peatfield
Alun Pedler
R M Pendleton
John Sidney Penn
Brian, Pauline & KathrynPhillips
M Piddock
Cyril Pile
Robert Piper
G John Pluckrose
F M Pollard
Stan & Joyce Pomfret
Mr Chris Porteous
Monnie E Potter
Jan & Chris Powis
Gerry Press
B & D Pritchard
Sharon Proudlove
Hugh R Pryke
Janet & Alec Ramage
Mrs Esmé Rand
Roy Randall
Paul & Denise Rason
Paul C Rayner
Mrs L R Read
Allan Redden
David C Redman
Arthur & Tess Reeve
John Reeves
Valerie Reeves
Colin Reffell
Kevin F Reynolds
Mrs I C Rhodes
Wendy A Richman
Pam Ridout
Wendy A Rickman
Trevor Robbie
Vera Roberts
Dennis Roberts
Ann Roffe

N S Rogans
Peter Rogers
Mrs R Rogers
Mrs W Rolfe
Martin Rolls
Joyce & Frank Rooney
Bertha Rose
Malcolm Round
Colin W Rumley
Cathy Ruskin
R D G Ruston
Joan Evelyn Sale
Valerie Salzer
Mrs Colleen Samarasinghe
John Sanders
Eileen L Sands
Robert Saunders
Brian A Sayer
Michael Scott
Mrs Rocky Scurr
Janet Seeley
Mrs J Sharp
Mary & Annette Shaw
M & P Shearman
Jackie Shearring
Mike & Tessa Sheeres
Maurice G Short
K E & B M Silver
Coral Simpson
Ron & Shirley Sinclair
Mrs E Sinstadt
Mr & Mrs J Smith
Mrs J Smith
Alan Smith
Miss P A Smith
Jim Smith
J R Spain
A J Spelman
Roy & Freda Spivey
Joan W Spreyer
Louise Spreyer
Nigel Steer
D G & C Stevens
Keith Stevens
June Stigwood nee' Marshall
Mr James Stock
Maurice Stocker
Ronald H H Stokes
Mrs I Streeting
Mrs Phyllis Streets
S J Stringer
Derek Sutton

Mrs Joyce Frances Tapsell
C H Taylor
S E Taylor
George Taylor
Hugh W Taylor
Valerie Thatcher
Miss M A Thatcher
Mrs Hilda Thickins
Frank M Thirkell
Mr Troye R Thomas
Ed Thompson
Paul Thompson
Miss Angela Thorn
LW & JG Thorne
Mr E A B Thorneycroft
Conrad M B Thrower
Mrs C A Tiernan
Graham Tippen
Roger Tolhurst
John R Toms
Michael J Tong
Eunice D Towersey
Mrs Norma Towler
Colin Towse
Mr Robin Tregunno
Vivienne & Brian Tremain
Miss J Tresize
Mrs Eve Tucker
Mike Tuckey
Ron & Doreen Turner
Gordon C Turner
D H W & P A Turner
Mark R G Turner
Timothy D J Turner
David W Twining
Miss B Twinn
John L Tyman
Mrs Stella D Underwood
C J Verdon
Brian Vinall
Marshall Vine
Mrs D Walford
Mr B A Walker
Johnny Walker
Mr P D Walker
Frere Wallond
Patricia Walsh
Jean & Tony Walters
Mrs A Wanstall
Philip Wanstall
John H Warner

K J Warrington
Michael J Waterhouse
Iris & Len Watkins
David Watts
Christine & Arthur Webb
Peter Webster
Alan Weeks
Mr S L Weller
Keith Wells
Colin Wells
Alan R Wells
Colin Westmancott
Mrs D Wheateley
Mr E Whitaker
Cedric White
Mrs E Whitehead
Gillian & Chris Whittingham
Frank Wicken
David Wickenden
Simon Wickens
Terry A Wickens
Don Wiffen
Alan Wilkinson
Jean Wilkinson
Geoffrey E Williams
John & Wendy Williams
Linda Williams
R M Williams
Derek & Hazel Willis
Sidney G Willson
Mrs S Wilmot
V & K Wilson
R A Wilson
Jack Wingate
Ronald Wingrove
Mr & Mrs PF & SM Winton
George & Mary Winton
David Witherspoon
Denzil, Susan, Jane & James Wood
June R Wood
Sylvia Wood
Christopher Wood
Lionel J Wood
Ron & Pat Woodgate
Miss M Wootton
John Edward Wratten
Patricia J Wright
Chris Wyer
Ivor Youngman

INDEX

FROGLETS BOOKS

BOB OGLEY is a journalist by profession, an historian by predilection and an author by courtesy of the greatest storm of the century. *In The Wake of The Hurricane* sold almost 250,000 copies, remained in the top ten bestseller list for eight months and changed his life.

Bob was then the editor of the Sevenoaks Chronicle and on course to remain so for a few more years. Today he is a full-time writer, the author of almost 20 other books and travels extensively in pursuit of information and photographs.

Many of his books about Kent have been county bestsellers. They include *Doodlebugs and Rockets, Biggin on The Bump, Kent at War, The Kent Weather Book* and, of course, his four-part *Chronicle of Kent*.

Bob, who was born in Sevenoaks and has lived in the county all his life, is in great demand across the south-east to tell his unique story.

On the charitable side his books have raised many thousands of pounds for such worthy causes as the National Trust and the RAF Benevolent Fund.